MEETINGS AND CONVENTIONS MANAGEMENT

MEETINGS AND CONVENTIONS MANAGEMENT

Marguerite L. Weirich
Meeting Management Consultant

DELMAR
CENGAGE Learning™

Australia • Brazil • Japan • Korea • Mexico • Singapore • Spain • United Kingdom • United States

Meetings and Conventions Management
Marguerite L. Weirich

Senior Acquisitions Editor: Mary McGarry

Project Editor: Andrea Edwards Myers

Production Coordinator: Sandra Woods

Art Supervisor: John Lent

Design Coordinator: Karen Kunz Kemp

Design Supervisor: Susan C. Mathews

Cover photo courtesy of Westin Bonaventure

Cover design by Juanita Brown

For product information and technology assistance, contact us at
Cengage Learning Customer & Sales Support, 1-800-354-9706

For permission to use material from this text or product,
submit all requests online at **www.cengage.com/permissions**
Further permissions questions can be emailed to
permissionrequest@cengage.com

Library of Congress Control Number: 91-3994

ISBN-13: 978-0-8273-4514-0

ISBN-10: 0-8273-4514-3

Delmar
Executive Woods
5 Maxwell Drive
Clifton Park, NY 12065
USA

Cengage Learning is a leading provider of customized learning solutions with office locations around the globe, including Singapore, the United Kingdom, Australia, Mexico, Brazil, and Japan. Locate your local office at **international.cengage.com/region**

Cengage Learning products are represented in Canada by Nelson Education, Ltd.

For your lifelong learning solutions, visit **www.cengage.com/delmar**

Visit our corporate website at **www.cengage.com**

Printed in the United States of America
9 10 11 12 13   17 16 15 14 13

TABLE OF CONTENTS

PREFACE

Meeting management is an exciting, challenging and fascinating career choice. Any book presenting the field to students should certainly reflect the creativity, glamour and total enjoyment that is intrinsic to the "business" of meetings. It should be presented from the viewpoint of experience and work in the field, rather than pure academia. The origination of this particular text began when I was asked to construct and instruct an introductory course in Meetings and Conventions Management. No text that I reviewed at that time seemed to capture the essence of the business nor to approach it from the industry side. Meetings and convention management is not a pure science, such as mathematics or chemistry, but an *art*. It has some basic required skills and talents; some desirable aptitudes and attitudes. But what makes the field intriguing is the freedom to imagine, create, develop, direct and execute a plan for each and every event, function and meeting.

This book therefore will endeavor to illustrate and exhibit to students the basic skills necessary to successfully work in the meetings "business," while also imparting a "feel" for the creative mental gymnastics and the opportunity to innovate that make meeting and convention management truly an art.

The text was developed as an introduction to the world of meetings, for those who have little or no knowledge of the field, and endeavors to give the student a comprehensive overview. It describes various kinds of meetings and some of the people and places involved in meetings. Through this overview, I hope to illustrate the hundreds of potential jobs available in the meetings business and those companies who work with and service the meetings industry; jobs which are intriguing, rewarding and monetarily satisfying.

Every business seems to have its own jargon. To help familiarize you with the terminology used in these chapters, there is included a glossary of terms. If you do not understand a word or phrase used in the text, look in the glossary for an explanation.

To enhance the readability of the text as well as to illustrate the "real world" of meeting management, I have included a few stories of actual incidents told by participants in various facets of the meetings and conventions business. These are true stories of some of the events in planning meetings, which have tested the creativity, sense of humor, equanimity and above all the professionalism of the people involved. At any gathering of meeting professionals, some of the most enjoyable moments are those times when each tries to "top" the others with tales of potential or actual disasters which have befallen them in this business of structuring and supervising meetings. It is also one of the best sources of continuing education to hear the solutions and incredibly resourceful reactions some of these "pros" employ.

For obvious reasons, some of the contributors of these stories have elected to remain anonymous — no one wants errors, mistakes or near-disasters made public. However, in those cases I have indicated the type of company involved and the position of the person writing the tale.

I hope that use of this text will encourage students to continue to seek out additional education in the field and to ultimately create their own niche in the industry — an industry which can be both intellectually and monetarily rewarding, while remaining an intriguing and joyous way to make a living.

Now, read, learn and *enjoy* — isn't that really what education is all about?

M.L. Weirich
Meeting Management Consultant

 # ACKNOWLEDGMENTS

My sincere and personal thank you to all of those people who contributed to this text, for both their gift of written knowledge and their encouragement of my efforts. A special thank you to Camille Stallings, Hospitality Department Chair at Pima Community College, Tucson, AZ; Phyllis Fetter, Director of Marketing and Sales at Westward Look Resort in Tucson, AZ; Marti Lorenzen, Manager, Internal Communications, Motorola Corporation, in Scottsdale, AZ; and Dr. H. Robert and Mrs. Jimette K. Baker, of HRB Arabians, Tucson, AZ.

I appreciate the contributions of Mark Mitchell, CPA, Managing Partner, Henry & Horne, Tucson, AZ; Charlotte St. Martin, Regional Vice President, Loews Hotels, Dallas, TX; Marilyn Reschmann, President of Ambiance Decorating, Tucson, AZ; and a sincere and heartfelt "thanks" to the many others whose advice and information I found invaluable, including the editors of Delmar Publishers Inc., particularly Mary McGarry, my senior editor and mentor in this endeavor. The reviewers of my manuscript and proposal deserve special mention: Sharon Giroux, University of Wisconsin-Stout, Menomonie, WI; Barney Klecker, Normandale Community College, Bloomington, MN; Anthony Strianese, Schenectady County Community College, Schenectady, NY; Diane Schaefer, Delgado Community College, New Orleans, LA; David Howell, Niagara University, Niagara Falls, NY.

 **1**

WHAT ARE MEETINGS?

OBJECTIVES

After reading this chapter, you will be able:

❑   To trace the history and evolution of the meetings industry
❑   To describe the beginnings of meeting management as a profession
❑   To define some of the terminology used to indicate various types of meetings

Throughout history, there have been numerous reasons for people to gather together or to meet. The cave men converged on a single hunting ground to kill game; women met in the fields to gather grain; Caesar gathered his military officers together for strategic planning; the mythical King Arthur assembled the Knights of the Round Table to plan the future of Camelot; these are examples of the earliest forms of meetings.

Only in the last thirty years or so have the multifaceted gatherings called "meetings" become a formalized industry. As meetings and the industries they serve become more complex, the need for specially trained professional planners becomes more evident.

It will be the purpose of this chapter to examine the anatomy of several kinds of meetings, from the skeleton of their purpose to the musculature of their structures, through their internal working mechanisms and concluding with a diagnosis of their differences. To do this, we have defined various words, which describe meetings, and have indicated some of the similarities and differences in these types of meetings.

THE EVOLUTION OF THE MEETINGS INDUSTRY

Until the 1960s, meetings were called by corporate or association executives, with the mechanics of putting together a simplistic program, the reservation of hotel space and the arrangement of a luncheon or dinner falling to a middle management executive or to the executive secretary of the "boss." Meetings were not as numerous nor as formalized and complex as they have become in more recent years. There were not as many people attending so many conferences, workshops, seminars or conventions with such complex legal ramifications, sophisticated audio/visuals (A/V), complicated tax considerations or immense budgetary expenditures.

Today, the over 950,000 meetings and conventions plus approximately 9,500 trade shows, held each year by organizations and corporations of the United States, represent an expenditure of an estimated $34.6 billion and an attendance of over 71.2 million persons. And this figure does not count the approximately 15 million unregistered spouses and children who enjoyed staying in the hotels and taking in the sites and the cities' attractions as a fringe benefit of meetings and conventions. Some industry experts estimate that in 1988 the total economic impact of this business of meetings, conventions and trade shows reached nearly $50 billion dollars, plus the personal spending of the delegates.

As meetings became an integral part of business and industry, corporate America began to understand their value and to comprehend that a meeting is a monetary investment expected to pay concrete dividends. As with any profit center, the operation of meetings now came within the purview of management. The business of putting together meetings, supervising their on-site operation and analyzing and evaluating their return to the company demanded more professional supervision. Thus meeting and convention planning became a formal position within the corporate structure, and the position of Meeting and Convention Manager was created.

Fig. 1–1. A convention general session in the Grand Ballroom, Loew's Anatole Hotel, Dallas, Texas.

FAUX PAS BY A NON-PRO

By: Marguerite Weirich
Meeting Consultant

Meeting planning certainly wasn't a recognized career or job description in the early to middle '50s. There may have been some people at that time who planned meetings for a living. But, if there were I didn't know about them. At the time, I worked as Executive Assistant to the President/Chairman of the Board of a chemical manufacturing company. We were mainly involved at that time in cosmetic chemistry, and thus were members of a number of industry associations. My boss, being the kind of man who couldn't say "no!" was often drafted to chair one meeting or charity drive or another. Being "the boss," he always delegated the duty down to me — this was many years before I ever dreamed of being in the business of running meetings.

I shall always remember the first time I was elected to set up all arrangements for one of the local major chemical association meetings. "This is a piece of cake!" I thought. "It will be fun and all I have to do is talk to the hotel people and let them do all of the work!" While this was partially true, I didn't know that whoever *plans* the meeting should ultimately be in control and is responsible for all decisions.

This all happened in the Chicago area, and I called the reputable and excellent Drake Hotel. I arranged for sleeping rooms for all of the out of town reps at a full undiscounted rate (I didn't know that special rates were offered for meetings.) I requested the kinds of meeting rooms we would need and obtained them at minimal *rates* (I didn't know that they could have been had for free). Murphy's Law was really operating. I met with the Banquet Sales person and we set up a scrumptious luncheon for the first session, consisting of a Hawaiian Ham Steak with all the trimmings (I hadn't realized that the predominant number of guests expected were Jewish, and because of religious restrictions, did not eat ham!)

The entire set-up for the meeting seemed to go this way, even though it sounds preposterous that one person could make so many errors! I managed! And at no time did I feel it expedient to run these "superb" plans by the boss or anyone else. This was my first lesson in meeting management; I really didn't know what I was doing. I retained my job only because I had a boss who was both understanding and empathetic. We made some adjustments, which were exceedingly expensive, and the meeting did go on.

From that point forward, I was much less confident that I knew all of the answers. I arranged a great many meetings after that: charity balls, fund-raising auctions, social dinner parties, business get-togethers. And, I might add, successfully, but I had learned the best lesson a potential meeting planner can learn: Experience is the best teacher *and* run your plans by someone who has done it before if you don't have the experience yourself! *Get help!*

Persons arranging meetings and conventions today have a great advantage, in that meeting planning has become a profession. There are schools at which to get the basic education and there are many, many professionals out there who will assist you if you ask.

Definitions

Let's look at some of the kinds of get-togethers that make up this business of meetings, their similarities and differences.

Meeting. A *meeting* may be defined as the coming together of a group of people with similar interests to accomplish some predetermined goals or purposes.

The "group of people" may be employees of a single company, members of the same association or participants in similar businesses. Their "similar interests" mean only that there must be some common strand pulling persons from diverse groups to attend the same meeting. All attendees may be stamp collectors at a philatelic meeting; sales people for one company; users of the same type of computer; members of a single religious persuasion; executives with the same position for different companies or associations (for example, meeting managers); franchise operators for a single product; et al. It is evident, therefore, that attendees may be from a variety of backgrounds, geographical areas, ages or sexes, who have come together because of a common interest.

To "accomplish some predetermined goals" indicates that all of these diverse individuals have attended a particular meeting to learn more about their common subject of interest; to be motivated to sell more for their companies; to socialize with their peers from other areas; to promote a piece of legislation which may impact on all members of a certain association; or to promote a new product. The predetermined goals can be as varied as the types of meetings which are held.

The term "meeting" is so generic as to indicate almost all types of get-togethers. There are some more specific terms to delineate or describe the many types of meetings. Let us look at some of the terminology commonly used, as defined by Webster.[1]

Seminar. "Seminar, n. A group of advanced students studying under a professor with each doing original research and exchanging results through reports and discussions; a course of study; a meeting for giving and discussing information."

Because of the exchange of information and attendee participation, seminars must by their very nature be smaller meetings. Most seminars are on very specific subjects, and conducted by recognized experts in the field and are attended by persons interested in the subject matter and who are willing to pay the required fee

---

[1] *Webster's New Collegiate Dictionary;* G. & C. Merriam & Co., 1980.

to attend and obtain the knowledge exchanged. There are usually questions and discussion from the floor as well as the expert presentation and therefore participation by attendees in a learning process.

Look in your local newspaper—frequently in the business section—to observe the proliferation of seminars being offered in today's market. You'll see advertisements for seminars on: Investments; How to Avoid Probate; Stress Management; Time Management; How to Handle Your Teenage Children; Obedience Training Your Pet; Entrepreneurship—How to Start Your Own Business. It seems there is a seminar offered on every phase of life or business. Direct mail addressed to an individual or even to "resident," is another favorite tool of some seminar marketers.

Workshop. "A usually brief, intensive educational program for a relatively small group of people in a given field that emphasizes participation in problem-solving efforts." While a Seminar has an expert in the field to present information for discussion, a workshop is a group of people in the field getting together to solve a problem or situation. For instance, a manufacturing plant finds that its production quotas are not being met. Management might very well pull together all of the executives and supervisors responsible for production to discuss the reasons for the drop in productivity and to seek solutions to the problem. In getting together the personnel involved with supervising production, the discussions reveal that the problem is attributable to a single shift in the plant. Perhaps there is assembly line resistance to a change in a foreman on a specific shift. The problem then becomes how to encourage employee cooperation and lift employee morale in that particular area. The group goes on to find solutions to the problem. This then was a workshop.

Conference. "A formal interchange of views; a meeting of two or more persons for discussing matters of common concern." We see that a conference implies participation, consultation and interchange of ideas by all attendees: a give and take of ideas and opinions. For these reasons, a conference must of necessity remain a small gathering, allowing for mutual participation in the process of idea exchange. Thus, we have a conference table, a work table around which a group of people may gather to confer.

For example, an association executive feels that in addition to active and associate memberships his association would benefit greatly from a student membership. He calls a conference of the association's Executive Committee. The Membership Vice-President objects to a student membership on the grounds that servicing another group, not directly engaged in the business of the association, would require more manpower, paperwork and supervision than the association can spare, while not producing a commensurate increase in membership revenues, since student members usually pay only nominal dues. The Executive Director points out that a student membership encourages active participation of students in association meetings and activities, thus increasing potential membership, building a basis for future strengthening of the association and creating a potential labor pool for the businesses in the association. Other concerned Vice Presidents express their thoughts on the subject. Thus we see that this meeting was a true conference requiring consultation, participation and discussion by all attendees. This group of people is discussing the proposal at hand, exchanging thoughts on the subject and providing food for thought to each other. They may reach a decision at this conference, or they may simply expose the group to the various ramifications of the proposal, to be decided at some future date.

Clinic. "A group meeting devoted to the analysis and solution of concrete problems, or to the acquiring of specific skills or knowledge in a particular field." Here the determining criteria seem to be "analysis and solution" of "concrete problems." For instance, meeting planners frequently schedule golf clinics as an extracurricular activity for their attendees. These clinics employ a golf pro to work with a group on a practice tee, to analyze each attendee's problem shots, to advise how to correct bad habits within their swing and, in general, to improve their game of golf. This clinic has a definite goal in analyzing the concrete problems of each participant, suggesting solutions and assisting every one to improve their specific skills.

Retreat. "A period of group withdrawal for prayer, meditation, study and instruction under a director." While this particular nomenclature is often used when referring to religious retreats, it too is employed to delineate a very specific type of meeting in the corporate, association or educational world. A retreat may be beneficial when an organization's employees are under severe pressure or stress and facing burnout. A corporation might call all top management personnel to an "off-the-beaten track" location, where privacy and quiet can be assured. The retreat usually is a mix of business and relaxation, without telephones or normal business interruptions. In addition to discussing and perhaps solving those problems causing stress, the group as a whole, or individually, might be counseled by a psychologist on methods of learning to personally handle stress and pressure. In addition to instruction and discussion, a retreat usually provides some time for quiet contemplation, outdoor walks or even quiet group activities. The entire atmosphere is one of calm serenity, actively promoting the idea of a complete change of scenery.

Convention. Although Webster says that a convention is "an assembly of persons met for a common purpose," in today's usage a convention usually consists of a dual meeting encompassing both the business for which the convention is called *and* a social interchange between attendees. Conventions are often held annually, calling for more intensive planning due to their larger size and the fact that the Meeting Manager must organize not only the business of the convention, but also an extensive social program. This can mean creation of cocktail parties, theme-dinner parties, tours and often spouse and children's activities, as well as participatory sports: mini-olympics, golf tournaments, tennis matches, skeet and trap shoots or perhaps swimming contests and games. With the inclusion of spouses, partners and sometimes children, the organizational process becomes more detailed and intricate, as the planner must include programs and/or tours and excursions for the spouses and appropriate entertainment and supervision for children.

Conclave. "Conclave: A private meeting or secret assembly." This is a less frequently used term, perhaps because it implies secrecy. The gathering it is most apt to bring to mind is a very unique one—the gathering of Cardinals of the Roman Catholic Church for the purpose of electing a new Pope. The Cardinals meet in conclave, a totally secret meeting when all participants are actually locked in the Sistine Chapel. The term, however, may be applied to any totally private and secret meeting. Another such example might be a corporate Board of Directors conclave to discuss the crisis impending due to a take-over attempt. These are both meetings with serious purpose, held in total privacy and thus termed a "conclave."

Assembly.   "A company of persons gathered for deliberation and legislation, worship or entertainment; a legislative body." We commonly hear this word refer to the gathering of representatives to a state legislature, but another more familiar usage is the calling together of a student body in school, particularly high school assemblies.

Class.   We frequently forget that a class is "a body of students meeting regularly to study the same subject." Thus even this group learning about "meetings and conventions" is actually a meeting of sorts.

Congress.   The term "congress" is most commonly used in describing international events, particularly in Europe. A congress is similar to a convention and is often used in scientific circles, particularly in medicine. Only here in the United States is it used to designate a legislative group.

Press Conference.   A very specialized kind of gathering where members of the media (newspapers, magazines, radio, television) are invited to a gathering to be given information on some new event or development. Corporations call press conferences to tell the press about a new product, about new officers or any other event which can be considered news. The purpose of the press conference is not only to inform the public, but to obtain unpaid publicity for the corporation or organization. The press conference is of a specific duration, at a precise time of day. Press kits of basic information must be prepared beforehand, containing background information, stock photos, brochures and of course the "press release" to be specifically discussed at the press conference. If the press conference is held as an event within another meeting, the meeting planner must often provide a press room equipped with computers, typewriters, fax machines, teletype machines, photocopiers and any other office equipment indicated. For television crews, sufficient and appropriate power and lighting is important; sometimes a satellite dish must be made available for national and international transmission. Therefore, when planning a press conference, it is important to discuss with the invited media representatives just what their needs might be. As with all other meetings, consideration of room size, ventilation, comfort and line-of-sight to the speakers is imperative.

The press conference is most frequently visible in the televised gatherings of press representatives at the White House. Here the President makes a brief speech transmitting some new information to the country and the Press may ask questions of the President after the announcement.

Forum and Symposium.   These two meetings are similar, though the symposium is perhaps the more formal of the two. Both employ discussions led by speakers or

Fig. 1–2. The use of the term *congress* is more prevalent in European countries than in the U.S. Here the Grand Duchy of Luxembourg uses it to promote their tiny nation as a prime meeting destination. (Courtesy of the Grand Duchy of Luxembourg.)

panelists and allow for questions and comments from the floor. There is usually a moderator to lead the process and summarize the business at hand at the end of the meeting. Town meetings are examples of forums.

Lecture.   A lecture may be a part of the program of another type of meeting, or it may be a session unto itself. This is a formal presentation by a single person, generally on a single subject. Questions from the floor may or may not be encouraged.

Panel.   Most of us have attended meetings where a panel of experts with diverse views on the same subject present their ideas in turn, under the direction of a moderator. Questions from the audience are appropriate and requested just prior to a summarization by the moderator.

Trade Show.   Trade shows may also be termed "exhibits" and consist of a series of exhibit booths in which people show their wares, hoping to influence attendees toward ordering or purchasing. The Trade show may be an integral part of another type of meeting, or may be a free-standing event by itself. The types of trade shows and their peculiarities will be discussed in a later chapter, since they actually constitute a specialty within the business of meeting planning.

Incentives.   In addition to these basic divisions or definitions of kinds of meetings, we would be remiss not to mention *incentive* programs. An incentive program is *not* a meeting, *but* many meeting and convention managers are responsible for developing and operating incentives. For this reason we will include them in this chapter.

The word "incentive" denotes "something that incites or has a tendency to incite to determination or action." Programs are developed to encourage employees to increase sales or solve problems within a corporation. Incentive programs begin with the structuring of a contest, by which entrants may win rewards, and culminate with the awarding of the prizes. The prizes or rewards may be in the form of fiscal compensation (money, savings bonds, etc.), products (cars, television sets, compact disc players, etc.) or glamorous trips. These contests are held by organizations for many reasons, the most common of which are:

1.   To increase sales: All sales people are invited to participate and various levels of sales quotas are outlined. Those who produce sales at the top level may win for instance $10,000, or perhaps a two-week trip to the Orient, or even a new car. Those at a secondary level may win $5,000, or a one-week trip to Monte Carlo, or perhaps a pair of all-terrain vehicles. A third level prize may be offered which could award a $1,000 prize, or a weekend in New York City, or a bicycle built for two.
2.   To increase production: The same strategy may apply, with rewards being offered to those responsible.
3.   To improve quality control or solve other problems within the organization

Structuring of the actual contest and determining the mechanics of selecting winners, then promoting participation and monitoring the contest for a specific length

The Call Of The Sea Has Turned Ordinary Men Into Ruthless Opportunists. Try It On Your Employees.

Whether it's your dealers, salespeople or employees, you'll be astonished at how our incentive vacation will transform them. But it's only to be expected. For five years running, *Travel-Holiday* magazine has named Royal Caribbean "world's best cruise line." Our luxurious ships sail to a variety of exciting destinations, (Europe, Alaska, Mexico, Bermuda, the Bahamas, and, of course, the Caribbean) on cruises ranging from three nights to twelve. Perhaps most importantly, we offer a fully staffed incentive sales department. So harness the power of the sea to your company's advantage. Offer a Royal Caribbean incentive vacation.

ROYAL CARIBBEAN ✠ INCENTIVE VACATIONS.

CRUISING THE CARIBBEAN BAHAMAS BERMUDA EUROPE MEXICO AND ALASKA

Ships of Norwegian, Liberian, and Bahamian Registry.

Fig. 1–3. Incentive meeting destinations must be attractive, unique, and even exotic. This ad for Royal Caribbean Cruise Line plays on the idea that employees will try harder to achieve if the incentive is an exotic cruise to any number of destinations on one of their luxurious ships. (Courtesy of Royal Caribbean Cruise Line.)

of time (perhaps as long as a year), is a specialty in itself. The Meeting and Convention Manager usually is brought into the picture to select and operate any trips which are part of the reward. These can be some of the most interesting meetings to operate, since the trip, as a reward, generally carries a fairly large budget.

Incentives are a fast-growing part of the meetings business. According to *Premium Incentive Business* magazine, incentive travel expenditures in 1989 climbed to $5.1 billion in the United States.[2]

❑ *SUMMARY*

While meetings as a social gathering are an old story, the profession of meeting planner is a comparatively new one. Whether planning a conference, convention, conclave, congress, forum, lecture, seminar, symposium, workshop, clinic, retreat, press conference or incentive, the same basic principles apply and the same skills and talents for organization, creativity, flexibility and humor are required.

Meetings come in all forms and sizes, with attendees of all ages, from varying geographical locations and diverse backgrounds, who possess a wide range of interests and reasons for attendance. It takes the ingenuity of a professional planner to organize and supervise the operation of so many varied gatherings; to make them successful and monetarily worthwhile. To the planner, however, the procedures for producing each of the sessions defined above is much the same. The kind of meeting will definitely impact upon the choice of location and site, the kinds of meeting rooms and equipment needed, but the step-by-step organization, preliminary planning and on-site supervision will follow the same general format.

❑ *PROJECTS*

1. List below the kinds of meetings which you or a friend have attended and indicate into which definition they fit, and why.

---

[2] Gralla Publications, *Premium Incentive Business*, Vol. 49 No. 7, pg. 23, July 1990.

2.   Call a local university or college, or some companies in your town, and ask if they hold meetings and do they have a full-time professional meeting planner? Report to the class on how each responded to your questions.

3.   Check your local newspapers and see what kinds of seminars are currently being offered in your area. Notice the variety of their subject matter. Cut out and bring to the next class any ads or promotional items you can find.

4.   Call your local meeting and convention bureau. (If you don't have one call the chamber of commerce.) Ask how many conventions or meetings are held in your city and how many persons attend annually, then report back to the class.

5.   With what trade shows are you familiar? Have you ever attended one in your town? Are there any being advertised in your local newspaper or on your local TV stations right now?

❏ *DISCUSSION QUESTIONS*

1. For how long have corporations and associations recognized meetings as a formalized industry? Prior to that time, how were meetings generally organized?

2. As meetings became "big business," how did corporate America begin to consider meetings?

3. How is the word "meeting" defined?

4. Explain the differences and similarities between a seminar and a workshop.

5. List the differences and similarities between a clinic and a retreat.

6. Why are the terms "assembly," "conclave," and "congress" heard less often than other meeting titles?

7. Explain the differences and similarities between a lecture and a panel presentation.

8. What is Webster's definition of "incentive" and how does that translate into an "incentive program"? Why is it called an "incentive program" and what is the usual involvement of a meeting manager?

9. **What are five major considerations in selecting a destination for an incentive program?**

10. **What skills and talents are mentioned in the Summary as required of meeting planners?**

2

WHAT IS A TRADE SHOW?

OBJECTIVES

After reading this chapter, you will be able:

❑ To illustrate the sophistication and complexity of today's trade shows
❑ To differentiate between the types of trade shows
❑ To demonstrate the responsibility of the planner to creatively develop methods of insuring good traffic flow through exhibit areas

Trade is defined as the business or work in which one regularly engages. A trade show is often called an exhibit and does, indeed, consist of a series of exhibit booths, in which people show the wares and services which they hope to promote to attendees.

Picture an immense room, segmented by brilliant blue draperies, flashes of color, neon lights, video presentations, models in sequined gowns, men and women in business attire and in the aisles, crowds of people of all ages in varied attire strolling and stopping frequently to view the booths. This would be a typical trade show. What is seemingly a random gathering of action and bodies, is in reality a carefully choreographed production. An air of excitement is deliberately created by the exhibit management company and exhibitors are encouraged to present a "show."

A great deal of time, thought, design and money goes into trade show booths. Gone are the days when a company entered an eight-foot draped area, with only a banquet table and a couple of chairs, and set up wares to display! Today's exhibitor hires a commercial designer and artist to create an attention-getting backdrop for a product, many times complete with pulsating laser beams, moving video images, sophisticated audio productions and even live entertainment! We can conclude from the hefty expenditure of monies for these backdrops and booths that "selling" on the trade show floor certainly pays off for the exhibitor. The business of designing and constructing display booths for trade shows has become very big business, involving immense dollar expenditures.

A trade show can be an integral part of a meeting or convention. (Less often, small trade shows are held in conjunction with a seminar or conference or other smaller meeting, but this is the exception rather than the rule.) At other times, the trade show stands on its own, and is considered a "limited" or "public" trade show.

TRADE SHOWS AS A PART OF A MEETING

The trade show or exhibit floor can be a critical part of a convention or meeting. In today's economy, corporations and associations are looking at costs more closely than ever. A bright, innovative meeting manager can contribute even more to the profit of the company or association, by intelligently scheduling a trade show as an important part of the meeting or convention. The trade show is held in conjunction with a convention for several good reasons. The convention meeting manager may very well want to partially underwrite costs of the meeting. By selling exhibit space to suppliers to the industry, the manager can cover the costs of some of the meal functions, the meeting space, the entertainment or other expenses, thus reducing the fee that must be charged to attendees. From the reverse point of view, exhibiting at a trade show allied with a convention, permits the supplier to have

Fig. 2–1. This photo of the trade show floor of the Las Vegas Convention Center is used to promote the city as a meeting destination. The center has over 1.3 million square feet of floor space. (Courtesy of Las Vegas Convention & Visitors Authority.)

access to a great number of potential buyers all in the same location at the same time.

For example, at an international meeting of Meeting Planners International (MPI), a concurrent trade show will have booths representing the tourist bureaus of countries throughout the world, the convention and visitors bureaus of major meeting cities, most of the large hotel chains, resort properties from all over the world who specialize in hosting meetings, companies selling advertising specialties as giveaways for meetings, airlines, bus companies and tour bus operators, journalists from many of the trade publications, organizations who sell various types of convention badges, and many other companies who deal in products of interest to meeting planners.

We have established that the trade show can be profitable to both the meeting manager and the exhibitor; but just how does a meeting planner go about putting together a trade show?

The first consideration must be just why a trade show or exhibit makes sense in conjunction with this particular meeting. The nature of the attendees' affiliations or interests must indicate that they are all interested in products or services in the same general area; there should be enough of these potential customers to benefit the exhibitor; the location of the trade show must be easily accessible and, ideally, directly adjacent to the meeting rooms; sufficient time must be allocated during the meeting for people to attend the trade show—and the meeting planner must encourage such attendance. If these criteria are met, then exhibitor purchase of booth space can contribute substantially to the income or assist in defraying expenses of the meeting.

Once the decision to hold a trade show is made, the planner must compile a list of all of the companies that could possibly profit from the exposure of their products or services to this group of attendees. These must be companies with goods, machines, products or services that these particular attending companies or associations would buy in the daily course of their businesses. From this we can see that the trade show or exhibit must be profitable not only to the company or association, but also to the attendees and to the exhibitors as well.

Logistics

The planner/manager will then get together with a good show booth company to discuss the logistics and costs of setting up booths and any electrical, furnishing and signage services that might be required. The show booth or exhibit company will undoubtedly have preprinted mailout registration materials to be sent to potential exhibitors. While these are excellent and give the required information on booth sizes, furnishings, available power, etc., the manager should incorporate into the packet specific information on why the exhibitors *must* be a part of this particular trade show; point out the advantages to the exhibitor and especially *spell out in detail* who the attendees at the convention will be and just how all attendees will be force-fed into the exhibit areas.

DRAPES DO DROOP

By Jimmette K. Baker, V.P.
Arizona Connection, Inc.

Our Company was an independent meeting management company, acting as meeting planners for a number of corporations and associations on contract. In the course of our regular business we were hired to plan, coordinate and supervise a meeting of the International Association of Goldsmiths. Each of these superb artisans would bring their most prized work for display, and we arranged for a number of their suppliers to participate in a mini-trade-show in conjunction with the meeting.

Since this was an association on a fairly limited budget, we endeavored every way that we could to save expenses for the group. Since setting up 8′ × 10′ exhibit booths, with simple pipe and drape dividers and skirting tables with prepleated skirting, could not be so difficult, we decided to save the expense of a professional exhibit company and rent and set up the booths with our own very experienced set-up crew. However, they had never set up exhibit booths before.

If you have ever put together a child's Christmas toys, with part A fitting into Slot B, etc. etc., then you know that it is not as simple as it looks or sounds. However, we did manage after much trial and error (and entirely too much staff and crew time) to get the pipes fitted into their bases and the cross pieces afixed —now, for the drapes. They threaded neatly onto the pipe, but they were so wrinkled from storage, they *drooped!* The only solution we could devise was to send all of our staff home for their steam irons. Then we plugged in four or five irons at a time (by then it was well past midnight) and ran the steam up and down each drape until the wrinkles disappeared. It was about 2 A.M. when we finished, and the group's "welcoming breakfast" was scheduled in exactly 4½ hours!

On conversation with the exhibit company personnel later, we found that they essentially do the same thing, but they have large steamers made for that purpose, and accomplish the whole job in a matter of minutes. If we had added up the total cost of our staff time in setting up those booths, it would certainly have been less expensive to hire an exhibit company to do the entire job in the first place.

With each meeting or event, even the experienced planner learns something new!

Traffic Flow

Proper management of the traffic flow through the trade show exhibits is critical to its success, and increases the meeting planner's chance of continuing to attract exhibitors for future meetings by strengthening the meeting manager's credibility with exhibitors. There are many ways to create this traffic flow, for example:

1. Give all meeting attendees a card with a block indicating each numbered booth in the show. Attendees who have all of these blocks paper-punched by the exhibitors may have their cards deposited into a drawing for a major prize (or prizes). The prize has to be large enough and attractive enough to make attendees want to visit all booths in order to be eligible. A car, substantial amount of cash, or computer and printer, are some examples, and depending upon the type of show, may even be a product being displayed, which an exhibitor might be willing to donate.
2. Coffee breaks can be held in the center of the exhibit area. Each time a session of the meeting or convention breaks, the attendees are encouraged to pass through the exhibit booths to get to the refreshment area.
3. A cocktail party can be held on the exhibit floor; perhaps even sponsored (paid for) by the exhibitors. Free refreshments will always draw a crowd at a meeting, and while circulating during the cocktail party, the attendees are continually passing exhibit booths.

Encouraging Attendance

Each meeting/show planner strives to come up with new, different and creative ways to encourage attendance at the exhibit booths. Exhibitors themselves try to use some lure to entice attendees to their particular booth. Most have giveaways (called advertising specialties) such as pens or pencils, golf tees, lighters, coffee mugs, baseball caps, visors and etc., all bearing their corporate name and/or logo. These serve a dual purpose: Attendees will tell others where they got that particular giveaway, thus encouraging additional people to visit the booth; and those who take home some item with a corporate name or logo will be reminded of that company again and again in the future. For this reason, exhibitors put a great deal of time and money into devising a giveaway that is unique and useful, and will attract attention.

Another gambit used by exhibitors is the participatory game. Most people love to compete, so by setting up a golf-putting hole, a dart board, jars of gumballs (to guess the number contained), archery targets or some other competitive endeavor, the exhibitor assures that people will be drawn to his or her booth. Again, the prizes must be something for which every attendee will wish to compete or perhaps that every competitor wins. Some booth-lures used by exhibitors are unique rather than competitive: a polaroid camera with each attendee's picture taken with a hired celebrity; or perhaps not even a celebrity—one western theme park at a travel show took pictures of all attendees with a company sales manager costumed as a prospector with a full-pack donkey. Nearly everyone likes to have their picture taken, and it's better still if they can take that picture home. The gimmicks used are as varied as the companies exhibiting.

Advantages of Trade Shows/Exhibits

Let's look again at the advantages of a trade show/exhibit to all concerned:

1. Through the sale of exhibit space, the meeting planner for a corporation has been able to pay for the meeting coffee breaks, one cocktail party and one luncheon. By figuring the per-booth cost of renting the exhibit hall, hiring the exhibit booth company to set up booths, powering and lighting each booth, and supplying a minimum of furniture (then marking up that figure sufficiently to cover the coffee breaks, cocktail party and one luncheon), the planner has reduced the amount of money that meeting attendees must be charged.
2. Meeting attendees pay a lesser rate for the meeting registration when part of the basic costs have been covered by exhibitors to the trade show portion. Also, attendees will have an opportunity to see the newest in equipment, supplies and/or services being offered by suppliers to their industry, and to become acquainted with new vendors.
3. Exhibitors have a chance to exhibit their wares and services to their current and potential customers all in a single location at one time. Visualize the savings in time and travel expenses derived from working a trade show vs. flying to each of these customer's places of business in order to sell products.

The key to any successful trade show allied with a meeting or convention is that the meeting planner *knows* how to produce a good exhibit. Exhibitors invited and induced to participate must have a direct connection to the types of businesses represented at the meeting. Exhibit space must be clean, attractive and well-planned, and be provided with good light, power and ventilation, with traffic patterns well-delineated. Attendees must be induced into the exhibit areas and encouraged to visit each booth to give exhibitors a chance to sell their wares. With good planning, the show should be a win-win situation for everyone.

THE LIMITED TRADE SHOW

Trade show management can be a career in itself. Many trade shows stand alone and are not held in conjunction with meetings and conventions.

One such show is the limited trade show. This is an exhibit in which the product or service is directed at a special segment of people and the show is produced for these people on an "invitation only" basis. Attendance is thus controlled and *limited* strictly to those persons who are serious prospective buyers.

This control may also be exercised by publicly inviting only those persons who work for certain firms, or are in certain industries which use the exhibitors' wares.

Admission then is by business card or other proof that the attendee is employed in the targeted industry.

There are many *user groups,* an alliance of people all of whom have purchased and are using a particular product (such as a certain brand of computer or a particular car). If you are the company selling that computer or that car, or if you sell computer programs for that machine or accessories for that car, what better group to invite to a limited trade show than the user group for your product? These groups may be invited through their user association, through mailing lists purchased from companies who compile such lists or through a publication circulated in the trade.

Certain countries, or regions of a country, or even a single destination city, hold limited trade shows for licensed travel agents only. The governmental agency (national, state or city), the hotels and resorts, many restaurants, visitor attractions, et al, all combine monies and energies to produce a trade show, in order to acquaint travel agencies with the locale so that they might be interested in introducing the destination to their clients for vacations or meetings. One of the largest of these was produced by the United States in cooperation with private industry to convince foreign wholesalers and travel agents to sell destinations in the United States to their clients. This was the DATO (Discover America Travel Organization) Pow Wow, which has since been renamed, Travel Industry Association Pow Wow.

One of the largest limited trade shows is the Premium and Incentive Show, now held in Chicago's McCormick Place each fall. This group exhibits all of the advertising specialties used by exhibitors at other shows and the premium and incentive gifts used in incentive programs or as general business gifts. These gifts may also include incentive travel destinations or the use of airlines or bus/tour companies.

The aforementioned are all examples of the limited trade show. Attendance is limited by the producers.

THE PUBLIC TRADE SHOW

Most people have at one time or another attended a new car show, a boat and travel show, a mobile home show or the like. The largest and fastest growing segment of the trade show business is the public show. As the name implies, this exhibit is open to the general public, and as such is widely advertised through both the print and television media. The success of these shows is measured by the vast numbers of persons who will pay an admission fee to see a large display of some product or item in which they are interested. Other than cars, boats and mobile homes, some of the most popular shows exhibit recreation vehicles, vacation destinations, housewares, jewelry—gems and minerals—coins, stamps and, of course, computers.

These very large trade shows are produced by professional show managers and producers. An admission is charged to the general public to see what's new. If the trade show is competently produced it can truly be an entertainment extravaganza! The attraction for the various exhibitors is the large numbers of people to whom they are able to show their products, all in a single location.

❑ *SUMMARY*

Therefore, we see that trade shows are multipurpose exhibits. They make money for the producer, whether a professional show promoter or the meeting planner of a convention; they enable the attendee to view new, innovative products from many suppliers, in a single area; and they provide access to vast numbers of potential customers for the exhibitor. Properly run trade shows represent a win-win situation for both the exhibitors and attendees.

❑ *PROJECTS*

1. List the trade shows which you have attended and indicate into which category they fit. Now add to that list all of the trade shows you might have noticed in local newspapers, on TV or heard about from friends.

2. Call some hotels or resorts in your community and inquire as to whether they cater to groups who have exhibits or trade shows connected to their meetings. If so, ask if you might visit the hotel and see the exhibit space. While at the hotel, note the proximity of exhibit or show space to the meeting rooms. Ask the hotel if they will give you a list of the companies or associations who will be holding exhibits in their hotel this year. Bring the list to class to discuss the kinds of meetings/exhibits that will be held.

3. Check the telephone book to see if you have any exhibit companies in your area, and call and ask if you might have copies of their promotional brochures or printed materials. Or you might call your local chapter of HSMA (Hotel Sales and Marketing Association), and ask with which local exhibit companies they do business.

4. Call a local advertising specialties company and ask if you might have a copy of their catalogue. Notice all of the items that might be used as giveaways in a trade-show booth.

5. If there is a show management company in your locale, call and ask if you might have a copy of their promotional brochure. Notice the kinds of services they advertise and what they are offering to their customers.

6. If you have a community center or convention center in your town, visit and notice the variety of possible exhibit spaces. Generally, they will have one large arena or exhibit hall and several smaller locations. Again, ask for any literature they might have.

❑ *DISCUSSION QUESTIONS*

1. What is meant by the word "trade"? How does this translate into the term "trade show"?

2. How does one go about setting up a booth for a trade show? What kinds of things are involved in an exhibit?

3. What are the three basic kinds of trade shows named in the text?

4. Why does a corporate meeting planner want to hold a trade show or exhibit in conjunction with a large convention?

5. Name the first thing to be considered by the planner when thinking about holding an exhibit with a meeting.

6. Once a decision is made to hold a trade show in conjunction with a meeting, what is the next step?

7. Explain the function of an exhibit company (also termed show booth company).

8. Why is management of traffic flow through trade-show exhibits critical to its success? Discuss some of the ways to control and direct this traffic.

9. **Explain some of the ways exhibitors strive to pull traffic to their booths.**

10. **List the advantages of a trade show with a convention to:**
    a. The meeting planner's company or association

    b. The meeting attendees

    c. The exhibitors

11. **How does a limited trade show differ from one held in conjunction with a meeting? Describe some possible kinds of limited shows.**

12. How does a public trade show differ from the prior two? Discuss some of the public shows you have heard about.

13. What is the attraction for various exhibitors to be part of a public trade show?

3

WHY ARE MEETINGS HELD?

OBJECTIVES

After reading this chapter, you will be able:

❏ To show why meetings must have an expressed reason for being held
❏ To demonstrate the variety of rationales for calling meetings
❏ To briefly discuss the idea of meetings as a social phenomenon

In previous chapters, we have discussed the anatomies of various kinds of meetings and trade shows. In so doing, we have talked about the terminology used to describe meetings. There is still another method of defining the types of meetings, and that is by the reasons for which they are held. The idea has often been expressed that perhaps too many meetings are held with insufficient reason, wasting both corporate and association funds and the valuable time of those who must attend. The conclusion then is obvious that every meeting must have a concrete reason.

Therefore, we pose our next question: *why?* Why do all of these people get together? For what reasons do corporations or associations fund meetings and why do the attendees go?

Every meeting *must have a concrete reason.* Every time an executive decides to call a group together, whether it be for a simple project discussion or to establish major corporate policy, there has to be a reason! When a meeting is being planned and the person responsible is asked what is to be accomplished by that meeting, if a specific goal or objective cannot be delineated, the meeting manager should reply, "Then don't hold the meeting!"

There are some *very good, solid reasons to hold meetings.* These might include a simple get-together of department heads to discuss the potential establishment of a new position, a conference to discuss the new budget projections which are due or the introduction of a new product line to the sales department. Whatever the goal someone wishes to accomplish, it should be a logical reason to call people from their busy schedules and ask them to spend time for a specific cause.

From this *reason* or *cause* the meeting manager can derive the *type* of meeting to be constructed, the site where it should be held, the persons who should attend, the speakers who should be invited to participate, the amount of money that should be spent to accomplish the task, and whether or not any time and/or money should be spent on entertainment or leisure activities. From this you can see that the *why,* or reason, for the meeting is *all important* to the planner. Let's look at some of the reasons why meetings are held and how this will influence the planner's task.

SALES MEETING

Most product-oriented companies hold semiregular sales meetings to motivate their sales force, to set goals for the season, to reward past performance or perhaps to instruct salespersons about a new product or service.

These meetings are working sessions, with programs usually constructed by the Director of Sales or Marketing and conducted only for those people directly involved with the promotion of a product or service. Depending upon the purpose and the length of the program itself, the meeting may range in length from one hour to several days.

Since attendance is mandatory, all costs are paid by the company for transportation to and from the site, housing, food and direct costs of the meeting itself. Spouses and children are usually not invited. The planner must then seek out a meeting site with a working atmosphere for this is not a meeting at which the participants will be entertained. Major considerations should include the site, meals and, most importantly, the program and speakers.

For instance, a local automobile dealer just prior to receiving the new model cars for the coming year, may take all of the sales force to a nearby hotel to introduce them to these new models. An engineer from the manufacturing company may be asked to attend in order to present in detail the advantages of the new engine modifications and any other technical amenities of which the salespeople must have knowledge. The sales manager will present the dealership's marketing plan for the coming year, and discuss pricing, commissions, required down payments and financing as it applies to this local dealership. The sales force will also be given copies of the brochures, advertisements or other selling tools to be utilized. The automobile dealer will, of course, pay all costs attendent to this annual sales meeting.

STOCKHOLDER MEETING

Corporations are mandated by their articles of incorporation to hold at least one stockholder meeting per year, and many do so quarterly. These meetings are called to inform the investors as to the status of the business, to report on plans for the coming year, to discuss any problems, or perhaps to elect additional members to the Board or new corporate executives.

Generally, stockholders attend these meetings at their own expense. Others may simply send in a proxy form permitting the corporate officers to act on their behalf, in order to acquire a voting quorum, thus eliminating the necessity for

e hammered out our business plan,
turned our sales force into tigers, showed our clients
a whale of a time, then slipped away
for dinner on the bay.

Just another beautiful day in ***San Diego.***

Fig. 3-1. San Diego uses the nostalgia of a paddlewheeler to draw attention to their availability as a destination for sales meetings. (Courtesy of San Diego Convention & Visitors Bureau.)

personal attendance. However, should a corporation be in the midst of a merger plan or a "takeover" bid by another company, the attendance at the annual stockholders meeting can increase considerably. Everyone who is an investor may want to attend to voice their opinions on the upcoming changes in the corporation. The meeting planner, aware of this possibility, will want to look very hard at potential meeting sites, to be sure that they can handle a larger number should attendance suddenly boom.

Since the stockholders meeting represents attendance by people who have invested money in the company, it should be structured carefully. Site selection should be meticulously orchestrated. Of course the meeting manager wants to select a fine property to illustrate concern for the stature and the opinions of the investors and to demonstrate the success of the corporation; however, the site cannot appear to be foolishly luxurious or unnecessarily costly. Here the planner must walk a fine line.

MANAGEMENT MEETING

Top corporate officers often find it advantageous to gather together, away from the place of business, to consider the "state of the business," to discuss successes and problems, to construct a plan for future growth, or sometimes to have a free-wheeling, brainstorming session to arrive at diversification, new products or services, or simply a new slant on present business.

This type of meeting is generally held at a more secluded, quiet location where the group can be more or less encapsulated, without distractions. Of course all accommodations are generally first class and the company pays the bill. Again, this is not a meeting where entertainment is primary, but perhaps a round of golf or a set of tennis will refresh participants for the next session.

BOARD OF DIRECTORS MEETING

These are generally faced by every meeting planner. While they are usually comparatively small meetings, they are nonetheless important to both the company and the planner.

Very often the Board of Directors will meet casually over lunch or dinner at a local club, hotel or restaurant, but sometimes the meeting will be a two or three day session at a more exotic destination. Here, the planner must carefully ascertain just what the corporate management has in mind. What image do they wish to project to the Board? Then, through other executives of the corporation, from records of past meetings, or from the secretaries of the board members themselves, the planner should ascertain some of the members' primary likes and dislikes about locations, food preferences and outside activities or interests. It is important to know whether each individual member will be impressed by being picked up at the airport in a Rolls Royce Silver Cloud with a uniformed driver or dismayed by this gesture, preferring to be met by a member of the executive staff in an ordinary sedan.

Fig. 3–2. An elegantly appointed board meeting room set-up at Loew's Santa Monica, California. The polished marble conference table, comfortable leather chairs, subdued appointments on the walls and around the room, plus excellent lighting, are all conductive to high-level discussions.

Another important consideration is budget. Just how much does management wish to spend on this board meeting? From all of these considerations, the planner can begin to make decisions on site, meals, amenities and leisure activities. The business program and its participants will be dictated by the reason for the meeting.

As in all meetings, one of the secrets of success is: *know as much as possible about your attendees.* This may entail a little detective work before the meeting, but it will pay off in the enhancement of the planner's reputation as a professional.

 THE LURE OF LOOT

**Anonymous
Corporate Meeting Planner**

While handling a sales meeting for a large major corporation, the attendees of which consisted of 150 outgoing, lively, independent and highly successful sales types, I learned not only the value of "offering the carrot" to induce groups of people to behave in the fashion which you expect of them, but also to *know* our attendees and choose the site for a meeting with great care and in consideration of the kind of persons attending.

This was a very intense, compacted course on "Overcoming the Objections of Potential Clients." The company had allocated a very large budget to hire the most prestigious sales presenters in the country and elected to fly all of their salespeople to a luxury resort/casino in Las Vegas, Nevada by private jets. I felt that the program of work, the sophisticated audio/visuals, the exquisitely produced four-color handouts, the sumptuous meals and the extracurricular private shows we had scheduled in the three-day meeting were first-rate as well. We were in one of the most exciting cities in the country, we were ready for the meeting and all was well with the world!

However, I hadn't counted on human nature. Although the Company was paying the entire tab, and these were some of the most successful, serious-minded salespeople around, the click of the dice and the whirring of the wheel were just too much. During the first break of the first meeting on the first day, about one-third of our attendees disappeared. After lunch on that day we lost another 40 or 50, which meant that the afternoon session held less than 100 persons. As the planner of record, I felt that I must do something to assure better attendance for the balance of the meeting. Evidently, our "super-duper" programming, "name" speakers and even the innovative food and beverages served at our breaks were not enough with this group of "free spirits."

Obviously, because of their top-of-the-line reputations as salespeople, these attendees weren't worried about their jobs or the reaction of their Directors of Sales/Marketing to their defections from the meetings. So, the solution for this particular type had to be of the same ilk as the siren song which had lured them away in the first place.

Bright and early at breakfast the morning of the second day, we announced an attendance prize. All attendees were asked to drop their business cards in a champagne punch bowl at the rear of the meeting room for each and every session, of which there were four more. At the conclusion of each session we would draw one business card and that person would win an all-expense three day stay-over, including $200 in gambling chips, at the Las Vegas property. Then, all cards would remain in the bowl and at the end of the total meeting we would draw one card and that lucky person would win an all-expense-paid one week trip for two, plus $500 in gambling chips, to a prestigious Monaco resort/casino.

We had decided to fight fire with fire, and it worked! For the balance of the meeting we had 100% attendance. The "lure of the loot" was the "carrot" that these particular attendees needed.

As a footnote: This *was* an expensive solution, but the program material was important to the company! We held the costs down somewhat by negotiating with the Las Vegas resort for special rates for our giveaway, and by dealing with both the international airline and the Monaco resort for attractive rates. In all cases, these were hotel companies and an airline with which the company did a great deal of business, so they were amenable to giving us a break. It also afforded the management and the planner an educational experience, in that it taught us to *know* our attendees and their potential reactions to the site being selected.

ASSOCIATION ANNUAL MEETING

Members of a single profession or industry often belong to an association with local chapters and a national or international membership organization. In addition to monthly meetings of the local chapter, and perhaps quarterly meetings of the chapters within a region or state, there will be an annual meeting of *all* members. These association meetings can range from a hundred or so attendees to several thousands of persons. Generally, these annual meetings are held to elect new officers, review legislation impacting on that particular profession or industry, exchange information and ideas, and renew old and make new acquaintances.

Often, with this type of meeting the national organization's planner will be working with a committee of the local host chapter (that is, the chapter of the organization located in the city where the annual national meeting will be held). Attendees will be paying their own expenses (or their individual companies may pick up the tab) and therefore attendance promotion becomes a major factor in the early planning stages. An annual association convention will require attractive leisure activities as well as educational sessions and a solid basic program. The meeting may well require multiple hotels of different price levels because of the meeting's sheer size and diversity of attendees. This will then entail the planning staff to handle the housing of attendees.

EDUCATIONAL/TRAINING MEETING

This particular brand of meeting is truly a specialty. There is even an association of people who plan such sessions, ASTD (American Society of Training Directors). The planner for these types of meetings often has a background in education.

There are several types of educational/training meetings:

New Employee Orientation

This meeting is generally a "command performance" to the new employee. When someone is hired, the truly professional personnel executive will see that he/she is properly introduced to the company, told the overview of the corporate purpose and structure, shown a copy of the organization chart, advised of the company's policies and rules, and then is probably assigned to a trainer for his/her particular department or division for more specific instruction in the job.

Because of its very nature, this type of meeting is usually held at the place of business. The purpose is to introduce the new employee to the company and what better place to accomplish this than at the company office or plant? The chief speaker at this meeting is usually someone in an executive capacity in the personnel or human resources department. Therefore, two of your major costs are already decided: free meeting space and a speaker already on the company payroll.

If the company is large enough that the orientation runs for a full day, the company will undoubtedly have to pay for lunch. This may be done by an in-house food service (company cafeteria) or may be catered by an outside contractor. After a group luncheon, the new personnel will usually be divided into groups by the departments in which they will work. This will then call for smaller meeting rooms for each group (these are called "break out" rooms), each of these groups will be instructed by an executive from the department to which they are being assigned. Again, these speakers are free because they already work for the company.

For meeting planners, this is one of the easiest meetings to plan because it is inexpensive and simple, and the program itself is constructed by the Human Resources Department together with the departments involved.

On-Going Training Programs

Most sizeable companies plan continuing, in-house educational programs for their employees. This will reinforce the original instruction they receive, instruct in new policies or procedures, bring employees up-to-date on any changes or innovations, and help prepare them for advancement within the company.

Although corporations sometimes hire outside speakers from the industry or professional trainers, these meetings are still rather simplistic, held at an office or plant with perhaps only a coffee break or a luncheon involved. Since they are repetitive and are continuously held, once the format has been established it is fairly simple to repeat the same meeting (with different participants) time after time.

MOTIVATIONAL MEETINGS

Often, when a company has encountered a problem or finds its sales or production gradually or dramatically declining, the decision is made that its employees must be *motivated* to produce or sell more, hold down costs more stringently, or simply develop a better on-the-job attitude or morale.

Such efforts to motivate often take the form of a professional motivational speaker who will put together a half day or a two or three day seminar to try to impart the importance of a certain attitude on the part of the employees to their own futures and that of the company. This motivational subject matter may be stress or time management, solutions to sales objections or even a more specific topic which fits the company's current problem.

Here again the attendees are already chosen by management and it's up to the planner to determine the best site at which the company's *reason* for holding this meeting will be best served.

Obviously, this is not a meeting at which the participants will be entertained, so the major considerations will be site, meals, program and speakers.

INFORMATIONAL MEETINGS

These are similar to new employee orientations except that they are aimed at a specific group of employees. For example, if management decides to introduce a new product, begin a new process, develop new health plans or pension programs or other benefits for employees, or even find it necessary to cut the work force, decrease wages, drop all bonuses, get rid of all company cars or other "perks," these bits of information must be conveyed to the employees involved. While sometimes it can be done through the use of an employees' newsletter, often the company deems it more expedient and more personal to gather the affected employees together and share the information more directly.

This kind of meeting can be a critical one for both the company and the planner. The task of imparting new information—good or bad—to employees can be a touchy one, and must be done with tact and diplomacy. All speakers must have the ability to divulge the information in a way to encourage the employee to understand and even empathize with the company position, even if the information is not to his or her liking.

If the Executive Vice-President of the company is a boring and uninspiring speaker and has an abrasive platform personality, it will be up to the planner to tactfully and with great diplomacy arrange for another person (perhaps even an outside professional) to be the major messenger of ill tidings at the meeting. In addition, the group may have to be fed, housed and educated, all of which falls ultimately to the expertise of the meeting planner.

MEETINGS AS A SOCIAL PHENOMENON

For whatever business reason a meeting is assembled, the fact remains that people *like* to meet. From time immemorial, the human being has been a social animal, assembling in groups to exchange ideas, communicate information and, perhaps most important of all, to socialize and be in personal contact with other persons.

With today's newer technologies for meetings, the teleconference has received a great deal of press, causing many hoteliers to fear the decline of the multi-night-stay conference or convention, a lucrative segment of the hotel industry. While teleconferencing has most definitely found a place in our industry, it will not, in the foreseeable future, supplant most of the meetings held in a hotel setting with real-live people sharing the presence of other persons with similar interests and listening to speakers and programs presented in person. In a later chapter, we will discuss the place of teleconferencing in the industry.

To the corporate employee, there is something complimentary about being included in a forthcoming meeting, particularly if it is being held in a hotel and requires overnight stays. Since most meetings are paid for by the employer, they have come to be viewed as a special perk for those who participate. They symbolize the employee's "arrival" as an integral member of the company. He or she has become one of the "in" group.

There can be an extra benefit to the company, as well, in the socialization of its employees. By sharing experiences of a conference or meeting, people can be brought closer together as a team or unit with the interests of "their" company at heart. Hopefully, this air of camaraderie and team effort will carry over to projects within the workplace. This feeling of team "esprit de corps" can be contagious and can strengthen morale within the entire company.

❑ SUMMARY

Every meeting must have a reason for being scheduled. It is up to the meeting manager to see that the reason is developed in concrete terms and expressed to all potential attendees. The variety of reasons for meeting is as broad as the kinds of companies or associations holding meetings, and the reason for a meeting will impact on the meeting manager's decisions as to budget, site, program and activities. While new technologies are evolving to allow the substance of meetings to be delivered in a teleconferencing format, the need for people to get together, socialize and receive information in person, will limit the kinds of meetings for which this new format will be utilized.

❑ PROJECTS

1. Talk to your family and friends who are in the work force. What kinds of meetings do their companies hold? What kinds of meetings have they personally attended? List them here.

2. If you have a job, full or part-time, what kinds of meetings does your employer hold? Did you attend any kind of orientation meeting? Does your company have on-going training programs? Describe them.

3. Think about all of the meetings you have listed above. What were the reasons for calling these meetings?

4. Most community newspapers list meetings being held in town. Look through your paper and categorize the meetings listed by reasons for holding the meeting.

5. If you have attended any meetings—of a company or of an organization to which you belong—did you enjoy them? How did you feel about being included in the meeting? Does your experience reflect the thoughts expressed in the section on "Meetings as a Social Phenomenon"? Explain.

❑ DISCUSSION QUESTIONS

1. **Give three reasons why it is important to have a reason for calling a meeting?**

2. **Name and describe two types of educational/training meetings.**

3. **The board meeting—what is it?**

4. **Discuss site selection and budget, and why you should know your attendees for a board meeting.**

5. **The motivational meeting—Why is it held?**

6. **The informational meeting—What is it?**

7. **Discuss why it is often better to "meet" than to impart information in an employee newsletter?**

8. **Discuss site selection, program and budget for an informational meeting.**

9. **What do we mean by saying that meetings are a social phenomenon?**

10. **Why** *won't* **teleconferencing replace meetings? Discuss.**

11. **What benefits are derived by the company from meetings?**

WHO HOLDS OR CONDUCTS MEETINGS/TRADE SHOWS?

OBJECTIVES

After reading this chapter, you will be able:

❑ To illustrate the differences between corporations and associations and their meetings
❑ To delineate the various levels of jobs which are performed by the meeting manager and meeting planner and their staff
❑ To outline the mechanics of the pre-con, post-con, and evaluation of every meeting

In parts of this text, for the sake of brevity, we simply refer to some phase of meetings as being held by a corporation or company. However, most of the same material, ideas, comments, statements are applied also to those gatherings held by associations. For our purposes in this material, a company or corporation is a *profit oriented business,* while an association refers to those groups of people with similar interests, allied in *a non-profit organization;* for example, the Dallas Oilmen's Club; the New York State Association of Dentists; the Western Regional Association of Orthopedic Surgeons; the National Society of Travel Writers; the International Association for the Promulgation of Widgets. From these examples you can see that such organizations may be local, state-wide, regional, national or even international in scope.

Some associations in the meeting planning business are: Meeting Planner's International; Professional Convention Management Association; International Association of Corporate Meeting Planners; International Association of Religious Meeting Planners; and International Association of Insurance Meeting Planners, to name but a few. For names and addresses of these and other trade associations, see the list in the Appendix A. In this chapter we will discuss in greater depth these two primary groups who do hold meetings (corporate and association).

CORPORATE

As we have seen in previous chapters, the company or corporation holds meetings for a variety of reasons, in a number of locations, for different lengths of time and with varying attendees. For these reasons the corporate meeting planner's position is a job demanding a person of thorough professionalism, great creativity and flair and an understanding of the corporate structure and its goals and purposes. The planner must have the knowledge necessary to structure meetings from the original decision that a meeting is required, through the budgeting process, the meeting plan, the coordination of the program, site selection, hotel and supplier contract negotiations, supervision of the meeting on-site and finally the evaluation of the entire process in a final report to management.

In smaller businesses, meeting planning is often left to a middle management executive or an executive secretary because the company "powers that be" do not understand that a meeting is an *investment* that must pay *dividends* to the company. Luckily, this situation is becoming more and more passé as corporations comprehend the knowledge and expertise that is required to successfully plan, construct and execute a *profitable* meeting within budget and to accomplish preset goals.

In corporations with separate in-house meeting-planning departments, there are several levels of job descriptions. Since most companies do not have huge meeting departments, many of these jobs will rest with one person, but this division will serve to illustrate the various levels of tasks for which a meeting manager is ultimately responsible.

The Role of the Meeting Manager

The *meeting manager* has the primary, overall responsibility for every meeting that is assigned to his department. This job should be a top level executive staff position, commanding a salary commensurate with the responsibility attendant to it.

The executives of the departments on which a particular meeting will impact get together with the meeting manager. Together they determine the reason for holding a meeting, the subject matter to be covered, the goals to be accomplished, the people who will be invited to attend, any specific speakers to be employed, an outline of the program as envisioned by the other executives, the length of time the meeting will take, and a ball-park idea of the budget to be allocated to the meeting.

With this information in hand, the meeting manager confers with the staff meeting planners and together they structure an exact agenda for the meeting, the precise budget required and an estimated time-table outline for each moment of the meeting. At this point, one meeting planner takes over. The meeting manager continues to be the guiding hand and the person ultimately responsible for the whole meeting. In the meantime, however, the meeting manager is busy at the inception of other meetings within the corporation, and must turn the responsibility for the details of one particular meeting over to a meeting planner.

The Role of the Meeting Planner

The *meeting planner* (sometimes referred to as the facilitator) first confers with the meeting manager on this particular meeting, as outlined above. The planner then contacts sites which fit this specific meeting, conference or convention, paying strict attention to the goals of the meeting, geographic considerations, the facilities' ability to meet the needs of the meeting, and finally the costs of rooms, meals, transportation and entertainment (if any) at those particular sites. When potential sites have been narrowed down to one, two or three (by their suitability), the meeting planner will make site-selection trips to the final competing sites.

On this site-selection trip, the meeting planner will be responsible for the contract negotiation, one of the most critical duties of meeting planners. With each potential site, hotel, resort, conference center or cruise ship, the planner obtains commitments for bottom-line rates and availability of the required numbers of sleeping rooms and public space needed for this meeting. Then the planner begins using the "art of negotiation." One of the catch phrases in the hospitality and meeting industry is that "Negotiations must be a win-win situation." This means that the final contract must have advantages for both the property and the meeting planner. Anytime you negotiate so toughly that the property feels taken, you can bet your bottom dollar that sometime during your meeting the hotel will "get even" so that their bottom line does not reflect a badly negotiated contract. Both the company holding the meeting and the hotel property providing the space are in business to make money. It is therefore important and advantageous for all con-tracted parties to cooperate in producing the finest meeting possible at a price profitable to all concerned.

In negotiating with a hotel, the planner does not concentrate on driving the hotel to a unprofitable room rate in order to get the business, but works to obtain concessions or "freebies" on other items the hotel can afford to give. For example, with a large group, and/or for potential continuing business, the hotel will probably negotiate on a free welcoming reception or cocktail parties, upgraded rooms and/or complimentary suites for VIPs or hotel rooms for the planning staff. (The usual ratio for complimentary rooms is one per fifty on each room night.) Perhaps free office space near the meeting rooms during the meeting, a free room for the meeting planner and maybe for one or two coordinators or travel staff can be negotiated. It may be possible to negotiate for complimentary wine for a major dinner function, or even theme decorations and centerpieces for another function at no charge. The thing every meeting planner must remember is that the total monetary expenditure within the hotel during the meeting must warrant the hotel's concessions in any of these areas.

All of these negotiations with the hotel are dependent upon the bottom-line total amount of money that the meeting will bring to the property. If several very expensive dinners and all luncheons are being provided, and perhaps one or two theme parties, the total billing will be higher and represent a very lucrative piece of business to the property, thus strengthening the bargaining power of the planner. However, if this is a tightly budgeted meeting, where attendees will be left on their own for many of the meals, and where no frills are possible within the budget, then the bargaining power of the meeting planner is certainly weakened because the total bottom-line expenditure for the meeting does not leave the hotel much room to grant concessions.

On the site-selection trip, the planner will also want to contact local Destination Management Companies (DMCs) in each of the potential sites and obtain firm prices on airport transfers, any tours or spouse activities which may be planned, decorations for any parties on the agenda and costs for participatory sports. The planner must also investigate A/V companies regarding availability and rates on microphones, projectors, sound systems, video cameras or any other A/V equipment that may be needed. Printers, florists, photographers, temporary help agencies, transfer companies and attractions are only a few of the companies from whom the planner will want to obtain firm prices and availabilities. Each meeting has its own profile and potential needs. For each meeting under the direction of the planner, there will be different and unique requirements.

After the site-selection trip, the meeting planner will return to the office, compare the various properties, their facilities and costs, the ease of transportation to the various locales, the activities and attractions which are in the area, the availability and fees of other suppliers, which may be needed. Only after all research is completed is the planner ready to decide which site best fits the meeting, and to recommend it to the meeting manager. Together the meeting manager, the meeting planner and perhaps some representatives of corporate management make the final decision on the site city and property.

From the job descriptions above, we see that the meeting planner is the one who develops the program and is responsible for its creativity. It is the planner who recommends (and in some cases actually selects) the site and all of the suppliers who will be used. The planner negotiates and signs all contracts and directly supervises the work of the personnel who will work on the meeting, both in the office and on-site. The planner will also be in attendance at the actual meeting. A meeting planner must be creative, experienced, flexible and above all *very detail oriented*. No small point can be missed in putting together a meeting; and the planner should always have an alternate plan ready in case of a minor disaster.

In addition, the planner must have a broad overview of the entire meeting and of how it will appear to the attendees. This may be an appropriate place to mention another thought: Although the meeting planner must be detail oriented and aware of all of the myriad of pieces that fit together to make a successful meeting, the planner must not allow a small glitch on-site at the meeting to destroy his sense of humor and proportion. Most minute details that do go wrong will never be noticed by the attendee and the planner should keep his or her sense of perspective and not create a disaster out of something that can be covered or solved with no one but the staff members the wiser. A whole meeting must be supervised on-site and one small omission or error must not destroy the efficiency of the staff for the balance of the meeting.

I have discussed the work originated by the meeting manager who then hands the project over to the meeting planner who in turn creates the detailed meeting plan, determines the site hotel and other subcontractors to be used and negotiates the working contracts. At this point, another member of the meeting staff enters the picture.

The Role of the Meeting Coordinator

The *meeting coordinator* takes over once the site has been selected and the agenda layed out in detail. This individual will notify the property that they have been selected and return the final contract with the meeting planner's signature. The coordinator then proceeds to put all of the pieces together, contacting all on-site suppliers (or the DMC if one is being used) and "nailing down" the details: selecting menus for all meals, arranging for hotel registrations (either directly by the registrant or by a total rooming list which the coordinator and clerical staff will prepare) and contacting the speakers and program participants. Speakers can be a very critical area. All participants must be notified of the date and time of the meeting, their exact place in the program, time allotted for their presentation, when rehearsal time is planned, how their A/V (if any) will be handled, how they are to get to the property from the airport and the arrangements for their return. Every minute detail must be communicated and any required input or information from them ascertained.

The coordinator is then responsible for disseminating information to the potential attendees about the date, time, place and reason for the meeting, and advising as to how they must register for both the meeting and accommodations. If there are any options in the program (for example, golf, tours, discretionary dinners, elective workshops, etc.) the coordinator must solicit their participation and the attendees must advise whether or not they will be participating.

All of this is done under the direction and with the cooperation of the assigned meeting planner, who is still responsible for all of the details, and in turn must report to the meeting manager.

The Roles of the Travel Staff

Travel staff is generally the on-site workers who see that all of the details within the meeting plan (plus any and all changes, alterations and last minute additions) are carried out. If the meeting staff is very large, these people do nothing but travel from one meeting site to the next, and working from the detailed meeting plan are the on-site crew. Depending upon the size and organization of their meeting department, they may or may not have worked on or even seen the details of this particular meeting prior to arriving on-site. From this it becomes very clear as to why the meeting plan must be complete to the last tiny detail.

Generally, the meeting planner and the travel staff are the only members of the meeting planning department to travel to the site for the meeting. The meeting manager will have gone on to organize another meeting or conference and the meeting coordinator's job is finished once the final meeting plan has been completed; then coordinating the next meeting is begun.

On-Site

One of the first activities is the *pre-con* or *pre-meeting-conference.* At the gathering, all members of the meeting planner's staff, all involved hotel personnel, representatives of the DMC, A/V companies or any outside contractors meet to go over the meeting plan and every detail of the meeting. This serves to imprint into everyone's minds all of the activities that will take place, and to discover if anyone has missed any detail important to the meeting. Some planners do not hold pre-con meetings, however, this meeting planner feels that it is one of the most important parts of any meeting, in that it serves to head off potential omissions by persons on the planners staff or by that of the hotel or other contractors. It also allows all participants in the planning process to offer possible suggestions or to correct or adjust details in their own meeting participation. In addition, it enables every participating entity to view their part in the overall picture of the meeting.

After the Meeting

Planner and travel staff settle all accounts on-site or arrange for future billing. Gratuities are distributed to individuals, or given to the hotel conference coordinator for distribution. Planner and staff pack up all materials for return to the home office. The meeting planner will have arranged with the hotel to have what is called a *post-con* (post-convention or post-conference) *meeting* with the hotel personnel who were involved with the meeting, and may include representatives from the DMC and/or any other outside contractors who participated. The purpose of this post-con is to obtain input from everyone involved as to how the next meeting could be improved. The meeting planner will first thank the hotel personnel for their assistance and cooperation and commend them for all of the things that went right at the meeting, then outline any procedures which could be changed to make a meeting run more smoothly. Finally, the planner will discuss frankly any major errors or omissions made by hotel staff on this particular meeting. If there were any major catastrophes caused by the hotel staff, this would be the place to bring them to light, but discussion of any penalties or reparations you feel appropriate should be postponed until after the post-con meeting when the meeting planner can discuss this in private with the hotel management. Matters of this kind should *not* be fully aired with outside agencies present.

The meeting planner should then ask the hotel conference coordinator for the input of the hotel personnel. The planner should keep the tone of the meeting to one of a mutual effort to improve performance on the part of both hotel and corporate representatives to attain a *mutual goal* of producing better meetings.

At this point, the hotel personnel indicate their appreciation of the corporation bringing the meeting to their property, thank the planning staff for their organization and professionalism and for any courtesies extended to the hotel. Then it is time for suggestions as to how the corporate planning staff could make the hotel's performance smoother by better premeeting communications or on-site considerations, and perhaps to bring up some demands made upon the hotel staff that were considered inappropriate or "impossible." The hotel may also wish to defend its position or delineate reasons why the "catastrophe" outlined by the planning staff happened. Again, this is not the place for any discussion of reparations. The hotel conference coordinator must also keep the tone of the post-con one of mutual cooperation, not of recriminations and blame. The hotel coordinator takes this opportunity, again, to thank the corporate representatives for the business and to urge them to return to the property for another meeting soon. The meeting is then turned over to any DMC representatives or other outside contractors who participated in the meeting.

The DMC (or other outside contractors) representatives then discuss what was done well in their part of the program and offer suggestions for making airport transfers, tours, theme parties, etc., run more smoothly and be more enjoyable for the attendees. The Destination Management Companies work meetings for hundreds of different clients and therefore may have some valuable comments of benefit to both the hotel and the corporate meeting planner. The same is true of the audio-visual companies, temporary help agencies, transportation companies, decorators and anyone else who may have been involved in this corporate meeting.

When everyone involved has spoken, the hotel sales manager recaps all comments which were made, indicates his appreciation for the input of all parties, thanks the outside contractors for their assistance and expresses the hope that they may all work together on this corporation's next meeting, and again thanks the corporate people for the business, inviting them to return. All participants are then dismissed, with the request that the corporate meeting staff remain for a moment. If the hotel general manager is in attendance (and it is a concerned and smart GM who *does* attend) he/she also remains to discuss any adjustments that may have to be made and to personally express his appreciation for the selection of this hotel as the meeting site. A side benefit of the general manager's attendance is that management will be aware of all that happened at this meeting and understand where his staff may have been either brilliant or less than perfect.

Meeting Evaluation

Meeting evaluation is the culmination of the months and months of work that went into producing the event. The evaluation is an analysis of the entire meeting from the original planning through the final gavel. The post-con meeting was the beginning of the evaluation and constituted input from the operational participants. But, perhaps even more important is: What did the attendees think of the meeting? Often a form is distributed to attendees to gain their opinions and suggestions and these, too, are incorporated into the final evaluation. Close critical attention must be paid to things like attendance at the entire meeting, attendance at various meal functions and activities, effectiveness of speakers and other program participants, appropriateness of the site selected together with the kinds of cooperation and service received, and answers to questions such as: Was the meeting enjoyed by attendees? Was it effective in reaching the goals set? Did it accomplish the original purpose? Was it cost effective? The evaluation then goes from the meeting planner to the meeting manager and subsequently to the executive staff of the corporation. The meeting evaluation is critical in that it demonstrates the effectiveness of the meetings department to the management of the company, it lets them know just what meetings are accomplishing, and in the final analysis, it tells them what *dividends* their meeting *investment* is paying.

Thus, we see that there are four distinct activities involved in planning a meeting, whether these are accomplished by one person or by a staff of many persons.

Meeting manager has overall responsibility for all meetings within the company, interfaces with management, and develops the general outline, purpose, goals and budget for every meeting.

Meeting planner is the "hands-on" developer of the total meeting. The planner establishes precise budget, handles site selection, negotiates all contracts, creates exact program and timing, writes the meeting plan, oversees the coordinator, travel staff and clerical assistants in their duties, supervises the entire meeting on-site and puts together all evaluations into a comprehensive overview of the meeting; and, of course, in all of this, reports to the meeting manager.

Meeting coordinator takes the meeting planner's preliminary meeting plan and contacts all properties and subcontractors to finalize all details and costs of the program. The coordinator fills in all details and schedules in the meeting plan, contacts all program participants and meeting attendees with information and sees that negotiated contracts are signed by all parties.

Travel staff is responsible for following the meeting plan and handling all details of the meeting on-site, working under the direction of the meeting planner.

ASSOCIATION

Meeting planning for an association has a slightly different scenario, although the parts of the plan are pretty much the same.

As we have seen earlier, the association is an organization of persons with similar businesses or interests, each paying dues for membership and being *responsible for having their companies (or themselves) pay for their attendance at any and all meetings.* This is an all-important point in understanding association meetings.

Large associations may very well have a separate meetings department, very similar to the one described for the large corporation. But in most associations, the Board of Directors expects the association executive (the hired CEO—Chief Executive Officer—of the organization) to be responsible for instituting and planning the meetings. If the association has the budget for it, the association executive may hire an outside independent planner with a staff already in place, who then becomes the meeting planner for the association on this one-time basis. More frequently, however, the association executive, with the association's clerical staff, goes through all of the steps described in the corporate planning section, with *one important addition.* Because each individual (or his/her company) is responsible for paying for all meeting expenses, the association planner will have to convince the members that this meeting is important and that there is sufficient reason to attend and reap its benefits, that the person be willing to "lay out" the money necessary.

This means that *strong promotional materials* will have to be designed and multiple mailings made to the membership, plus articles and information disseminated through the trade newsletter or magazine. While the corporation can dictate who *must* attend a meeting, the association must lure its members to the gathering. That means that the program must be structured to the interest and benefit of the membership, a site must be selected that will encourage people to attend, and the extracurricular activities, spouse programs, sports tournaments and tours must all be designed to make attendance at the meeting an attractive option. Many associations mail preconference information to the individuals' homes, trying to elicit the assistance of the spouse in encouraging the member's decision to come to the meeting and bring the spouse and children (if children are welcome). Here the association planner must truly be a marketer and salesperson.

In addition, the planner must structure the registration fee so that it covers all expense. For purposes of maintaining control, the association planner usually elects to have all registrations for both meeting and hotel come through his office. Therefore, the processing of sign-ups for hotels, meals, activities and spouse programs is usually a paperwork nightmare. Of late years, computer programs have been designed to take much of the hassle out of this facet of planning.

Thus we see that in addition to running an organization, worrying about membership growth and retention, local monthly or quarterly meeting programs, legislative lobbying on city, state and national levels, operating a home office with its staff, obtaining high visibility through the media and conducting the business of that particular organization, the association executive often puts on the hat of meeting manager, meeting planner, coordinator and travel staff. If the organization does have a full-time meeting planner, the problems are much the same as those of the corporate meeting planner, with slightly different emphasis and some added considerations.

INDEPENDENT MEETING MANAGEMENT COMPANIES

Another entity responsible for holding meetings is the independent planner. Companies, which specialize in managing meetings for other corporations or associations, offer excellent career paths for potential employees or for the entrepreneurial in spirit. The planner who elects to organize an *independent meeting management company,* must be ready not only to manage meetings for others, but to set up a company with all of the attendent problems and headaches. The entrepreneur must understand capitalization of a company, management, accounting, personnel administration and perhaps most important of all, the marketing of a service to potential customers. Once the company is set up and operating, the independent must develop and maintain a reputation for excellence, dependability, creativity, honesty, integrity and complete ethical behavior. Because the independent planner is working for a number of different clients, the staff must be entirely trustworthy and not discuss one client's business with another, even in passing conversation. Once services are sold to a client, the independent planner must do some research to learn about that company/client, its philosophy, product and personnel. To learn about prior meetings—their successes and failures—the independent planner contacts the convention bureaus, hotels, DMCs and other suppliers who have served the client in the past. Through thorough research, the independent may be able to avoid the varied problems and pitfalls, which have resulted in the company seeking out their services.

Once the client has been sold upon using the services of the independent planner and the research has been done, the organization of the meeting and its planning and execution become much the same as that required of an in-house planner. In the same way, final evaluations are critical, for they will often determine whether the planner will be hired for future meetings. There are a few considerations which should be mentioned here. As an outside planner, the independent must be sure that he/she has a clear understanding of the parameters of the job. What are the expectations of the client? The responsibility for producing the meeting is probably clearly the independent planner's, but what authority is being granted to the planner by the company? May the independent planner execute contracts in the client's name or will his function be that of negotiator of contracts for approval by someone within the corporation? Will budgeted funds be placed at the planner's disposal or will invoices need to be submitted to the company for payment? Will all liability insurance protecting the company also cover the independent planner and will the company add the independent meeting management company to its policy for the duration of this event? Independent planners, as a matter of course, must carry liability insurance, performance bonds, insurance for errors and omissions committed by its employees, workers' compensation insurance, et al, but by arranging for the client to cover the independent under their policy, the independent can reduce his overhead insurance costs considerably. Details of necessary insurance protection will be discussed at length in a later chapter.

❏ *SUMMARY*

In response to the Chapter Title question, *Who Holds or Conducts Meetings?* we have discussed the corporation and its staff, the association and its meetings and the independent meeting management company. Each has a common responsibility for planning and executing meetings, but each also has its different priorities and operational methods. The information in this chapter, as previously stated, is based on a large firm with a multiperson meeting staff. In most medium-sized corporations or associations, or in those with fewer or smaller meetings, the jobs of each of the meetings staff herein described may be accomplished by only one or two people, or even by an outside independent meeting planning company. Nevertheless, no matter who does the job, an idea is given of the levels of planning, coordinating and on-site work, which every meeting entails. It is also stressed that the pre-con, and post-con and evaluation sessions with all operational participants are critical to the success of not only this particular meeting, but of future meetings and the continuing professional development of the meeting planning staff.

This chapter serves to demonstrate the wide variety of careers possible in the business of meeting/convention planning. Future chapters will expand upon this information, broadening the scope, by discussing many more positions and jobs available in businesses servicing the meetings industry.

❑ *PROJECTS*

1. Do you or any of your acquaintances work for a profit-oriented business? For a non-profit organization? List the kinds of companies and associations that you or they work for.

2. Do you belong to an association? Perhaps you have been a Boy Scout, a Girl Scout, a member of Junior Achievement? What are the similar interests held by the members? Are these local, state-wide, national or international groups?

3. Have you heard of any of the meeting planners' associations? Go to your local library and see what you can find out about each — their membership makeup and their goals.

4. What associations are there which were not mentioned in the text?

5. Call your local convention and visitors bureau or chamber of commerce and find out which companies in your area have meeting planning departments? Are there some who use an executive or executive secretary to arrange meetings?

6. In your area, do you have any independent meeting management companies? If you do, talk with the chief executive and find out how many planners are on their staffs, how many coordinators they use and how large a travel staff they employ. Ask how you can get a job with that company and what is the road to advancing to meeting planner with their firm.

7. Think about all of the jobs within a meeting planning department or company. Which of these jobs would appeal to you? What would you like about each of the jobs? What would you dislike?

❑ *DISCUSSION QUESTIONS*

1. In this chapter, how is a company or corporation described? An association?

2. What are the two primary groups which hold meetings?

3. What does the chapter list as job demands for a corporate meeting planner?

4. Who may plan meetings for a smaller business? Why is this practice becoming passe?

5. **What four jobs are described within the corporate meeting planning department? Describe the duties of each.**

6. **Name the eight items of discussion between the corporate management executives and the meeting manager when first putting together a meeting.**

7. **With the information from the prior question, what is the meeting manager's next step?**

8. **Who bears the ultimate responsibility for the whole meeting?**

9. **What is another name or title for the meeting planner?**

10. Name some of the duties assumed by the meeting planner from the meeting manager?

11. What is meant by a site-selection trip? How does the meeting planner decide where to go?

12. On the site-selection trip, what is the meeting planner looking for?

13. Discuss precontract negotiations. What principle must the planner bear in mind while negotiating with the potential site hotel?

14. What kinds of things are negotiable with a hotel? Explain.

15. **What is the usual ratio on complimentary rooms that a hotel will give?**

16. **What is the hotel's major concern during negotiations? What factors must the sales manager take into consideration during the negotiations?**

17. **What other suppliers might a meeting planner contact on the site-selection trip? What kinds of services might they supply?**

18. **After the site-selection trip has been made, and final suppliers determined, who is then responsible for putting the detailed pieces together?**

19. **What are some of the details that must be conveyed to program speakers or other participants?**

20. Who is responsible for disseminating information to potential attendees? What kinds of information must be provided to each?

21. Who usually travels to the meeting site?

22. What details are handled by the planner and travel staff after the meeting?

23. Describe a post-con meeting. Who is involved and what is its purpose?

24. Who generally ends up as meeting planner for an association? Why?

25. **What single basic factor within associations impacts most on the association meeting planner's job?**

26. **What two tasks are more apt to apply to the job of the meeting planner and coordinators for an association than for their counterparts in a corporate meeting?**

27. **What is an independent meeting management company? What additional skills must an independent meeting manager possess?**

28. **For whom do independents hold meetings?**

WHO ELSE HOLDS OR CONDUCTS MEETINGS/TRADE SHOWS?

OBJECTIVES

After reading this chapter, you will be able:

❏   To discuss the special considerations involved in religious meeting planning
❏   To be familiar with the specialties of fund-raising meetings and special events
❏   To illustrate the differences between for profit and non-profit fund-raisers

We have learned from the last chapter about the various kinds of meeting planning jobs, which are involved in putting together meetings, conventions, conferences, seminars etc., within the structure of corporations and associations. Although these next events are generally covered within those descriptions, they are rather specialized and we feel deserve a separate section of discussion.

RELIGIOUS ORGANIZATIONS

More and more in the last few years, religious denominations are holding annual get-togethers of their members and followers. These meetings often involve men and women from all over the world, both adults and children, and therefore are very large and diverse in attendance.

Because of their size, these meetings utilize large convention halls and community centers, with hotel accommodations being city-wide, representing a broad range of types (from roadside motels to luxury resorts) and prices. Individual attendees often drive to the meeting site, which makes travel for the entire family less costly. Therefore, planners need not worry about mass transportation from so many hotels to the convention hall (although most *do* provide some shuttle bus transportation from four or five designated convention properties). The meeting headquarters is generally in the convention center or hall.

Need we say more?

The Colorado Convention Center is a reality. With all the features meeting planners asked for and a lot more.
• 2-level design with all exhibits on one floor, all meetings on the other.
• 4,000 committable hotel rooms within 5½ blocks.
• Another 13,000 hotel rooms within 20 minutes.
• 300,000 sq. ft. of contiguous exhibit space.
• 100,000 sq. ft. of meeting space.
• 44 total meeting rooms on a single level.
• 35,000 sq. ft. column-free ballroom.
• 100,000 sq. ft. additional space in adjacent Currigan Hall.
• 24 loading bays for fast set-up.
• 65,000 sq. ft. of registration space.
  Don't make plans without us. Send for our free Denver Convention Planner. It's everything you need to make your next meeting part of our Grand Opening celebration. Call 1-800-888-1990 for details.

DENVER METRO CONVENTION & VISITORS BUREAU
225 W. Colfax / Denver, CO 80202 / (303) 892-1112 (FAX: 892-1636)

Fig. 5–1. Convention centers, like the one in this ad for Denver, offer the kind of floor space needed for many large religious conventions. (Courtesy of Denver Metro Convention & Visitors Bureau.)

Some religious organizations receive tithing (10% of gross income) from their members and in turn pay for expenses at the annual meeting or convention, therefore assuring very heavy attendance of the membership. Some families plan that this trip will do double duty as the family vacation for the year. Other religious organizations charge registration and hotel fees to their members, some with a markup to make a slight profit for the organization. However, in all cases the religious meeting is generally kept to a fairly economical one, and in the interest of economy is frequently held in summer, in a winter resort location. Summers are also the times when children are out of school and this enables the entire family to attend. These organizations are excellent business potential for hotels, resorts and convention halls during their off-season. Although kept to a strict budget, the seasonality of religious conventions makes them prime business.

The meeting manager and/or meeting planner for such organizations must then be prepared to deal in very large attendance numbers, to negotiate city-wide hotel rates (often with the help of convention and visitors bureaus), and to structure their meeting program and activities in a large convention hall, with very large arena facilities, plus many break-out rooms. The very size of these arenas makes selection and operation of audio/visual equipment one of the prime concerns. People in the far corners of a vast hall must be able to see and hear clearly. The planner must also be ready to handle the traffic patterns of assembling masses of people, of arranging for coffee breaks and luncheons for large numbers with expeditious service, and structuring orderly adjournments. Very mundane considerations, which are critical to a successful meeting, like sufficient rest rooms, strategically located water stations, very specific signing, and an efficient and knowledgeable registration crew become responsibilities of the meeting planner. Because of the large numbers of attendees, most planners arrange to have emergency first aid stations; sometimes well-staffed message centers become crucial.

Since the number of attendees are so very large, many religious organizations run simultaneous trade shows where vendors of all types of religious articles, books, statues, instructional tapes, religious music discs, etc. display their wares. This then calls for the solicitation of exhibitors, the set-up of large booth areas and the planning of a traffic flow through the exhibits. Booth fees from the vendors are set high enough to make a profit for the religious organization.

The religious meeting planning staff is structured just like those for corporations or other associations, with some added special problems and considerations; for example, how do you create a church, chapel or just a contemplative atmosphere in the middle of a vast arena?

FUND-RAISING FOR PROFIT AND NON-PROFIT ORGANIZATIONS

Those special planners who deal with fund-raising meetings, seminars and special events have an entirely different outlook on their meetings and may work for either profit or non-profit organizations. Their primary consideration is to promote attendance in order to raise money. As we explore the structure of these fund-raisers, let's understand just what the *for profit* or *non-profit* designations mean.

For Profit Meetings

For profit seminars or meeting fund-raisers are structured by a planner who is in the business of making money directly from the meeting for their company. The primary example of this is in the company who structures seminars by well-known speakers on subjects of general interest like "Stress Management," "Time Management," "How to Handle Your Teenagers," "Substance Abuse," "Recognizing Mental Depression," etc. Here, the company is in the business of making money; to do so they will book a particular speaker to do a multicity tour of one to three day seminars. In each target city, the company planner runs public advertising in the newspapers or direct mail to a specific segment of the community (for example, to all doctors and other health professionals). Fairly generous fees are charged to attend the seminar; sometimes the planner makes additional monies by marking up the room rate on all sleeping accommodations booked for the seminar, letting the hotel do all of the work of rooms registration.

The for-profit gatherings can also take the form of public trade shows; for example, a boat show; a recreational vehicle show; a gem and mineral show, an auto show.

Non-Profit Meetings

Non-profit seminars or meeting fund-raisers/events are structured by planners who are raising monies to support an organization or cause (like the Cancer Fund, the Heart Fund or funds for abused children), but who are not attempting to make a profit for a business. All monies from the fund-raiser (after expenses or "seed monies" for the next event) go to a specific charity. One of the more popular fund-raisers seen over the past ten years has been the TV telethons, pleading for call-in pledges from the television audience.

Here, although the planning steps are much the same, the professional planner is working for a volunteer group—either the Board of Directors of the charity or a fund-raising committee of local, civic-minded citizens. While they have hired the professional for his or her expertise and reputation as a fund-raiser, they will nevertheless have to be handled tactfully and their ideas and "brilliant" suggestions considered. Never forget that this group *does know* the local scene and can be invaluable to the planner in advising who will give how much and for what reasons.

Another facet of charity fund-raising is in the keeping of very precise, detailed, honest and accurate records of all monies either received or expended. The Internal Revenue Service will care, the local citizenry will care and the Board of Directors of the organization will certainly care. The planner's entire reputation can rest on the honest accounting of funds being raised for any charitable cause, and complete and accurate bookkeeping will be imperative.

The professionals who plan and run fund-raisers are specialists in knowing how to promote a very special event at an inflated price and encouraging people to buy tickets (or pledge monies) for their special cause. These events often take the form of specialty style-show luncheons, large carnival-like events, very formal theme dinners or celebrity auctions where all merchandise has been donated by well-known persons, thus allowing greater monies to be collected for the cause. The format can be as varied as the creativity of the hired planner.

Specialty events, commanding the services of expert, professional planners are many: state fairs; political conventions (both local and national); public relations events and promotions like grand-openings and ground breakings; marathon television fund-raisers; awards programs like the Oscars and Emmies; and political events such as state dinners. While all of these special events and fund-raisers require some extraordinary planning, the basics of good meeting planning do apply to all of them. This merely opens up another varied, and very intriguing avenue of meeting planning for exploration by the novice planner.

❏ *SUMMARY*

The professionals who run all of these religious conventions, fund-raisers, trade shows, and special events must be proficient meeting planners, particularly when dealing with public masses of people. It takes a real tactician to keep crowds moving when you want them to move, and where you want them to move, yet still having them go away feeling that they received value for their admission price or registration dollars.

The planners who are involved in fund-raising meetings or special events, are really specialists within the meeting planning community. Some special events, which offer intriguing job possibilities, are the state fairs, political conventions, Olympic competitions, and most certainly the protocol-heavy meetings between diplomats and heads of state.

❏ *PROJECTS*

1. Do any religious organizations that you know about hold annual conventions? Have you ever attended one? Talk to friends and list all religious conventions you hear about.

2. Consider any largely attended gatherings you have seen (even rock concerts, sporting events) and describe the traffic-flow problems they created.

3. Call your local community center or convention hall and find out if they host any religious conventions. If so, find out what time of year they are held, where attendees are housed and what special challenges are involved for your city.

4. If you watched the Democratic and Republican national political conventions on TV, discuss some of the obvious logistics involved.

❑ *DISCUSSION QUESTIONS*

1. **What is the one major consideration in planning a religious convention? What kinds of problems must be taken into consideration?**

2. How are some religious conventions paid for?

3. What kind of trade show might a planner develop with a religious convention?

4. Why do fund-raising professionals have a different approach to meeting planning?

5. Name some of the for profit money making events.

6. **How is a for profit seminar series constructed?**

7. **Describe the "professionals" who plan and run fund-raisers.**

8. **For whom does the professional non-profit fund-raiser usually work?**

9. **Why is accounting so important for a fund-raiser?**

10.   **Name some specialty events which command the services of expert meeting planners?**

11.   **Would this kind of meeting planning interest you? Why or why not?**

WHEN ARE MEETINGS HELD?

OBJECTIVES

After reading this chapter, you will be able:

❑ To discuss when meetings are held and the importance of this decision
❑ To illustrate that the "when" of meetings effects the planning process
❑ To show that the "why" and "when" of a meeting are intertwined and impact upon the "where" and "how" of that meeting

Meetings are held every year, in every season, on all days of the week and at any time of the day. We will now take a look at what determines when a specific meeting is held and what considerations impact upon this decision.

FOR AN ORGANIZATION'S REASONS

A time may be determined for reasons of the corporation or organization. This only means that the company or association may find it necessary to hold a meeting at a specific time for their own reasons. For instance, a board meeting of the corporation is set annually on a specific date from the inception of that corporation, by law. Therefore, while the company may elect to hold a number of special board meetings during the year, that one Annual Meeting *must* take place, for example, on January 5th (or some other specific date), because it is so stated in the Articles of Incorporation.

If the organization's busy season runs from June through December, perhaps because it retails back-to-school items and then Christmas wares, obviously a meeting would be called sometime early in the New Year to introduce the new items for the following season to its sales staff. For example: Lionel's Toy World, Toys "Я" Us,℠ F.A.O. Schwartz or any other store chain whose heaviest sales season is the Christmas market will have meetings in late winter or early spring to introduce Christmas merchandise. By the same reasoning a meeting wouldn't be called from June to December about Christmas merchandise, since this busy season would be nearly upon the stores and all decisions would have been made much earlier.

Perhaps awards or bonuses are given out at a dinner at the end of each fiscal year, which, for a particular company, may end June 30. This then would indicate that the awards dinner meeting would be held in early July.

Thus we observe that the company or association may have its own reasons for the dates on which it decides to hold certain meetings.

TRADITION

Tradition can carry a lot of weight with some organizations. For example, if a particular training meeting was originally held in October because that was the time when most hiring had been done, then the annual get-away training seminar, which has been held for the last twenty-five years every October, would no doubt continue to be scheduled at that time. It has thus become traditional to hold that particular meeting every October. This date could be changed, but both management and employees have come to expect the tradition to continue.

Perhaps a college alumni association has always recognized Founder's Day, the day on which the college was first chartered. Then that particular date would be the only day on which the founding of the college is celebrated.

A religious organization may hold an Annual Lenten Retreat over a three-day weekend. Since the dates of Lent are dictated by religious tradition, the annual retreat will traditionally be held at that time. A good example of the traditional meeting, is the annual Christmas party for employees and their families. The company could hardly produce the Christmas party in August! The same holds true for companies who hold annual employee family picnics on the Fourth of July.

EMERGENCIES

Emergencies can also be the determining factor in calling a meeting. A sudden increase in an order from a government contract can be one of the "good emergencies" which would require a get-together of an entire production staff. The serious illness of one of the principles of a business could warrant an emergency meeting of the other executives to divide up the responsibilities of the ailing member for the time being. A national emergency such as war, a major famine or flood, destruction by a tornado or hurricane, may well impact on certain businesses and require its top executives (who may be spread throughout the country) to gather for a meeting.

A drop in the Stock Market may require a meeting of brokers; or, as occurred during the "Black Friday" stock market fall in October of 1988, meetings may be cancelled in such an event, because brokers are too busy to travel away from the office at such a time.

Emergencies come in many forms that may require the immediate structuring of a meeting.

CORPORATE NEEDS

Corporate needs may also dictate the time of a meeting. For example, the company introducing an innovative marketing plan for a new product may call a meeting of the entire marketing and sales force. There may be two influencing items in this decision. First, the item will have to be introduced to the sales team prior to the dates it will go on sale to the customers. Secondly, most businesses have a peak season, and generally a new product would be introduced at the beginning of the primary sales time.

The resignation of a key officer, such as President or Executive Vice-President, may require a Board decision for replacement. The date of effectiveness of the resignation would then determine when the Board must meet to name a successor.

A major slump in sales, may dictate calling of an immediate meeting of the sales executives for a brainstorming and evaluation session.

Any major disaster that impacts upon the business of the company may very well call for an unscheduled meeting. These disasters may be financial, personnel-related, market-oriented or even caused by nature (such as an earthquake). The "corporate needs" timing for calling a meeting can be as varied as the kinds of problems that can occur in a business. And, you will notice that there is a fine, and some times undistinguishable, line between *reasons of the corporation* and *corporate needs.*

SEASONAL CONSIDERATIONS

A particular season may be a reason for calling meetings and this can occur in several guises. The corporation or association that is extremely cost-conscious, may hold meetings in a warm climate only in the summers in order to take advantage of off-season rates.

Hoteliers who run winter resorts, certainly do not meet from January through June because they are too busy conducting their own businesses. Large produce companies would not call a meeting during a harvest season because no one could get away from their farms to attend. Teachers' associations might meet over weekends, in summer, or during other school vacation periods, when faculties are not involved in regular school sessions.

In other cases, associations may always hold their annual meeting at a fine resort in the winter, which would serve to encourage attendance; and then conduct a week-long training meeting at a university during the school's summer vacation to save money.

Many corporations, particularly with regard to incentive programs, prefer to hold their meetings at a very fine resort in high season. That is, at a ski resort during the winter ski season or at a golf resort in the south when it's too cold to golf back home.

Fig. 6-1. Cold weather in many of the other 49 states may well cause a planner to choose Hawaii as an ideal meeting site. (Courtesy of Hawaii Meetings & Conventions Department.)

COSTS

Costs are important to all meeting planners, whether they are working with an enormous budget or eking out expenses on a shoestring. Those who have larger budgets will spend a great deal of money but expect to get their money's worth in product and service. Those on a shoestring must be more creative to produce a meeting at the lowest cost possible and still have that meeting accomplish the goals set forth in the planning stage.

For a planner who is timing a meeting, the "when" to hold the meeting can have a terrific impact on the total costs. One of the primary ways to control costs is in site selection, and this can impact in two ways. First, the site should be close to the majority of attendees to hold down airfares or other transportation costs. The planner should also investigate the possibility of any excursion or special air fares, which might be available at certain times of the year. Second, although the site must fit the meeting's needs, many hotels or resorts have off-season or "shoulder-season" rates, or even lower rates for certain days of the week. This might dictate the "when" of a meeting.

MISCELLANEOUS REASONS

Miscellaneous reasons cover all of the other causes for the "whens" of meetings. There are less purposeful reasons, such as the Chairman of the Board's decision to hold a meeting at a certain time because it fits best with his schedule, or even the meeting planner's option of a date for a meeting because it falls between two other major meetings already on the planning schedule. Sometimes the primary speaker for a meeting may be of such importance to that particular session that the whole meeting is scheduled around his availability. An example of this might be a banker's convention being arranged in order to accommodate the Chairman of the Federal Reserve as keynote speaker.

WHAT DETERMINES THE "WHEN" OF MEETINGS?

1. Reasons of the Corporation
2. Tradition
3. Emergencies
4. Corporate Needs
5. Seasonal Considerations
6. Costs
7. Miscellaneous Reasons

THE IMPORTANCE OF THE "WHEN" OF MEETINGS TO THE PLANNER

The vital nature of the timing of meetings is evidenced in many ways. Let's consider just what the "when" means to the job of putting together the meeting.

Although the corporation or association determines the "when" of meetings, consideration must always be given to the attendee. In conjunction with other determining factors, the attendees' needs and wants must also be figured into the equation, for without attendance there is no meeting. When a corporation is involved, attendance is mandatory and paid for by the company, nevertheless the work schedules of employees and convenience of the meeting's timing must be taken into consideration, as it may well impact on corporate operation. When the meeting is being produced by an association, attendees may elect whether or not to attend and therefore the "when" must be compatible with their needs and wants in order to encourage their presence.

Hopefully, the meeting manager will be in on the decision as to the "when" of meetings. At the preliminary management meeting, where the reasons for a meeting and its goals and purposes are discussed, the "when" will most certainly be one of the points considered and the meeting manager will be a part of that determination. The timing of the meeting can impact on costs, site selection, participant availability and meeting planning staffing requirements.

When the meeting planner is handed the basic requirements of a meeting by the meeting manager, one of the first considerations will be the number of staff hours necessary to produce and oversee this particular meeting. If the meeting is held at a time when there are few or no other meetings in progress, more staff can be made available. Should the "when" of this meeting be overlapping one or several other meetings, then staffing can become a problem. Personnel can either be spread very thinly, with people doing double duty, or additional personnel may have to be acquired from other departments or even from an outside meeting management company. Often the decision to spread the in-house staff too thinly can be a mistake, in that the potential for error multiplies. Independent meeting management companies will have staff experienced in all areas of meeting production, and therefore are often the best answer to a deficit in staff.

The "when" of a meeting can very well impact on its cost. If the decision is made to hold a meeting during the January to June period, the meeting planner may look for a northern site where hotels and resorts are not in "high season," unless the goals and purposes of the meeting demand a "high season" location. Or on the flip side, if management decides to hold a meeting during the summer, the planner might look at southern sites, who are in their "low seasons," in order to obtain better hotel rates, and perhaps even better air fares.

Once a location has been determined, the planner must deliberate on the choice of a particular hotel property. Here, the nature of the meeting will help eliminate some hotels and bring others to the forefront of preference.

Site selection is thus impacted by the "when" of a meeting. Some hotel properties will negotiate better rates if the meeting is being held over a weekend. Or perhaps a certain property may have just the space you need between two other major meetings. The hotel sales department is always anxious to negotiate to fill a "hole" between other groups, therefore the planner must search for a property for whom it would be advantageous to host the meeting at the selected time.

In cases were the "when" of a meeting is specified, you might find that your preferred hotel is out of space and unable to accommodate your meeting. This may force you to choose a property with less desirable rates or even less than perfect meeting amenities. We see then that the "when" can impact on both cost and quality. If the "when" of the meeting is predetermined, the meeting planner may have to be doubly creative in developing promotional materials, in order to encourage attendance. If the timing of the meeting is less than the "perfect" time for potential attendees, pre-mailers and promotional brochures will have to create very strong incentives for people to come.

If the "when" of the meeting is flexible, the planner may find bargains out there by moving the meeting dates by only a day or two.

❏ *SUMMARY*

Timing of meetings can be determined by any number of factors. As we have seen, reasons of the corporation, tradition, corporate needs, emergencies, season and costs can impact on the decision as to when to hold a meeting. Once that decision has been made, other considerations come to the forefront for the planner:

Costs — Staying within budget and negotiating prices
Staffing — Finding sufficient numbers of planning staff
Site Selection — Finding the appropriate city and property
Attendance — Creating a desire to attend

The "why" and the "when" of meetings are demonstrably intertwined and will have an effect on the "where" and "how" of a meeting.

❏ *PROJECTS*

1. In mid-January XYZ Corporation, located in Oak Park, Illinois (a Chicago suburb) has announced to you, the meeting planner, that a Board of Directors' meeting must be called immediately, due to the death of the Vice-President of Sales. Board members all reside in the Northeastern United States. Under which determining factor was the decision made as to:

    a. Why a meeting would be called

    b. When the meeting would be held

    c. As the meeting planner, where would you elect to hold the meeting and why?

2. Look through your local newspaper for notices of meetings. See if you can determine from the type of meeting what determined the "when" of each particular gathering.

3. Think about various traditions and how they might impact on decisions to hold meetings. Can you list some traditions that are not mentioned in the text?

4. Consider some of the meetings held by organizations to which you belong or of which you have some knowledge, and see if you can determine the reasons for their timing.

5. In this chapter, I've talked about seasons. Consider your community: Do you have a "high season"? If so, what is it and why is this so? Is this season attractive for meetings? Why?

❏ *DISCUSSION QUESTIONS*

1. **What is meant by "reasons of the corporation"? Define this and give examples.**

2. **Explain what is meant by "corporate needs" in selecting dates for a meeting. What examples are given in the text? Can you think of others?**

3. **What kinds of emergencies might call for a meeting?**

4. What do we mean by stating that "when" a meeting is held can be influenced by season?

5. What does the "when" of meetings have to do with costs?

6. What problems can the "when" of a meeting create for the meeting planner?

7. List some of the considerations that are impacted by the "when" of a meeting, which the planner must deal with when choosing a geographic location.

8. **Illustrate how site selection is affected by the "when" of a meeting.**

9. **Discuss how the "when" can favorably affect a certain property's selection.**

WHERE ARE MEETINGS HELD?

OBJECTIVES

After reading this chapter, you will be able:

❑   To discuss the geographic reasons for determining the "where" of meetings
❑   To illustrate the various kinds of hotel properties and how each lends itself to certain types of meetings
❑   To show how a site-selection trip is handled and the criteria to be considered when selecting a property

Sometimes the "where" of holding meetings is entirely up to the discretion of the meeting planner. This occurs when the decision is made to hold a meeting for a specific purpose, the budget has been developed, and the outline of a program devised; then the planner may choose a site to fit the criteria of that meeting. Sometimes, however, the nature of an organization, such as a state association, may dictate the locale of the meeting.

LOCAL MEETINGS

Local meetings are held by trade association, civic organization or social-group chapters in the particular city where their members are located. For example, a short weekly staff meeting is generally called by the chief executive and is held within the offices of the company. Similarly, a weekly or monthly sales meeting is called by the Director of Sales and can be held in the office or at a local hotel or even in a local restaurant over lunch or dinner.

These "local" meetings are generally those which are of short duration and involve people living and/or working in the same city or area. Therefore, by holding them locally, no travel or hotel room costs are usually incurred; attendees come to the meeting and then return to their local office or home with perhaps the only expense being a coffee break, luncheon or dinner and maybe audio/visual equipment or printed handouts. Thus, local meetings eliminate the need for many of the most expensive items in the meeting budget.

Occasionally, meetings are held locally in the interest of time and costs, even if they are of more than a day's duration. Since these are generally meetings which are "strictly business," there is no need to go further afield to entertain the participants or impress them with overnights in an expensive resort.

Some examples of these local meetings might be the Rotary Club in a particular city, a duplicate bridge club, a Boy Scout troop, the marketing and sales department of a local hotel or the Association of Certified Public Accountants of Boise, Idaho. Whether each of these "local" groups, like the duplicate bridge club, belongs to a regional, national and perhaps even an international association (the local hotel is probably a part of a national or international chain), the local entity holds meetings regularly in their own city or town.

STATE MEETINGS

State meetings are held by associations with several chapters within a single state or by corporations with more than one office within the same state. These meetings allow business people or members within the same geographic location to get together and discuss mutual concerns and problems.

An example of a state meeting would be the Arizona Association of Dentists holding a state-wide meeting for all member dentists within the state. Those from Phoenix, Tucson, Yuma, Flagstaff and all of the smaller cities in Arizona would gather for this meeting. Undoubtedly, these same dentists would also belong to the Regional Association, and the National Association, but the State Association meeting would be held within the State of Arizona.

REGIONAL MEETINGS

Regional meetings are also held as a matter of routine in some businesses and associations. For instance, the local chapter of a trade association is usually a part of a regional division, which in turn belongs to the national or international organization. These regional divisions will hold meetings quarterly or semi-annually, between the national or international conventions or conferences. The city chapter of an association like the Hotel Sales and Marketing Association, will belong to a western, eastern, southern or Midwestern region, as well as to the international association. Therefore, when the regional office holds a meeting it is generally held within that region. The meeting planner may have the option of several states and/or cities in which to structure the meeting, but almost always it must be held within its own region.

Many corporations have offices spread throughout the country or world. For greater control and organization, the company is then divided into several regions. The regional sales manager, for instance, being responsible for sales within a certain region, will call together the sales people from his or her entire area for a sales meeting, and it only makes sense to hold that meeting within the region. This will save transportation costs, and more importantly the time of the sales personnel involved. Many may even elect to drive both ways the day of the meeting.

NATIONAL MEETINGS

National meetings are obviously those which involve people from throughout the country, and therefore the choice of meeting place becomes much broader. The meeting planner has much greater latitude and the choice is not restricted to a single state, region or locale. For the national meeting, the choice of city and site must be based on other considerations, which we will discuss later in the chapter. However, briefly, you would look at the various areas from which the attendees would be coming. If the largest number of employees, or members, are from the Midwest it might very well be wise to concentrate on cities in Minnesota, Illinois, Wisconsin or other Midwest states. This would encourage attendance because the attendee would have a minimal expenditure on air fare or other transportation and would have to spend less time getting there.

Other national organizations make it a practice to rotate the location of their meetings so that branches or chapters in all sections of the country have an opportunity to host the meeting. In this case, the locale would be dictated by which area was in line for the next meeting.

Because many local chapters are anxious to have the national convention held in their town, and consider it an honor that will mean a certain prestige for their hometown group, the local chapter will put together a complete presentation on their city's desirability, to be shown at the current year's national convention. The local Shriners, for instance, might create a 12 minute film about their city and state, its weather (at the time of the national convention), its excellent hotels and resorts and its attractions. This part of their presentation may be produced with the help of the State Office of Tourism and the local convention and visitors bureau, because of the financial impact that a national convention would have on the local economy. To this A/V presentation, the local Shriners group may add what is termed a "dog and pony show" including their best clowns or musicians, together with some kind of souvenier handouts depicting their city. This Shriner group would undoubtedly be competing with five or six other groups to lure the national convention to their city. After all five or six cities have made their presentations, a committee of the national convention would vote on which of the competing cities will be chosen. This process usually takes place from three to five years before the convention year which is being discussed.

INTERNATIONAL MEETINGS

International meetings' locations are determined by many of the same criteria as those listed previously under "National Meetings." But, there are a few considerations which might impact on the international meeting, which are not a factor in any other kind. Language has to be a major determinant in planning a meeting. Do a sufficient number of employees or members speak the language of the potential meeting locale to assure a comfort factor? Does the area under consideration have employees in shops, hotels and restaurants who speak English? And, will the convention sales and service people in the site hotel be able to communicate in English? If not, are there people on the planning staff who speak, read and understand fluently the language of the potential site country? Does the meeting facility have simultaneous translation equipment? Is there any health hazard in the area that requires immunization shots for travel to the country being considered? In the more cosmopolitan areas of the world, these factors will not present a problem, but should an event be planned in a newer, more exotic destination, language and health hazards must be taken into consideration.

The monetary value of various currencies could also reflect on the decision to hold an international meeting where inflationary factors or instability of the local currency would make it a problem. For instance, during 1985 when the Mexican peso was so unstable that its value was changing hourly, there was no way to predict costs of a meeting in Mexico in advance, and no meeting can be sensibly planned when a budget cannot be at least estimated *closely*.

Tax laws bearing upon deductibility of expenses of a meeting abroad need to be seriously considered, whenever the planner is considering an international meeting. And this consideration must be of the tax laws of all countries from which attendees might be expected to originate.

The *culture* of a region can be an intriguing promotional tool for an international meeting; but culture can be a double-edged sword if the planner is not aware of the pitfalls. When planning any foreign meeting, advice should be sought on the customs of the intended site. A good source of this information may be your local university languages department, or even the tourist department of the government in the country in which you intend to meet.

Once manners and acceptable behavior or attire for the area are determined, the information should be disseminated to potential attendees. This may be accomplished by holding a mini travel seminar prior to the departure date, or if this is impractical, the planner should see that a brochure or letter is composed to send the information with other literature promoting attendance at the meeting, and again, with registration confirmations.

Customs in other countries can be very different from ours. For instance, never give a gift wrapped in white paper to a person who is Japanese — white signifies mourning or death. In many traditional Arab countries, alcohol may not be served nor consumed (even in the privacy of your hotel). If you request a napkin in an English restaurant, you may well receive a baby's diaper — or an odd look in response. In France, don't get burned by the water faucet — "C" stands for "Chaud" or "HOT"! European hotel floors are numbered from the floor *above* the lobby, therefore, when meeting someone in the first floor dining room, remember that it's one floor *up* from the lobby. If you want ice in a beverage in Europe you will have to ask for it — most Europeans don't think chilled drinks are good for the stomach. While there are no divisions in European restaurants for smokers and

We've been creating vacation palaces for over 1,000 years.

From the romance of ancient Mayan palaces to elegant hotels that fulfill every vow of luxury, Cancún can make your honeymoon unforgettable. So come and celebrate your future together on an island that's the perfect marriage of past and present. Call your travel agent or write: P.O. Box 9018 BRD, East Setauket, NY 11733-3453 for a free brochure.

© 1990 The Cancún Trust

CANCÚN
The Caribbean island of legendary pleasures

Fig. 7–1. The image of Mayan royalty depicted in this ad lends a certain intrigue to Cancun as a destination. This Mexican Caribbean island is using its centuries-old culture to lure meetings and visitors. (Courtesy of the Cancun Trust.)

nonsmokers, never light up a cigarette at a formal dinner in Great Britain before the toast to the Queen. In most other areas of the world, people are not as informal as Americans, so call business acquaintances "Mister," "Misses," or by their appropriate title, but never by their first names until requested to do so. These are but a few of the "good manners abroad" that will keep the planner and his/her group from being considered "ugly Americans." It is therefore up to the planner to see that a group has been fully apprised of local customs before embarking to a foreign destination.

Terrorism is a fact of modern life in our world. No planner would want to schedule an international meeting in a potentially dangerous world location. Some areas of the Middle East, for example, have proven to be unsafe locations for American tourists.

SITE-SELECTION CRITERIA

In past paragraphs, we have seen how a specific country, region or city might be pre-indicated as a site for a meeting. Now, let's look at some of the many considerations that must be examined in deciding upon a particular property.

Types of Properties

Prior to the actual physical site inspection, and the question of what properties might physically best fit the needs of a specific meeting, it should be determined just what type of property will best serve the attendees and the goals and purposes of the meeting.

Inner-City Hotels.   Inner-city hotels have many amenities to make them appropriate for a business meeting. They are usually business-oriented and equipped to handle commercial meetings. Since they are located downtown, many business offices, restaurants, community centers and entertainment sources are within walking distance.

If a specific meeting requires a visit to a place of business or downtown area plant as part of the program, the inner-city hotel may well be perfect. When the meeting consists of a series of seminars and break-out sessions, with some attendees having breaks between sessions, downtown is convenient for them to shop or stroll in their leisure time. If many nonattendee spouses will be in attendance, downtown enables them to have something to do close by, while their spouses are in meetings. If it is a very large meeting, or if it has an attendant trade show which demands usage of a community center, downtown may be the most convenient location to the community center and the hotel headquarters.

Airport Hotels.   These have become more and more popular as the business community has become more airborne. With the advent of more convenient flights, "hub city" scheduling and more economical air fares, additional airport hotels have been built.

Fig. 7–2 A & B. Hotel chains often offer the best of many worlds. These two ads from Penta Hotels promote the attractions and conveniences particular to their locations. (Courtesy of Atlanta Penta Hotel and Orlando Penta Hotel.)

If a meeting involves calling in attendees from many distant areas of the country, it may save hundreds of cumulative hours to have them fly into a centrally located airport and take only three or four minutes to arrive at the meeting location. Also, at the termination of the meeting, attendees can be at the airport ready to board home-bound flights within minutes. Most airport hotels have been built to accommodate small to medium-sized meetings. Many such airport hotel meetings are structured to be short meetings of a few hours, or a single overnight stay; this type of facility is certainly convenient.

Resort Hotels.   They have become more popular with commercial business and association meeting planners as attendees combine vacation time with a business trip. As more spouses are invited to meetings and included in incentive trips, the resort offers a more active destination. Many times the selection of an attractive and glamorous resort property, with multiple activities on property, can improve attendance.

The resort can offer the planner a wider selection of moderate to luxury accommodations, several sizes and designs of suites, and large meeting and public room areas, in addition to the amenities of golf, tennis and/or racquetball. Also the resort usually boasts several kinds of food service from coffee shops and poolside snack bars to exquisite, formal, continental dining rooms. And many today offer full spa services.

Often meetings include golf and tennis tournaments, "olympic" games, swimming pool contests and activities, exercise classes, participatory rodeos, skiing competitions and other events, which resorts are fully equipped to handle. With today's accent on physical fitness, corporations and associations are more attuned to planning active, competitive contests for attendees.

In choosing the site for a meeting, planners are well aware that the selection of a fine, well-appointed luxury resort property, may increase attendance measurably. Some people might never book a luxury resort for their personal vacation, but for a meeting with group room rates already negotiated for them, they might very well bring the family and stay a few extra days. In this case, the experienced planner will solicit attendance by sending information and brochures to the home where the spouse and children become "promoters" of the meeting.

Suburban Hotels.   These are popular with the planner who wants to keep attendees at the hotel, and attendant to the business at hand, but who needs neither the amenities, the leisure activities nor the cost of an outlying resort. Also, a number of plants and factories have been built in the suburbs of large metropolitan areas, and often personnel from these businesses are the hosts of the meeting, or the attendees will be visiting their facilities as a part of the meeting. If, for some reason, this site is convenient and the price is right, it should be the meeting planner's choice.

Conference Centers.   In the past several years, conference centers have come into their own as complete meeting facilities. Their numbers and complexity have steadily increased. This type of property offers not only fine, luxury accommoda-

Fig. 7–3. "Open spaces" for recreation and facilities for "open minds" for business are offered by this ad for Keystone Conference Center. (Courtesy of Keystone Resort, Colorado.)

Fig. 7–4. A beautifully appointed meeting room at Loew's Anatole Hotel in Dallas, Texas, is set up for an executive conference and exemplifies the type of luxury resort chosen for many corporate meetings.

tions and dining, but also a complete, fully trained meeting staff. They are totally self-contained properties dedicated to organizing and operating entire meetings, providing all required meeting amenities and every assistance to the planner. A conference center accepts no other hotel business and dedicates all of its efforts to serving the meetings and conventions market. This is an excellent choice for the planner with minimal or no staff or the newcomer to the business who will appreciate the direction and assistance that the center's very professional personnel can offer.

Cruise Ships.   As we mention in other chapters, cruise ships are another option for the planner. The very idea of a sea cruise seems exotic and exciting to attendees, and the all-inclusive price makes budgeting an easy task for the planner. For the right size group, this "encapsulated" environment may well be an excellent choice.

Once the decision has been made as to what type of hotel fits a specific meeting, the planner will of course plan a site-inspection trip to decide which property will get the business.

Fig. 7—5. Conference centers are very special properties. This one has the added attraction of being adjacent to a magnificent national park in the middle of wide-open Big Sky country in Montana. (Courtesy of Big Sky Ski & Summer Resort, Montana.)

Availability of Properties

The availability of properties can be determined by several methods. If the planners are not personally familiar with the country, region, state or city to be considered, then they must depend upon information from other sources. One of the primary places to obtain information is a tourist information office of the country or state where one is considering holding a meeting. By writing or calling the Director of Tourist Information, the planner can obtain a very broad picture of the kinds of properties available for a specific type of meeting. Convention and visitors bureaus are generally located in cities that are major convention or meeting sites and they too can provide general information. Your local library may have information on cities under consideration. Contacting other meeting planners (perhaps through one or more of the meeting planner organizations) will usually result in a more detailed look at the capabilities of properties in the area under consideration. From them, a true picture should evolve of the kinds of experiences they have had with

Fig. 7–6. Cruise ship in port at Cabo San Lucus, Baja Sur, Mexico.

specific properties. Once it has been determined just what might be available to a group, it is time to look at other criteria.

Availability of Needs

The phrase "availability of needs" is rather awkward, however, it is a term used in the industry and indicates that the planner must look at the requirements (or needs) of a meeting before booking a potential hotel.

Accommodations.   First and foremost, does the property under consideration have sufficient sleeping rooms to contain all attendees? Or if it is a very large meeting, are there several hotels within close proximity, which together can contain all attendees?

Is this hotel (or hotels) of the quality or standard that the members or attendees will expect? For instance, if the meeting involves the very top executives of the organization, they would anticipate much more luxurious accommodations and appointments than would a middle management or supervisory group.

Meeting Space.   Next, what kind of meeting space will the group need? Does the ballroom hold enough people for both opening and closing general sessions? Does the hotel have sufficient break-out rooms for concurrent, smaller meetings? Check on the acoustics of each of the rooms, does it have posts or pillars that would reduce seating capacity or interfere with planned A/V projection? Is the heating and/or air conditioning in perfect working order and can it be regulated within the area itself? Is the lighting in the room adequate and can it be darkened properly for possible A/V presentations if desired? Is the seating provided in the meeting areas comfortable and in good condition? Does the shape of the room lend itself to the seating patterns which have been devised? And, of course, will all of the meeting space required be available and will the hotel block out specific areas for the meeting upon negotiation of the hotel contract?

Fig. 7—7. "Break out" room at Loew's Ventana Canyon Resort, Tucson, Arizona

Public Areas.   Look carefully at the public areas. Do they create the impression upon arrival at the hotel that should be conveyed? If this is a serious study session, does the hotel seem to have the privacy and quiet atmosphere conducive to serious learning? For a large annual convention, does the hotel convey an atmosphere of fun and bustling activity? Is the lobby large enough to handle group arrivals of the size of the group? Will the hotel have sufficient front desk personnel to facilitate check-ins? Are there enough bell desk personnel to move luggage in and out quickly?

Are the hotel restaurants and dining areas of sufficient size to handle the group? This is particularly important for early breakfast, to be sure attendees can get in and out of the dining room in time for the meetings. If there is any question of this, will the hotel cooperate in setting up some sort of separate, buffet arrangement in a private area?

Where are the restrooms in the public areas? Are they well maintained, attractive and are there enough of them?

While not always informed, the planner may have potential attendees with physical handicaps. Does the hotel have handicapped and wheelchair accessible sleeping rooms? Are their dining rooms, lobbies, meeting rooms, public areas (particularly restrooms) accessible to those with crutches, walkers or wheelchairs?

Other Considerations.   Does the hotel property handle its own audio/visual equipment? If not, is there a reliable A/V company that they regularly use and will that company keep operators, repair crews and extra equipment in the hotel for emergencies during the meeting?

Fig. 7–8. Promoting services and experienced personnel, highlights Anaheim's ad. (Courtesy of Anaheim Area Visitor & Convention Bureau.)

Double check the type of security employed by the hotel. Is the safety of guests in case of fire, theft or personal injury of prime consideration to the hotel management?

If the group is into golf, tennis or other sports, does the hotel/resort have such facilities on their own property or are such facilities available and easily accessible to hotel guests? Will the hotel make the necessary arrangements for attendees and can such charges be added to hotel accounts? Can transportation be readily provided?

Once it has been determined that the hotel/resort meets the needs of the meeting, the planner should discuss the group with the convention services director. From answers to specific questions, and from the questions asked by the convention services person, it can be ascertained just how knowledgeable this hotel contact is going to be during the meeting. Although site selection by personal inspection of the physical facility is important, remember that hotel personnel working with any meeting are critical and can mean the difference between a smooth, professionally conducted meeting and one that consists of one emergency after another.

Forms used for site selection vary from meeting planner to meeting planner. However, each should carry the information which will impact on your meeting. One form is filled out for each hotel under consideration. Information is gathered on the form to facilitate the decision-making process once the site-selection trip has been completed. See the Site-Selection Data form in Figure 7-9.

PROPERTY SITE-SELECTION DATA

Once a geographic site has been selected, the planner must then consider what type of property has the availability of needs, and the type of property that fits the meeting must be chosen:

> Inner-city hotel
> Airport hotel
> Resort hotel
> Suburban hotel
> Conference center
> Cruise ship

At this point, a site-selection trip is in order, which will enable the planner to personally see and compare the hotels or resorts, which comprise his or her final list of potential sites. In addition to seeing that the property has the necessary availability of needs, the planner will also meet with the hotel management team, the sales department and the convention coordinator before making a final selection.

```
                    SITE SELECTION DATA FORM

COMPANY/DEPARTMENT: _____   DATE OF INSPECTION: _____

TYPE OF MTG.: _____

ANTICIPATED ATTENDANCE: _____   AVAILABLE MEETING DATES:

HOTEL NAME: _____       _____

CITY: _____        _____

TRANSPORTATION TO SITE CITY:

      PRIMARY AIRLINE:_____

TRANSPORTATION AVAILABLE FROM AIRPORT: _____

_____

      TRAVEL TIME:         COST: _____

_____             _____

_____             _____

ROOM REQUIREMENTS:

SINGLES: _____  COST QUOTED: _____

DBLES:   _____  COST QUOTED: _____

SUITES:  _____  COST QUOTED: _____


DAY    TIMES   EVENT   RM.   SET-UP   #S    AVAILABILITY

(THIS INFORMATION IS FILLED IN FOR EACH MEETING ROOM WHICH WILL
BE REQUIRED, EACH DAY OF THE MEETING.)


GENERAL IMPRESSION OF MEETING AREAS:

   APPEARANCE:              SUITABILITY:

   LIGHT/SOUND/HEAT/AIR CONDITIONING:

HOW MANY DINING ROOMS?      ARE THEY ADEQUATE FOR GROUP?
```

Fig. 7—9. Site Selection Data Form

LOCAL DESTINATION MANAGEMENT COMPANIES AVAILABLE:

HOTEL CONVENTION COORDINATOR:

  NAME: _____

  PHONE: _____

    KNOWLEDGEABLE?

    COMMENTS: _____

_____

_____

    GOLF ON PROPERTY? _____

    TENNIS ON PROPERTY? _____

    QUALITY OF SPORTS FACILITIES: _____

_____

    HOTEL SECURITY?   ADEQUATE? _____

    IS EXTRA SECURITY AVAILABLE IF NEEDED? _____

_____

    ARE PUBLIC AREAS ACCESSIBLE TO THE HANDICAPPED? _____

    DO SLEEPING ROOMS HAVE WHEELCHAIR ACCESSIBLE BATHROOMS?

_____

_____

    IMPRESSION OF HOTEL IN GENERAL:

      STAFF PERSONNEL: _____   PUBLIC AREAS: _____

      ROOMS: _____   DINING AREAS: _____

      RESTROOMS: _____

COMMENTS: _____

(ALWAYS HAVE EXTRA SHEETS OF PAPER FOR COMMENTS/OBSERVATIONS.)

Fig. 7-9. Site Selection Data Form (Continued.)

SITE SELECT BECOMES VETO VISIT

By Phyllis Fetter, Director of Marketing, Westward Look Resort, Tucson, Arizona

As is customary, we at the resort answer immediately any requests that come in from planners who have seen our ads in trade publications. This one came from an ad in *Successful Meetings,* one of the better meeting publications — and so we assume inquiries come from serious planners who are interested in our resort.

We sent the typical response, lauding our resort (but not pretending to be anything we are not), explaining the facilities and services that we have to offer, *and* inviting the planner to visit us as our guest. Little did we know that the planner was well on his way to our property when our letter was received in his office.

Obviously we like to make the arrangements for a meeting planner to visit us. We "meet and greet" and make sure the person has a room that we like to show off, invite the person to dinner in our fine dining room, give a tour of the property, including other rooms and meeting rooms, discuss the planner's meeting needs, etc. When planners come unexpected without notice, we can only hope to accomplish the above. On the other hand, we should expect our property and services to meet expectations. *Sometimes this doesn't happen!*

Upon the arrival of this planner, the monsoon season had taken down our sign at the foot of the road so he passed up our resort two or three times. When he finally registered, the front desk gave him (unwittingly I might add) the best room available in the house at the time, but his wife objected to the distance from the main lobby and dining room, so the front desk re-assigned them to another, closer in. Guess what? The computer did not perform and the guest was sent to a room that was occupied. On the third try, the guest was placed in one of our older rooms next to the middle pool. Consider that we had just experienced multiple monsoon storms, which resulted in desert critters being driven in — to our visiting planner's room! Bugs don't like to be outside in inclement weather either.

In addition, the gentleman of the family went out the next morning to take his exercise in the middle pool, stepped on a piece of glass and cut his heel. We had had another storm in the night and only God knows how a piece of glass was on the walkway from his room to the pool. Actually, our grounds maintenance is excellent!

Well, when something goes wrong in the hotel business, Murphy's Law takes over with a vengeance, and everything *will* go wrong. Needless to say this man was not impressed by our resort. Upon returning to his office, unknown by us to have visited our property, he found our glowing letter introducing him to the resort and inviting him to visit. Need I tell you what he wrote across the letter and sent back to us? Dirty words should not be a part of this text.

We win some and we lose some — and in this case a site select turned into a visit veto.

❑ *SUMMARY*

The process of site selection can be one of the most critical decisions made by the meeting planner. First, the geographical location that best fits the needs of this particular corporate or association meeting must be selected, and this might also include a mobile site, like a cruise ship. Once the locale has been decided upon, the planner must consider convention centers, conference centers, cruise ships, resorts and downtown, suburban, and airport hotels and decide which type of property is required. Having narrowed down the selection to the *type* of property, the planner still must select the one best property for the meeting.

❑ *PROJECTS*

1. You are the meeting planner for The MPQ Corp., and have been asked to select a site for the meeting. The information which has been given to you is:
   a. The meeting will involve the top-echelon management team of the corporation, which is located in Teaneck, New Jersey.
   b. Mid-February has been selected as a convenient time.
   c. The purpose of the meeting is to interview and socialize with five candidates for the position of Vice-President of Marketing for the corporation.
   d. The meeting will be of four days duration.
   e. Attendance will number twenty-two, plus the five candidates who will be invited for the first two days only.
   f. All members of the management team are avid golfers.

With this information in hand, you are given the following list of potential sites and asked to select one. Which would be your choice and why?

❑ A mid-town, five star hotel in New York City
❑ An airport meeting hotel in Denver, Colorado
❑ A five star luxury hotel on the Gold Coast (in town) in Chicago, Illinois
❑ A plush resort near Dallas, Texas
❑ A golf resort near Quebec, Canada
❑ An executive conference center in Minneapolis, Minnesota

2. Visit the various hotels/resorts in your locale. From their locations within your community, from the amenities they offer, and from their advertising, categorize each as to whether it is an inner-city hotel, a resort property, a suburban hotel, an airport hotel or a conference center.

3. Think about the organizations or clubs to which you belong. Do they hold meetings? If so, are they local, regional, state-wide, national or international? To this list, add the organizations or associations with which you are familiar even if you are not a member. How do these meetings fit the descriptions in this chapter?

4. Talk to some of your hotel convention services people. How do they find out what the meeting planner is looking for? Ask if they are instructed or trained by their hotel management to be aware of the meeting planner's needs. What kind of training do they receive?

❏ *DISCUSSION QUESTIONS*

1. **Describe how the nature of an organization may dictate the general locale of a meeting.**

2. How does the chapter describe "local meetings"? Who holds them?

3. Describe "regional meetings." Who might hold them?

4. What is a "national meeting"? Who would hold one?

5. What is an "international meeting"? Think of some organizations who might hold one. What unique problems might they face?

6. Where would you look for information as to availability of properties in a potential meeting location?

7. **What is meant by "availability of needs"?**

8. **What are some of the criteria (or needs) to be considered in looking for a property? What other considerations of the hotel or hotel personnel will impact on the site-selection decision?**

9. **Name the types of properties and describe the characteristics of each briefly.**

10. **List some of the reasons for choosing a resort hotel.**

11. **What does the text say about resort hotels and attendance?**

12. The text mentions "keeping attendees at the hotel." Why would this occur in a suburban hotel? Why might it *not* occur at a resort hotel? Do you think this would occur at a casino/resort?

8

WHAT KINDS OF MEETING PLANNERS ARE THERE?

OBJECTIVES

After reading this chapter, you will be able:

❑ To describe the three major types of meeting planners: corporate, association and independent

❑ To illustrate the similarities and differences between planning for corporations and for associations

❑ To discuss other persons who perform some of the same functions as the meeting planner, and how they fit into the industry

All types of people plan meetings, from the bosses' secretaries to the large corporate meeting managers and some professional planners whose titles don't indicate this function of their jobs at all. These people come from different corporate levels, diverse educational backgrounds, widely varying experience and many levels of income. It will be the purpose of this chapter to illustrate the various planning positions and just how they are similar or different from one another.

THE CORPORATE MEETING PLANNER

As illustrated in earlier chapters, there are many levels of meeting "planner" within the corporate meetings department; however all of them have things in common.

Corporate meeting planners structure meetings for a single company, with a set service or product. This means that although they may be doing meetings for many, many different departments, they still work for the same "boss" with the same philosophical bent. For this reason, many of the meetings will be repeats year after year, and some of the detail will become easier with each repeat. This same factor will, however, present a challenge to creativity. Although repetitious in structure, the planner never wants to allow the program, subject matter or even the entertainment to be a repeat of the year before. Because some meetings will have many of the same attendees, they should have a fresh, innovative and new approach.

"Alte Oper" Convention Center, Frankfurt

Germany

One of the world's most intriguing meeting destinations.

Where else can you confer in glorious castles, combine a high-tech symposium with a romantic trip on the River Rhine, and visit medieval fortresses as well as modern industry.

To organize successful meetings the easy way, turn to the German Convention Bureau (GCB). We plan it for you. And show how to further enrich your event with fascinating sightseeing, before and after conventions. In Germany, with all her incomparable attractions.

Get the facts now. From our Convention Planner's Guide to Germany. It's objective, informative and free!

FREE

⊕ **GCB**
German Convention Bureau–GCB
1640 Hempstead Turnpike
East-Meadow, N.Y. 11554
(516) 794-1632

German National Tourist Office

Please send me a free copy of the "Convention Planner's Guide to Germany".

I am organizing   a convention ☐
a meeting ☐
an incentive ☐

from _____ to _____
with _____ participants.

Name/Position _____
Company/Association _____
Street _____
City _____
State _____ ZIP _____

Fig. 8–1. Addressed directly to the meeting planner, this ad also offers a "Convention Planner's Guide to Germany." (Courtesy of German Convention Bureau (GCB).)

As a corporate employee, the planner knows that the company will be paying the bill and attendance will not have to be encouraged or promoted, because the personnel will be *told* to attend. However, this is where the planner must illustrate to top management that meetings are an *investment,* which will pay *dividends* to the company. The planner has an obligation and an opportunity to illustrate the value of the in-house planning department to the corporation, by developing innovative programs, selecting appropriate sites, and staying within predetermined budgetary guidelines, while accomplishing those goals and objectives set before the meeting.

THE ASSOCIATION MEETING PLANNER

In earlier chapters, it has been mentioned that meeting planning for many associations falls to the Executive Director. However, whether we are talking about a large association with a meeting planning department or one where the executives double as meeting planners, the job remains the same.

Meetings are *big* business with the 8,000 business and professional associations. They spent $24 billion in 1985 on 227,700 meetings that attracted an attendance of 31.6 million persons.[3]

The association planner is responsible for local, monthly membership meetings, which generally consist of a business program, an instructional speaker and either a luncheon or dinner function. Many organizations will have a contract with one single property for all of their meetings throughout the year, with the dates all reserved and menus selected far in advance. Each meeting format will be the same as the one the month before, with only the business to be discussed and the speaker changing. Others will select a different hotel or restaurant for each monthly meeting, thus spreading their business around, as well as accommodating members from all parts of the city.

Meeting notices must be sent out or published in the association newsletter, reservations received from members, phone calls made to all who have not responded in order to promote attendance, a registration desk staffed at the meeting and ready to collect fees from all who have not prepaid. The planner will have someone check the room set-up, the audio/visual equipment or microphones and the meal set-up, but all of this becomes routine, since it is just like the prior month. Someone will have to meet and welcome the speaker and reiterate when introductions will be made to the group and how much time has been allotted for the presentation. The association meeting planner may or may not have to develop an agenda and see that it is distributed to all participants.

Most associations will also have regular Board of Directors' meetings and these sometimes take place in a private room just prior to the general membership

---

[3] *LODGING:* American Hotel Association. Directory Corp., April 1988, p. 15, "Loews Anatole Positioning, Targeting the Most Significant Market."

meeting. Often these sessions are only an hour or two in lengths, with carafes of water on the tables being the only refreshment. The planner is responsible for scheduling these meetings with the hotel or other property, checking on the room set-up, notifying the board members either by telephone, mail, or newsletter and then perhaps assigning someone to take the minutes of the meeting.

Some associations also structure regular educational seminars; often quarterly ones. The association planner becomes responsible for putting together the physical aspects of these, and maybe consulting on the program as well.

The biggest job of the association planner will come with the annual convention. A planner for a national or international association headquarters assumes this job each year and the job involves invitations to members of all state and metropolitan chapters, a full program structure, budget development, establishment of registration fees, site selection, entertainment, transportation and all of the other details that fall to *every* meeting planner, whether association or corporate. Because members will be paying their own expenses entirely and making the decision whether or not to attend, one of the planner's primary jobs will be to encourage attendance with eye-catching mail-outs, attractive and appropriate site selection and solid programming.

The planner for a local chapter of a national association may become involved with the national convention only once every ten or more years when that chapter elects to host the convention in their hometown. At that time, the local planner will probably only assist the national planner and handle many of the local details. The local chapter will possibly become involved in the site-selection process and local ground transportation plus local input to the national program.

THE INDEPENDENT MEETING PLANNER

The business of independent meeting planning has evolved only since the mid seventies. These planning consultants conduct separate businesses, which sell their planning and coordination services to companies or associations. Their customers may be companies/associations who either can't afford a full-time meeting planner, or whose meeting activity is too limited to require full-time planning. Or perhaps their clients are large companies who prefer to hire independent planners to negate the necessity of adding to their payroll and paying the expenses attendant to having actual meeting department employees. One of the independent planner's other functions is to act as an addition to the staff of a corporate or association planner.

In addition to performing the same tasks as the corporate or association meeting planners, independents must also be both marketing and sales oriented. Before these planners can begin to plan meetings, they must first develop and market information about the availability of their services, then sell specific organizations on hiring them on annual contracts to run all of the groups' meetings. (This is the ideal situation, although some companies hire an independent meeting planner on a one time basis to run a single specific meeting.)

The independent planner will be working for several entirely different companies or organizations at the same time. In order to effectively assist in structuring a meeting, the independent must research the business of the client and know as much about their needs and expectations from the meeting as possible.

Once the independent has learned something about the business in which he or she will be dealing, the job of budgeting, structuring, planning and coordinating the meeting becomes much the same as that of in-house corporate planner. One major difference will be that in evaluating the meeting and its dividends to the client, independent planners must accurately report on the meeting, but manage to stress that the meeting was successful because of their expertise. It will probably be due in great part to that evaluation that the company will renew the contract for another year.

OTHER PERSONS IN THE MEETING PLANNING BUSINESS

Travel Agents

Travel agents by and large are *not* meeting planners. However, because they are already handling all of the transportation and travel arrangements for certain companies, they are beginning to try to diversify their efforts by doing the meeting planning for those clients.

The *best* of those agencies are smart enough to know that booking hotel rooms and making air reservations does not make one a meeting planner. They are therefore beginning to hire people with full meeting management experience, and setting up divisions of their travel agencies to do just that. Because they already have the confidence of their corporate clients, they have an edge in acquiring the meeting planning business. Being a planner for a travel agency can be fascinating work. There is diversity in the clients, and often inside knowledge of the best resorts, convention centers, and hotels throughout the world, both old and new. For a company requiring these services, it can be a good deal, because *everything* for their meeting, including transportation, will be handled by a single agency.

Directors of Convention Services

Hotel/resort director of convention services is another position of entree into the business. This person works for a single hotel or property. Once a group meeting contract has been negotiated for the hotel, the file is generally turned over to convention services. It is their job to interface between the client and the hotel, finely tuning their programming, helping them select menus and block out meeting space, aiding in setting up theme parties, golf/tennis tournaments, swimming pool games, and in general, obtaining as much of the peripheral activity of the meeting for the hotel as possible. In cases where the convention services person realizes that the client is set upon the idea of an off-property activity, the coordinator should then recommend either a destination management company to assist or just give the client the name of transportation companies, off-property dinner locations, et al.

Once the convention services coordinator has helped the client delineate the details of the meeting, it is then up to hotel personnel to supervise all of the activities within the hotel and to assure a smoothly run gathering for the client. The professional, successful, convention services director can help secure repeat meeting business year after year.

Two things for the meeting planner to remember as an outside planner depending upon the services of a hotel convention services director:

❏ Number one: The coordinator works for the hotel first and foremost! Of course the coordinator is concerned with helping the planner produce a professionally run, smoothly operated meeting, but the coordinator's first allegiance is to the boss, the hotel.

❏ Number two: The coordinator's job depends upon keeping the planner happy! This consideration is very true, however, his or her assistance will have to be within the constraints placed upon the coordinator as an employee of the hotel property. The experienced coordinator will do a good job for the planner-client. But the client must be wary of being talked into an on-property theme party, when what is truly called for is a total change of atmosphere for participants, with, for example, a beautiful soiree at the local zoo!

It is important that the hotel convention services personnel be thoroughly cognizant of what the meeting planner does, what the planner wants and how the planner will negotiate for it. Although the convention services coordinator represents the hotel instead of the attendees, to do a superior job for both the client and the hotel, the coordinator must know what the planners are going to expect from the hotel and what points any specific planner might consider negotiable, as well as those on which that same planner probably won't budge.

Destination Management Companies

Destination Management Companies (DMCs) are also getting into the business of meeting management. With the experience of doing so much of the coordination and supervision of ground transportation, registrations, activities, etc. on-site, many destination management companies have developed full meeting management divisions. They have hired experienced planners to join their staffs, giving them the capability of running full programs/meetings for their clients. Once the budgeting, premeeting planning and site selection have been accomplished by their meetings division, they can make tandem the ground-operations with their destination management section, thus expanding their business from two angles. Although part of a DMC, these planners are really a part of the independent meeting management industry. They must market their services to a wide variety of companies.

❑ *SUMMARY*

Meeting planning is accomplished by a variety of persons, some who are professional planners by trade and some who simply inherit the job of putting together conferences or meetings. The broad divisions of these planners may be described as: those who plan meetings for the corporations for whom they work; those who put together meetings and conventions for the association by whom they are employed; those coordinators who work for the hotel in which the client has booked space for a meeting; and those independents who plan for a wide variety of clients. Each of these areas presents employment opportunities for persons who want to work in the meetings and convention management industry. The people who find jobs in the conventions industry (other than meeting planning) attractive, might also do well to look at these alternative areas for positions.

Kinds of Planners

Corporate
Association
Independent
Travel Agency
Hotel Meeting Coordinators
DMC/Meeting Planners

❑ *PROJECTS*

1. In your city or locale, research the entrance requirements in experience and education for:
   a. Corporate meeting planners—Call some local companies and, if they employ a meeting planner, discuss the job with that person.
   b. Association meeting planners—Contact the Executive Directors of some local associations and ask what they require of someone who they are going to hire to plan meetings.
   c. Independent meeting managers—Check with your local convention and visitors bureau or chamber of commerce and inquire as to whether your town has any independent meeting management companies. If so, ask them what it takes to be employed by them.

2. Call some local hotels/resorts and ask how you prepare to work in their convention services department.

3. Contact some of your local travel agencies and find out how many, if any, are now in the meeting planning business. Are they considering such an expansion?

❑ *DISCUSSION QUESTIONS*

1. **Briefly, how does this chapter describe the corporate meeting planner's job?**

2. **Why is meeting evaluation of critical importance to the corporate meeting planner?**

3. **What does the text say about the year-after-year meeting sameness in some corporate meetings? How can it test a planner?**

4. **What one factor makes an association planner's job different from that of a corporate planner?**

5. **Describe briefly the various kinds of meetings with which an association planner is involved?**

6. **What do we mean by an "independent" meeting planner?**

7. **Why must an independent meeting planner be sales and marketing oriented?**

8. Discuss the variety of work done by an independent meeting planner which makes his or her job different from that of the corporate or association planner?

9. How does an independent planner use the evaluation of a meeting?

10. We usually think of travel agents as only booking airline tickets and hotel rooms. What do they have to do with meeting planning?

11. Why would work as a meeting planner for a travel agency be interesting?

12. What is a convention services director? For whom does he or she work?

13. **What is the value of a good convention services director to the corporate meeting planner?**

14. **What is the value of a good convention services director to the hotel property for whom he or she works?**

15. **Name the *two* things to remember when dealing with a convention services director from the hotel.**

16. **Why should convention services directors be thoroughly familiar with the meeting planner's job?**

SUPPLIERS TO THE MEETING INDUSTRY

OBJECTIVES

After reading this chapter, you will be able:

❑ To enumerate the suppliers who provide accommodations to the meeting industry
❑ To discuss the many suppliers who provide services to the meetings industry, and their importance
❑ To illustrate the development of theme parties and their place in complementing the theme of the total meeting

Suppliers are all of those people upon whose services and products the meeting planner must depend for the success of a meeting.

No matter how carefully the budget has been devised, how expertly the program developed, how creatively the promotional materials have been presented, the people who are supplying transportation, accommodations, escorts, guides, sports activities, theme parties, flowers, speakers, entertainment, audio/visual equipment, and all of the other parts that make up the whole, must be responsible, dependable and reputable in their own fields, in order to assure that the meeting goes off as planned.

One of the more critical operational considerations of all meeting planners must be, "To whom should all of those necessary addenda to the meeting be subcontracted?" If planners are familiar with the area and its businesses, they may already know who will produce results for them. But if they don't, then they must depend upon the advice of other meeting planners who have worked in the area, on the recommendations of the hotel convention services director, on suggestions from the local convention and visitors bureau, and probably most important of all, their own good judgement when meeting potential suppliers.

Just who are these people who can help make meeting planners "heroes" to their own companies, or negate all of the time and effort that has already gone into the planning process?

SUPPLIERS

Hotels

No meeting can be successful without the complete cooperation of the site hotel, and the assistance of all of its personnel. That is why most meeting planning courses will spend a great deal of time on the site-selection process. However, after the physical facilities have met all of the criteria, the planner must take a really hard look at the professional expertise of the people in the hotel with whom he/she will be dealing.

It is the hotel personnel who will see that:

- ❑ the proper reservations are accurately recorded
- ❑ the correct people are assigned to those certain rooms and suites
- ❑ the bell desk and front desk are properly staffed upon the group's arrival
- ❑ rooms are made-up on time
- ❑ all amenities are in the proper rooms
- ❑ meeting rooms are correctly blocked
- ❑ all menus have been transmitted to the banquet department
- ❑ all of the other requests of the planner or the guests are handled with efficiency and expedience.

It is especially important that the planner can get a "feeling" on the site-selection visit that the hotel convention services department is knowledgeable, professional and flexible.

Resorts

As suppliers to the meetings industry, resorts, like hotels, must have personnel who pay attention to all of the details of the meeting for which the planner has contracted. In addition, the resort will have had to carefully schedule many of the on-property leisure sports and activities. Their tennis and golf pros, spa attendants and concierges must all be attuned to the meeting and what it will require from their individual departments.

It is the duty of all resort personnel to not only see that the meeting goes without a hitch, but also to see that all guests truly have a wonderful time at their resort.

Conference Centers

Conference centers are very special properties, which have been specifically designed, engineered and managed especially to accommodate meetings. Their entire physical plant is dedicated to making the running of meetings smoother and easier. Their personnel too are carefully trained to assist the planner in conducting a professionally produced meeting.

WESTFIELDS INTERNATIONAL CONFERENCE CENTER

340 Rooms

WESTFIELDS
INTERNATIONAL CONFERENCE CENTER

Located just seven miles south of Dulles International Airport and 25 minutes from the nation's capital, The Westfields International Conference Center is specially designed to serve the most senior corporate, association and government meetings.

Expressing the charm of magnificent colonial Virginia estates, this Georgian structure conveys the elegance of the nation's capital in a comfortable setting accented by the judicious use of brick, marble, oak paneling and art.

The Rotunda is the focus of the public space which is dedicated to superb dining, social gatherings, and conference circulation to more than 40,000 square feet of meeting space in thirty meeting rooms.

Westfields is truly a special place capable of raising expectations which are met by its professionally trained staff.

SUBURBAN WASHINGTON D.C.

14750 Conference Center Drive, Chantilly, VA 22021. PHONE: (703) 818-0300; 800-635-5666. KEY PERSONNEL: Richard Thomas, Managing Director; Robert Parriott, Director of Marketing.

LOCATION/TRANSPORTATION FACTS – Executive conference center located on eleven hundred acre corporate office park in Fairfax County, VA. Seven miles south of Dulles International Airport and 25 minutes from nation's capital. Company owned limovans transport guests to and from airport, $8.50 per person, each way. Taxi to/from airport, $12. Westfields stretch limousine available on request, at a charge.

ACCOMMODATIONS – Georgian-style 5-story brick conference center, designed to reflect colonial Virginia estates, houses 340 rooms including 4 Presidential suites. All are soundproof and have individual air conditioning control, 3 direct-dial phones with 2 lines, message alert and bathroom extension, oversized beds and armoire with color TV, radio, and refrigerator. Suites have programmed music, balcony, oversized conversation area, wet bar. Groups are pre-registered.

DINING/ENTERTAINMENT – Three restaurants, two lounges. The Palm Court provides an elegant setting for gourmet dining with meals prepared tableside. The Fairfax offers buffet breakfast and lunch and evening menu service for conference dining. Wellington's Pub features light meals, snacks and specialty beers and ales. Lounges include Westfields Lounge and Wellington's Pub. Room service 6:30AM-1:00AM.

SERVICES/FACILITIES/SHOPS – Newsstand, florist, gift shop, pro shop. Airline ticket and car rental desks. Travel agency. Local tour desk. Physician on call. Staff fluency: French, German, Spanish. Free parking.

RECREATIONAL/AMUSEMENT FACILITIES – Heated indoor swimming pool. Health club with sauna and steam baths. 8 lighted tennis courts with ball machines, instruction and CCTV. Staff can arrange for tours of Georgetown, Washington, D.C. monuments, Smithsonian Museum.

RATES – Full American Conference Plan per person rates include guest room, 3 meals, 2 coffee breaks, meeting room, and FACP a/v package. May 18 to June 30: $275 single, $195 double; July 1 to September 4: $195 Single, $145 double; September 5 to November 17: $275 double, $195 single; November 11 to March 16, 1991: $225 single; $165 double. Special holiday rates offered at Easter, Thanksgiving and Christmas/New Years. Credit Cards: all major. For Direct Billing: file credit application in advance. Checks: cashed at front desk.

– Principal Meeting Facilities, Equipment and Services –

GENERAL COMMENTS – Thirty meeting rooms, including the Lincoln Forum Amphitheatre, are on the first two floors. Grand Dominion and Jeffersonian rooms can be divided into 6 each, and Washingtonian into 3. All have individual controls for climate, sound, 208V 3-phase electricity with multiple electrical/microphone/telephone outlets. The Lincoln Forum offers fixed seating for 200 people and has a permanent stage with a proscenium 24' wide and 15' high. Multilingual translation facility is adjacent. Lighting is computer assisted through 64 instruments and the sound is controlled by adjacent Media Center. Registration area, coat check and rest rooms, phones, storage. Direct truck access via door, ramp, dock. Freight elevator. Independent utilities on floor outlets include phone, broadcast conduits, CCTV, cable, water, waste.

Name of Room	Grand Dominion	Washingtonian	Jeffersonian	Treaty
Dimensions (LxWxH in feet)	115x80x16	80x95x16	60x80x16	22x38x16
Square Feet	9200	7600	4800	836
Floor Number	2	1	2	2
Floor Cover	Carpet	Carpet	Carpet	Carpet
Portable Walls	Yes	Yes	Yes	Yes
Capacity				
Auditorium	950	800	575	75
Classroom	650	500	260	40
U-Shape	375	300	70	30
Banquet	775	625	350	60

MEETING EQUIPMENT:

Supplied by the conference center's in-house Media Center – at no charge with *Full American Conference Plan:* 35mm projection, 16mm projection, overhead projector, flipcharts, podiums, microphones, house sound system, and staging–1 of each per 50 attendees. *At a charge:* full darkroom, computer graphics, multi image staging and production, 3/4" on line and off line A/B/C roll video editing, 16 track audio recording studio; video projection, argon laser light show, concert sound and lighting systems. (All according to a published schedule.)

MEETING SUPPORT SERVICES:

Provided by the hotel – at no charge: First Aid; Attendee Registration – at a charge: Electrician; Locksmith; Laborers; A/V Operators & Repairmen; Photographer; Messenger; Stenographer; Notary.

Provided by local vendors – Printer; Carpenter; Display Builder; Translators; Sign Painter; Paint Shop; Plumber; Musicians; Security; Decorator; Tours & Entertainment.

Fig. 9–1. This ad from *Meetings and Conventions* magazine details all the services provided by the Westfields International Conference Center. A conference center is a very special property for your very special meeting. (Courtesy of Westfields.)

From a conference center, the planner has every right to expect a very professional, dedicated staff and, generally, with the best ones this is true.

Universities

Universities are a real asset to the community which is a convention and meetings destination. Not only can they offer a planner inexpensive housing and meeting space during the summer hiatus and other school vacation periods, but they can offer a wealth and wide variety of expertise when the planner is searching for speakers on a special subject, entertainment from their drama or music departments, or even research and information.

The university students can also be a source of manpower to assist with registrations, perform as ushers and car valets for special events, or to direct foot traffic at a trade show or exhibit. If the university has a hospitality department, or even more particularly, if it offers courses in meeting planning, students from that department can be especially helpful, while they too can obtain "hands-on" experience in the business. This may even prove to be a source for future staff for the meeting planner's own department. Any place the planner needs nonprofessional personnel, students may be quickly trained to assist, and are generally delighted with the opportunity to learn.

Community Centers

Community centers are certainly a part of the meeting scenario, if the planner is running a very large meeting, or if a sizeable trade show is a part of the convention. While this property will have nothing to do with sleeping rooms, breakfast problems at the hotel or room amenities, they will have a great deal to do with the physical set-up of the actual meetings and/or exhibit or show. This is their business, and in most cases a convention center does employ a very professional staff. Their people will know how to set up a meeting room to best advantage, and they will have engineers ready to install and operate any audio/visual requirements that the planner may have (generally their sound and lighting technicians are the very best). Again, their expertise can be invaluable to the planner, but the planner must be entirely cognizant of what the convention center should do so that he/she remains the planner *in charge!* Although the convention center personnel are fully cognizant of the capabilities of their facility and may prove to have invaluable suggestions, the meeting planner is still the client and should "call the shots" when making final decisions.

Community centers will ordinarily have a reception area or lobby for registrations, a large arena for general sessions, many break-out rooms for smaller conferences and a large exhibit/trade show area for booths; in addition, they will have catering capabilities to take care of meal or break requirements. Thus all meeting functions may be held under one roof.

The New Unlimited Addition.

With the new 400,000 square foot addition to the Las Vegas Convention Center, the possibilities will be unlimited. That's because the Convention Center is already America's largest single level convention complex. Adding to the unlimited possibilities is the fact that Las Vegas is building over 15,000 new hotel/motel rooms over the coming year.

What does all this mean to the meeting and convention planner? Choice... Unlimited variety of convention facilities and guest rooms. Our size assures access to booking dates to accommodate your needs. If you have big plans for your next meeting or convention, give us a call.

Las Vegas Convention and Visitors Authority
3150 Paradise Road, Las Vegas,
Nevada 89109-9096
702-733-2244

Fig. 9–2. Existing convention centers are expanding, like the Las Vegas Convention Center pictured here. New centers are being built throughout the country to service the growing number of large meetings. (Courtesy of the Las Vegas Convention Center.)

Exhibit Halls

Exhibit halls are generally found in the larger metropolitan areas, and are quite specialized. Their expertise lies in operating trade shows and exhibits with booths or display areas. Ordinarily they do not offer meeting space. Their personnel will be able to tell the planner the electrical requirements of all types of equipment and the availability of that power to certain areas of the hall. They can advise on booth construction, set-up and breakdown, and will probably assist in setting traffic patterns and ideal times for a show. However, the planner cannot count on them to promote attendance, encourage exhibitor participation or to insure the popularity or success of the show; that is still the planner's job!

If the physical facility is adequate, well-maintained and well-managed, its personnel knowledgeable about their own property as a show hall and the various union rulings, fire codes and shipping information required, they will have done their job for the planner.

Cruise Ships

Cruise ships are the newer entrants into the convention and meetings industry. They come in all sizes, from the small ship that can be chartered for a private cruise-meeting to the enormous liners on which the meeting group will be just a part of the entire passenger list. The degree of luxury may be as sumptuous or conservative as the meeting budget will allow.

Some of the advantages the planner must consider are:

1. A single price package with the cruise itself, all meals, meeting space, entertainment and services included
2. Encapsulation of the group, where at sea everyone must stay within the confines of the ship
3. Ports-of-Call which will serve as off-property entertainment and give everyone a chance to tour exotic islands and cities while shopping (in many cases, duty-free)
4. Constant on-ship activities in which attendees may participate or not as they wish

With all of this going for the planner, much of the creative, extracurricular planning work is done by the cruise line. On most cruises the food is plentiful and excellent, and entertainment may include big-name stars and/or casinos. On-board activities can be varied, from swimming, shuffleboard and badminton, to golf driving ranges, tennis, and trap and skeet shooting. Most ships also offer some limited shopping in boutiques and gift shops on-board.

The cruise ship can be ideal for certain meetings, but once again the planner must be sure that the ship can provide the "availability of needs" for the particular meeting. The site-selection process should be much the same as for a hotel or resort on land.

PERFECT HARMONY.
THROUGHOUT EUROPE.

Soon, Crystal Cruises will bring harmony to Europe. It will be known as the Crystal Age. And it begins in April 1991 when the Crystal Harmony introduces a new level of luxury and elegance.

Starting with an unforgettable Trans-Atlantic crossing, our twelve to fourteen-day itineraries visit the classic ports of the western Mediterranean; the romantic, sun-drenched ports of the eastern Mediterranean and Black Sea; and the lively, picturesque ports of northern Europe and Scandinavia. Each voyage made even more memorable by this splendid new ship, the Crystal Harmony.

You will be inspired by her luxury and elegance—from the grandeur of her public rooms,

to the lavish appointments of her staterooms, to more choices in dining than any ship in the world.

You will find more rooms with private verandahs, an ocean-view spa and salon, Caesars Palace at Sea and Broadway musical revues. Dining alternatives abound. There's the sumptuous menu of the Crystal Dining Room, the authentic Oriental cuisine of Kyoto and the Italian dining delights of Prego. All at no extra charge.

And, of course, a European-trained staff that is sensitive not only to your needs but to who you are—our guest.

Crystal Cruises are booked exclusively through travel agents.

CRYSTAL
C R U I S E S

WELCOME TO THE CRYSTAL AGE · EUROPE · TRANS-CANAL · SOUTH PACIFIC

Fig. 9–3. One of the more luxurious cruise lines, Crystal Cruises, might be perfect for a high-level corporate meeting. Their recent ad in *Travel & Leisure* magazine emphasizes the elegance of their ships and service. (Courtesy of Crystal Cruises.)

Suppliers of Accommodations and Meeting Space

Hotels
Resorts
Conference Centers
Universities
Community Centers
Exhibit Halls
Cruise Ships

The properties and people I have been discussing as suppliers have a physical plant complete with the following elements to sell the meeting planner: sleeping accommodations, meeting rooms, dining rooms, exhibit and show halls, to name a few. And, even more importantly, they are responsible for having well-trained employees to successfully assist within the parameters of their properties.

The next suppliers to be discussed, have much less concrete merchandise to present, in that they will provide the knowledgeable personnel who can assist the planner in organizing a function and then will know where to find, in their communities, the items and services required. Much of this expertise the planner must buy on the basis of reputation, past performance, or recommendation of some trustworthy person, since their product is generally not one they can parade before the planner for personal inspection.

SUPPLIERS OF FULL SERVICES TO THE PLANNER

Ground Handlers

Ground handlers, as the name indicates, specialize in organizing and operating ground transportation. This involves supervising all transport needed once a group deplanes from the air carrier that delivers them to a meeting destination city. This service can be particularly valuable in providing assistance to the planner without an enormous travel staff at the destination.

When a group arrives at the site city, the ground handler will direct them to the baggage claim area, assist in retrieving luggage, and then escort the members of the group to whatever transportation mode has been provided to move them to the site hotel. Ground handler personnel will accompany the group to the selected hotel, perhaps giving general information and bits of trivia, folklore and historical data en route. Once a group has arrived at the hotel, the ground handlers' airport function has been completed. This facet of a ground handler's duties may seem pretty simple and easily executed; however, experienced planners will advise that, depending upon a group's specific arrival pattern, this function can be as intricate, involved and critical to the success of a meeting as any other single entity in the meeting plan. *The first and probably most lasting impression attendees have of a meeting site is the welcome and assistance (or lack thereof) that they receive at the airport.*

Where multiple arriving flights may be involved, it is the duty of the ground handler to provide sufficient, efficient and appropriate transport for the anticipated arrival pattern; *and* few groups ever arrive with every flight performing according to schedule! The ground handler then must have "plan B" ready to accommodate those flights, which arrive anywhere from a few minutes to several hours early or late, without holding those passengers in the terminal who have managed to be on schedule. This takes forethought, preplanning, good judgment, people communication skills and often "nerves of steel." This demonstrates that one of the prime requisites for selecting a ground handler is to ascertain that the company under consideration has had lots of experience in shuttling groups close to the size and nature of the group for which the planner is responsible.

The following figure illustrates a typical airport transport worksheet utilized by ground handlers together with the passenger manifest (list of arriving passengers by flight).

Time	Airline/Flt. #	No. of Pax	Vehicle
8:00 A.M.	TWA #242	16	Van #1
8:16 A.M.	AAL #116	4	Van #2
9:22 A.M.	AW #32	10	Van #3
11:42 A.M.	AAL #366	41	Bus #1
11:59 A.M.	AW #57	8	Van #1
3:37 P.M.	UAL #177	67	Bus #1 & Bus #2
4:07 P.M.	AW #44	11	Van #1
6:02 P.M.	NW #1244	6	Van #1

In this example, turn-around time for each vehicle from airport to motel and return is 1½ hrs. This illustrates how the ground handler used Van #1 multiple times, while releasing Van #2 and #3 after a single trip. When the passenger count warranted, Bus #1 was used again, adding Bus #2 to accommodate all passengers.

The figure above illustrates how the ground handler must utilize all vehicles, but if these are the only vehicles on hand, what happens when AAL#116 is one hour late? Each van handles only twelve passengers with luggage, but Vans #1 and #2 must be utilized on the first run and will not have returned when the flight finally arrives at 10:00 A.M. The van scheduled for AW#32 cannot be used as it must wait for its flight, therefore, the experienced ground handler will have "standby vehicles" on hand for just this kind of eventuality. Knowing how to "juggle" vans, buses and limousines is part of the expertise of a truly professional ground handler.

In addition to meet/greet and transport from the airport, the ground handler will arrange and coordinate shuttles for multiple hotel meetings, provide transportation to the golf course or to local restaurants, set up shopping shuttles or provide special transportation to a factory or office, which may be part of the meeting. As their name describes, they will "handle" all ground transportation vehicles whether that requires inter-city buses, airport vans, business sedans, or standard and luxury/stretch limousines. The professional ground handler knows how and where to obtain the best vehicles to provide for the meeting's needs at the fairest prices.

Destination Management Companies

Destination management companies (DMCs) are just what their name implies. DMCs are often employed instead of ground handlers when the meeting is large enough or has a multiple activity program.

The DMC has often been described by meeting planners as "an addendum to the planner's own staff"; "a right hand" necessary to the success of any meeting held outside of the planner's own familiar terrain; the vibrant, creative mentality behind some of the most innovative, successful theme parties. As the name indicates, a destination management company will manage any and all facets of a meeting from the time attendees leave their transportation of arrival, until they are expertly transported back to their departing transport. If a meeting is large enough or its plan is intricate enough to overload the planner's own staff, a DMC is the answer to a prayer!

In addition to performing the ground handler's chores, the DMC will also construct tours for attendees and/or spouses, develop interesting programs to entertain, instruct or amuse the group, provide additional staff to assist the planner on-site in the hotel, structure full golf and tennis tournaments, supply pillow gifts, prizes or other giveaways within the meeting budget. The DMC may suggest speakers or program participants and then hire them, supervise their part in the program, see that they are picked up at the airport, housed, fed, rehearsed, on time for their participation and then returned to the airport with paycheck, honorarium or fee in hand.

The DMC staff will also know where to find a proficient photographer, a local quick-print shop, secretaries, office equipment and people to operate same, florists, car rental agencies, local doctors, hospitals, churches, pharmacies and just about anything else the planner or meeting attendees may need on the spur of the moment.

DMCs are also often the source of truly innovative, imaginative, unique and fascinating theme parties. (These will be discussed in more detail in the section on suppliers of theme parties.)

Some DMCs charge for their expertise by billing the planner for all actual expenses, plus an hourly fee for their help. Others will work on the basis of a percentage charge on all activities in which they are involved. Whatever their charge, or however they arrive at the figure, the truly professional destination management company is worth every penny. They will take much of the load (and the "blood, sweat and tears") off the shoulders of the hard-pressed meeting planner. The good ones are creative, knowledgeable, ethical, professional and reliable.

The destination management company will interface with all of the other suppliers on behalf of the meeting planner. Therefore, the planner who is employing a DMC will have no need to contact any of the other suppliers we will be mentioning in this chapter, with the exception of the hotel convention coordinator.

Hotel Convention Coordinators

Hotel convention coordinator is just another name for the convention services director and the director's staff, which is generally made up of several convention services assistants, and a clerical staff. This group may be as small as two people or as large as the hotel's meeting and convention business demands. Once the sales department has sold the planner on holding a meeting in their hotel and the contract has been negotiated and signed, the coordination of all in-house functions for that meeting are turned over to the convention services department.

In most fine hotels, a single person will be introduced to the meeting planner as the contact for everything involved in that meeting. This individual is critical to the planner for getting things done within the property. The coordinator's job is to help the planner create the kind of meeting atmosphere he or she wishes to convey, while within the hotel confines. This staff will help the planner block rooms, select meeting areas, devise menus, plan in-house activities and then be there to supervise the hotel side of each event.

Many a meeting has moved from one hotel to another when an excellent hotel coordinator (convention service director) has changed jobs. Proficiency at the job is so critical that clients will follow a truly good coordinator from one property to another.

The sales manager who has obtained the business for his hotel property will generally outline the meeting with the planner. But once the planner has negotiated and signed the contract, all operations are turned over to the convention coordinator or convention services person. From that point on, the success of the meeting can depend greatly on that person's talents.

The convention coordinator's greatest assets are:

❑ A thorough knowledge of the hotel property
❑ The creative energy to work with a wide variety of planners
❑ Understanding of traffic patterns and flow
❑ A flare for menu selection
❑ Knowledge of the capabilities (and limitations) of the property's kitchen
❑ Information on food and beverage and costs
❑ A working acquaintance with local suppliers in order to know where to find A/V expertise and good sound and light technicians, a creative floral designer, musicians and good ground transportation

❏ Familiarity with the local destination management companies, decorators and tour suppliers

❏ Above all, the ability to know when a request can be handled by the hotel, and when to say "no" and suggest outside suppliers to the planner

To summarize, the coordinator must be knowledgeable about the hotel in particular and meetings in general, and must be amenable and, perhaps most importantly, must be flexible.

There are at least two reasons for the convention coordinator at a hotel to be proficient:

1. It is the job of the coordinator to work effectively with the planner, to provide everything within reason that is needed to make the meeting a success. If in the process he is able to upgrade or increase the expenditures of the planner within the hotel during the meeting, he has fulfilled one of his commitments to his employer, the hotel.
2. The coordinator's performance may well be measured by his or her superiors on how many planners are sufficiently impressed with the services in the hotel, that they book another meeting at the same property.

Therefore, we see that it is to the advantage of both the coordinator and the planner that the hotel coordinator do the best possible job.

The convention coordinator is a good person to befriend when booking a meeting into a property, but the planner must remember that, although the coordinator becomes a "friend," the coordinator still works for the hotel!

SUPPLIERS WHO PROVIDE ENTERTAINMENT

Agents

When trying to locate musicians, dancers, actors, models or other performers to add "pizzazz" to a meeting or convention, unless the planner is one of those rare people who really knows the entertainment business, a professional should be utilized!

The minute that word gets out that the planner is looking for a performer, or an entire show, agents will begin "knocking down the doors." An agent represents the artist and usually has a "stable" of performers to whom he or she is committed to find jobs, engagements or "gigs." For their services, the agents will receive a percentage of the performer's fee or wages.

Because agents are committed to finding work for those performers who have retained them, they are limited to supplying the planner with those people. If an agent happens to have just the right entertainer for the planner, that agent will be the best source. But, if his or her stable does not include the kind of entertainment wanted, the planner must look elsewhere. The agent is generally local.

The Booking Agency

A larger, more sophisticated version of the local agent, is the entertainment booking agency. Many of these companies have multiple offices throughout the country or even internationally. While these agencies do act for certain artists, they also have wide contacts in the industry and can obtain through other agencies any kind of performer or entire show that a meeting planner would like to hire and can afford.

They will research the meeting date and location, and tell the planner what "name" performer may be in the area at that time, and thus would enable the planner to save some of the time and travel monies that would ordinarily have to be paid to transport the artists. Or entertainers, in order to profitably use the time while in the area of a meeting, may perform for a reduced fee if they are already booked nearby.

With the large booking agencies, the planner can indicate which artists or name entertainers would be appropriate for the meeting or convention, and they will contact the performers' agents to determine their availability and cost.

When hiring through these booking agencies, the planner will still pay the artist the extra percentage to cover the agency fee. If the agency has obtained the entertainer through another agency, that additional agency fee will be added to the cost.

In dealing with agents or agencies, the planner should remember to ask if the quoted artists' prices include all backup musicians, required sound and light equipment, any transportation and hotel and meal costs. Sometimes these contracts will also include limousines to and from performances, rehearsal time, personal services like makeup persons, hairdressers and/or complete hotel suites for the "stars" and their entourages. These items can add considerably to contract costs, so the planner must be sure to ascertain that everything has been included in the amount of money quoted. Many a novice meeting planner has been disastrously surprised when the final billing was delivered.

One last comment on agents and agencies: They can considerably lessen the planner's degree of tension. The agent's representative will arrive on-site well before the performance is scheduled. It is an integral part of the job description to see that the musicians are on-property, their equipment set-up and inspected, in proper costume and ready to play when the planner has indicated. Because of their wide contacts, agencies will be ready to call in substitutes in the event of an illness, emergency "no show" or an unavoidable late arrival. With out-of-town performers, should weather or mechanical failure cause cancellation or delay of flights, or should a local traffic accident involve the planner's "show," the agent representative will be able to provide some sort of backup plan in a hurry. This factor alone makes the agent well worth his or her fee.

Individual Performers

Individual performers may well represent themselves and not contract through an agent. Particularly where the planner is seeking a local guitarist for background, a small chamber group, or a local dance trio or dance band, he/she may receive brochures, flyers or information direct from the performer. Generally, the local convention bureau will have released the information that a specific meeting is being planned and this triggers the flood of information to the planner, including data from entertainers.

Hiring an entertainer directly will save money, however, the planner should be sure to check with staff at the hotel, with destination management companies, and with bureau personnel to see if they are familiar with the performer and will recommend both his/her talent and reliability. It might even be possible to preview the talent, if they are playing elsewhere at a convenient time.

Without an agent or agency involved, the planner must remember to be sure the entertainment arrives on time, that sufficient time has been allowed for setting up instruments, sound and light equipment, etc. (How many times have attendees walked into a function to find the musicians still "tuning up"?) In the event of a "no show" or late arrival, it will be the planner's responsibility to substitute at the last moment. Is the planner prepared with an alternate plan? Is there someone on the planning staff who plays piano?

One final critical note for the planner: Most entertainers must be paid the night of performance, so the check book must be ready if dealing directly with individual performers!

Hotel Properties

In recent years, hotel properties have sometimes arranged all entertainment being booked into their hotel. If the selected site has this service, you may wish to allow them to book entertainment for the meeting.

In the event that the hotel is arranging entertainment, you should remember that they are adding their own fee for this service. *And* if the planner elects to have entertainment billed to the master account, another 15% is probably being added to the bill for this privilege. Hotels are in the business of selling sleeping rooms, anything else that they are requested to do is not gratis.

On the other side of the coin, if the hotel books the performers, it is now their responsibility to see that the entertainment shows up on time. And, since the property is interested in the planner's future business, their recommendations can usually be depended upon.

Destination Management Companies

As we discuss earlier in this chapter, DMCs can take over all arrangements for a meeting at their specific destination city; and one of these functions can be booking entertainment. The advantages of allowing a DMC to perform this task are much the same as those for using an agency: They become responsible for supervising set-up, arrival, performance, breakdown and on-site payment. And, as with any agency, their fee for services rendered will be added to the cost of the act.

Entertainment Bookers

Agents
Booking Agencies
Individual Performers
Hotel/Resort Properties
Destination Management Companies

Entertainment, whatever form it takes, is the focal point of many convention or meeting functions. Therefore, it is critical that the performers be good, professional, on time and as advertised. So, whatever method of hiring entertainment the planner chooses, the reputation of the performer, show and/or agent is of utmost importance. The planner should do as much checking as possible before hiring, then be absolutely sure that the contract is all-inclusive, including penalties for a no show, or lateness.

SUPPLIERS WHO PROVIDE THEME PARTIES

Theme Parties

Theme parties are those functions where a planner wishes to create an entire experience, through illusion. The theme must be carried out through site, decor, entertainment, menu, etc. It is possible for the meeting planner, with a large staff, to put together the theme party. However, in most cases, with the constraints of time and lack of knowledge as to what's available at the site city, the planner would be well-advised to hire someone to create this function.

If the meeting planner is using a destination management company to make all local arrangements, then this is the route to take. The DMC will probably have a large list of themes, which have already been created and run successfully, or they can often be the source of new, truly innovative, imaginative, unique and fascinating theme parties. The DMC will be able to produce an event that carries out the total theme of a meeting; develop a party to encompass an idea presented by the meeting planner; or come up with a totally new concept, complete with props, decorations, music, entertainment, costumes and even a complementary menu. One of the most elaborate themes might be a gorgeous Arabian Nights party complete with costumed Arabian horse show, exotic belly dancers, courageous fire eaters, unbelievable jugglers, enormous tents festooned with oriental rugs and silken hangings and complete with knee-high tables and accompanying velvet cushions for the dinner guests, all complemented by appropriate live music, foods and beverages.

Another exciting evening could be a "'name of the company' 500" — an event featuring 14″ race cars, remotely controlled by radios in the hands of attendees, racing on a 40' × 30' black turf oval track, complete with grandstands, gasoline alley with pit crews and smartly attired models to rescue those cars which hang up on the side bumpers or under the flower-bedecked bridges. The ballroom decorated with race banners, car tires, posters from oil and tire companies and 8' trophies. Each dinner table with a small golf-cart tire full of flowers and flying colorful pennants. One side of the room could be lined with booths for the purpose of paramutuel betting on favorite cars and "drivers" — with play money of course. This would be a favorite with competitive type groups who would rather participate in some activity than to be passively entertained.

A more elegant party — if not as active — is an around the world motif! Food would be served (with appropriate beverages) from a multitude of stations around the ballroom. Each station representing a country (or perhaps a city in which the host company had district offices) complete with backdrop, furnishings, costumed service personnel, and some type of musical or entertainment group indigenous to that area.

For instance, New Orleans represented by a backdrop containing wrought iron balconies over a typical French-Quarter hotel. In front of this, linen-bedecked buffets heaped with crayfish, jambolaya, prawns, blackened redfish and other Cajun delicacies and a bar station serving Sazaracs. A typical New Orleans jazz trio playing under street lights bearing "Canal Street" and "Bourbon Street" signs completing the atmosphere.

Another backdrop could represent Dallas, complete with corral fence and horses, hay bales and a huge barbecue grill serving steak fingers, mini bowls of Texas chili, corn cobettes, a bar with the expected "red eye" and a stetson-and-boots-clad western trio.

The Paris area, with a backdrop of Notre Dame Cathedral, could be fronted with a miniature Eiffel Tower and tables bearing every kind of French pastry and chocolate delicacy one could imagine, accompanied by fine coffee and Napoleon brandy.

The Japanese sector could boast a mini pool stocked with colorful Japanese Coy (a colorful, large Goldfish) under a cascading waterfall. A fine Suschi Bar and hot Saki served by kimono-clad servers would complete the aura.

This type of party has as many possibilities as there are cities. Each should have some sort of entertainment or music which should be put on a strict schedule to avoid a cacophony of sound. Each area is elegantly lighted to fit its mood and these lights become highlight spots as each booth's entertainment is featured. To successfully accomplish this, a technician with a good light and sound board is mandatory.

Decorators

Decorators are companies which generally have large warehouses full of props, together with the technical expertise to put them together, to create the illusion or theme to fit a particular occasion. Upon contact from a meeting planner, they will undoubtedly come up with a catalogue of descriptions, photos and costs on hundreds of potential themes. If the planner has some other theme in mind, they will also work up a price to create exactly the party wanted. By using one of their stock ideas, however, the planner can save dollars. The props necessary for the party have already been constructed or collected and used before; therefore, the planner will be paying a rental fee for the decor, instead of having to bear the cost of design, construction and materials for entirely new props which may or may not be used again.

For some reason, themes seem to run in cycles. The planner will find the very same themes being used in many cities across the country. For instance, with the popularity of the "M.A.S.H." television show, every decorator in the U.S. structured an entire "M.A.S.H." party, complete with tents, operating room "greens" for costuming, IV bottles as dispensers for beverages, and mess tent tinware for food service. Everpopular are the "Roaring Twenties" and "Sock-Hop '50s" parties. The decor, props, and entertainment have been packaged for almost every convention and meeting destination by decorating companies.

Cities in the South will present "Gone With the Wind" parties, the West offers "Cowboys, Indians and Gunfighters" as themes. And who would not enjoy a "Las Vegas Night" or a take-off on the "New Orleans Mardi Gras"? These types of theme parties are very popular because they can "fit" with the destination or locale in which the planner has decided to hold the meeting. The attendees feel they are getting a touch of local history and color.

Some of the individually created parties that have been produced were an "Alice in Wonderland" complete with Mad Hatter and March Hare, the Looking Glass and fancifully decorated toadstool-strewn garden paths leading to the ballroom; a "Moonscape Party," complete with artificial fog and futuristically costumed guests surrounded by mock planets; a "Toyland Party" with mechanically active Jack and Jill; Hickory, Dickory, Dock mice complete with grandfather clock; See-Saw Marjorie Daw and other celebrated nursery rhyme characters, all in motion. Guests at this one were asked to come dressed as their favorite nursery rhyme character. Party themes are limited only by the imagination of the creator.

All of these parties *must* be produced by a professional decorator, who can build the sets, drape the walls, design centerpieces, obtain costumes if indicated and alert attendees that they are to be costumed, create innovative invitations, develop a complementary menu and find the caterer to produce it (providing the party is *not* in a hotel), and then put together the music or show to complete the total experience.

Properties

Properties, that is hotels, resorts and convention centers, now maintain on their premises a few props for specific theme parties. Some have created special themes themselves, others have simply jumped on the band wagon of a particularly popular theme. For instance, in the southwest almost every hotel can come up with the component parts for a Mexican fiesta or a western cookout.

If your theme is to be held off property, or if you want a more elaborate, creatively different party, then work with a good decorator.

Fig. 9–4 A & B. A local hotel ballroom was transformed into a typical western town in about four hours for a "Western Hoedown," and a local resort became the site of an elegant "Mexican Fiesta" with adobe walls, a colorful tree-of-life, paper flowers, and multi-colored serapes and piñatas. Both were designed and created by Ambience Decorating of Tucson, Arizona.

Agents

Agents who book entertainment are beginning to build theme parties around their clients' acts or shows.

One popular show out of Phoenix, Arizona is based on the music of Fats Waller and the '20s era. The booking agent will not only sell you the one-hour show, but will also provide wall decor with period posters, table centerpieces, and dinner music, plus an after-dinner dance group.

Agents have found that many of their musicians and performers are more marketable if combined with a complete package of an evening's illusion.

A popular magician now arranges for tuxedo-clad tableside magicians to perform closeup magic during dinner, invitations to the party written in disappearing ink, his/her major illusionist show, magical centerpieces and music throughout the evening.

One of the currently popular murder mysteries is done entirely in music, can be hired with "Columbo and his basset hound" wandering around the cocktail party asking questions and taking notes, centerpieces containing clues to the murder, mysterious invitations, the full musical mystery presented during dinner, prizes for the guests who solve the murder, and again musicians for cocktails, dinner and dancing. All of this put together by the agent for the musicians performing the show.

Theme parties can add a memorable experience to any meeting or convention; however, the theme party should be in keeping with the overall impression the planner is trying to create. If the meeting stresses the future, very avant garde approaches to the company's next ten years, the planner won't want to include a "'50s Sock Hop" as the meeting's party. The theme party should be an integral part of the meeting and should *contribute* to its goals.

Theme Party Suppliers

Destination Management Companies
Decorators
Hotel/Resort Properties
Agents

SIGHTSEEING

Sightseeing is a part of most meetings. With leisure time between sessions, spouses in attendance and people combining meetings with vacations, meeting planners are more and more frequently providing tours to see local sights and attractions.

Sightseeing to some persons seems to dredge up visions of "little old ladies" trooping aboard an overcrowded bus for a boring afternoon of lectures by an overzealous tour guide. Nothing could be further from the truth. There is no better way to see a strange city and learn about its culture and points of interest than to take a tour escorted by a thoroughly trained, knowledgeable guide. However, for the more active and adventurous types there are other ways to structure the local tour. And these variations may be arranged by the meeting planning staff or by a destination management company.

Arrange to rent sufficient cars for the group, from a local car rental agency. (Perhaps even arrange for convertibles, weather permitting.) Equip each car with an unmarked road map and set of "road rally" instructions, plus a polaroid camera with lots of film. The "check points" on the road rally, are various attractions and points of interest in the area, each of which is listed in the instructions with exact mileage and estimated travel time. "Timers" from the meeting planning staff are stationed at each check point/attraction to check car times in and out and to be of general assistance. Luncheon can be a simple menu at one of the attractions on the route, or may be a glamorous, gourmet picnic catered "out in the boondocks." The proof that each car has kept to the itinerary and schedule is a combination of arrival/departure times kept by the "timers" and specific, required polaroid shots taken by the photographer in each car. Every participant can be provided with a road rally jacket and a car antennae can carry banners with corporate name(s) and possible road rally symbol. This requires some sightseeing, and provides great competitive fun. Winning cars and "race teams" receive prizes at the final banquet.

Jeep Tours/Scavenger Hunts

Another method of seeing the countryside is a scavenger hunt by jeep. Many cities now have jeep tour companies which will construct a full-day tour by jeep, including luncheon. Only imagination limits the activities that can be included, and competitions can be arranged between all of the jeeps on the tour. Jeeps provide an imaginative way to see some magnificent "off-the-beaten-track" scenery in even the roughest country.

Because it takes familiarity with the local environment, tours are best put together by someone knowledgeable from the site city.

Transportation Companies

Transportation companies, in order to broaden usage of their vehicles, construct tours which may be taken by the individual participant, or they charter out their vehicles and escorts to the meeting planner for a private tour.

Although the company will have stock tours, the meeting planner can get together with the sales department of the tour company and construct exactly the kind of tour attendees might enjoy, and arrange for pick up at the site-hotel instead of at the pick-up area of the transportation company. The tour may include several attractions, stops for shopping and arrangements for a luncheon stop or box lunches.

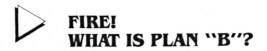

FIRE!
WHAT IS PLAN "B"?

Anonymous
Tours coordinator for a
destination management company

A major corporation was planning an incentive in our town and had selected our firm as their DMC.

A very comprehensive plan of activities had been presented to the company and they had accepted all of our recommendations with enthusiasm. They were particularly enthralled with a complete Mexican fiesta we had planned *in Mexico!* Since the participants were all from the east coast of the U.S., this would be a memorable experience.

Six well-appointed inter-city motor coaches in tandem would pick up the group at their hotel in the early morning. En route, two of our well-trained tour escorts on each motor coach, in full Mexican costume, would serve a truly gourmet boxed breakfast, complete with fresh fruit, sopapillas (delicate puffy pastries filled with honey), hot huevos rancheros (scrambled eggs served on paper thin flour tortillas topped with salsa, guacamole and sour cream), champagne, coffee, milk or tea. Stops en route would include visits to a 1700s Spanish Indian mission, where the indians also have puestos (booths) from which one could purchase all kinds of original Indian handicrafts; a pecan grove in the midst of full harvest (where we arranged for each person to be given a package of the fresh, succulent nut meats); an operating chile factory; and a private country club, which had been constructed on a rancho boasting an original Spanish land grant. At the club, we would enjoy a margarita or a cup of coffee, while seated at a bar equipped with hand-tooled Mexican roping saddles as bar stools. After this mid-morning stop, we would proceed to an artists' colony inhabiting what used to be a village around a Spanish presidio (or fort), where our guests could browse and shop for all kinds of crafts from sun-baked tiles, to fine wrought iron work, oil paintings, hand-woven designer fabrics and original hand-thrown pottery.

Subsequent to these sightseeing stops, we would proceed into Mexico, where luncheon had been arranged at La Caverna—a celebrated and marvelous Mexican restaurant, located in deep caves dug into the hillside. The caves had once housed a jail from which Pancho Villa had miraculously escaped. Here we would also have a full Mariachi band, and an exhibition of Folklorico dancing, while lunching on the freshest of shellfish from the Sea of Cortez and a selection of Mexican foods from both Sonora (northern Mexico) and the Mexico City area.

Participants then had the option of attending a real bull fight or using the time for browsing and shopping in Mexico, before the 90 minute trip home, during which we would have "show and tell," with each participant displaying and bragging about the bargains and purchases made on the trip. This would indeed be a trip to remember!

Just as the last coach pulled away from the hotel, I received a radio message from our office. La Caverna had experienced a major kitchen fire the evening before, igniting most of the interior of the restaurant. Most fortunately, no one had been injured, but this tragedy would put this landmark out of business for months to come. (As a matter of fact, they never were able to open again.) In the meantime, we had some 275 persons on the road, expecting luncheon at La Caverna—and where could we find a location, along the prospective route, who could handle nearly 300 persons for luncheon, with no more than three or so hours advance notice?

In situations like this, it's nice to have business friends who will go all out to assist! The Sheraton Rio Rico, sits just 12 miles north of the Mexican border, and they have a very large patio area and poolside, which could be set up for luncheon in a hurry. Because they were not prepared for 300 persons eating the *same* menu, we opted for a large and *varied* buffet (whatever they had on hand and could prepare in a hurry), with as many Mexican food touches as they could manage. They did have a supply of Guaymas shrimp, their chef could manage a complete salad buffet, fresh Mexican fruit and hot hand-tossed tortillas. In addition, good old American prime rib, sliced thinly and rolled in the tortillas with green or red chile salsa, trays of cheeses, and for the faint of heart, they would also add miniature hamburgers, tiny rolls and all of the condiments prepared on portable grills at the buffet. This part of the problem was solved—thanks to a very flexible and amenable chef at Sheraton Rio Rico.

Now, how to relay our brilliant solution to the group. Our radios could not reach the motorcoaches beyond a few miles. Staff members got on telephones and left messages at every stop en route to Old Mexico, and finally, one of the escorts called us back.

Although the group truly missed the experience of luncheon at La Caverna, they received a superb and widely varied buffet experience at an American resort and still proceeded across the border for shopping and the bull fights.

For every event, always have plan B! I don't know how you could arrange for a preplanned option B, when it entails food for 300 persons; I don't know of a restaurant or caterer who would agree to be ready for a large group if you happen to need them! I guess plan B in a case like this has to be: Know your area, and make good friends in all areas of the business, so that when you find yourself in a real bind they are willing to go the extra mile to be of help.

Attractions

Attractions are those commercial entities which offer some kind of sightseeing and/or entertainment. It may be a large theme park like Disneyworld®, a local art museum or a cave or other natural phenomenon. In order to attract group business from the meeting planner, the attraction may put together transportation, tour itinerary, escort/guide, admission fees and luncheons in a total reduced single price package.

This type of tour is slightly limited, however, since the attraction is putting together the package and probably will not include any other commercial entity. However, if the attraction is sufficiently interesting to be a "stop" in itself, perhaps you would not want to include anything additional, and certainly these people would put together the most knowledgeable tour of their own property.

Tour Guide Companies

Tour guide companies are organized to gather, train and provide attractive, uniformed, friendly and knowledgeable escorts and guides to local sightseeing and attractions. Generally they do not provide the transportation. Often these guides are also employed to meet/greet at the airport and accompany the transfer vehicles to the hotel — this can make the trip more educational and help make a long trip more enjoyable. If the planner has rented vans for usage during the meeting, he/she may make them available for a group of spouses and children to tour and shop, and, not knowing the area, it is usually wise to hire one of the guides from these companies to accompany the group.

Or, if the planner is working directly with a transportation company for airport transfers, he/she may want to charter their vehicles for sightseeing or transportation to a theme party, and then hire an escort/guide to go along and make the trip more interesting. Sometimes the tour guide companies will also make their personnel available to staff registration desks or act as general assistants to the meeting planner during the meeting. If the planner is short on staff, this is an excellent way to add extra personnel.

☐ *SUMMARY*

In this chapter, I have discussed the various types of suppliers who assist the planner in putting together the on-site portions of his or her meeting. In addition to those mentioned, the planner also may depend upon florists, printers, temporary personnel companies, office supply stores, computer rental companies, and many, many others in the community. The types of suppliers may be as varied and many in numbers as the meeting plan demands.

The meeting planner must depend upon subcontracted suppliers for many, many portions of a meeting. The types of suppliers can be divided into two major segments:

1. Those who supply accommodations and meeting rooms
2. Those who supply a multitude of services

The first division includes hotels, resorts, conference centers, universities, community centers, exhibit halls and cruise ships. The second group is comprised of ground handlers, destination management companies and hotel convention coordinators. It also includes the various agents who supply entertainment and theme parties, decorators and a multitude of persons offering sightseeing options, as well as florists, printers, temporary employee agencies, A/V equipment suppliers, caterers, attractions and all of those persons offering any of the many services used in producing a successful meeting.

❑ *PROJECTS*

1. Look around your own community and see if you can identify all of the hotels, resorts, conference centers, universities, community centers, exhibit halls and, if you happen to live in a coastal region, cruise ships that might act as suppliers to a meeting planner. Find out from each of them just how one goes about getting into their end of the business. What education or work background do they require?

2. Contact a local DMC (if your area has one) and ask just how they feel about their performance as suppliers to the meetings industry. Ask the DMC persons that you contact how they got into the business. What background in experience and education did they offer?

3. Call a local resort or hotel convention coordinator or convention services director and find out how that department acts as a supplier to the meetings industry. Again, ascertain just what background experience and/or education is needed to break into this part of the business.

4. If you have a booking agency in your area, find out if they work with meetings and meeting planners and just what their service entails. How do you obtain employment in a booking agency?

❑ *DISCUSSION QUESTIONS*

1. How does the text define "suppliers"? What is their impact upon the planner's meeting?

2. Describe the hotel as a supplier. What makes the resort a more comprehensive supplier?

3. When would a planner elect a community center as a supplier? What do they do for the planner?

4. How does an exhibit hall differ from a community center? In what way are they suppliers?

5. Give several reasons why it may be smart to use a supplier in obtaining entertainment.

6. Give the pros and cons of using an agent to obtain performers.

7. What does a booking agency do and how do they differ from the individual agent?

8. In dealing with entertainment, name some of the extras that should be listed in the contract.

9. When would a planner book an individual performer directly?

10. Just what is a "theme party"?

11. Who puts together theme parties?

12. What is the major function of a decorator? Other than strictly room decor, what will a decorator supply?

13. How does a hotel property get into developing theme parties? What kinds might they be able to handle on behalf of the planner?

14. **When would you *not* use a hotel property to create a theme?**

15. **Why do entertainment agents get into theme parties? What kinds of themes might be built around their performers?**

16. **Why have sightseeing tours become such an integral part of many meetings?**

17. **Describe the "road rally" as a sightseeing tour. What other means might there be of structuring tours that are different?**

18. **How do transportation companies fit into tours/sightseeing? When might a planner hire a transportation company for tours?**

19. **Why does an attraction get into the business of structuring tours?**

20. **Name some ways a planner can make tours more individualized?**

21. **When would a planner *not* want to use an attraction as a tour company?**

22. **What is the function of a tour guide company? Name several ways a planner might use their services.**

10

PUTTING TOGETHER THE BUDGET AND THE MEETING PLAN

OBJECTIVES

After reading this chapter, you will be able:

❏ To illustrate how the planner controls the costs of a meeting through a financial plan
❏ To explain the budgeting process
❏ To demonstrate the construction of income and expense budgets and the accompanying spreadsheet
❏ To illustrate the necessity of a comprehensive meeting plan
❏ To show how the progress chart relates to the meeting planning process

The business of meetings and conventions continues to grow by leaps and bounds. According to *Meetings & Conventions Magazine,* May 1990, pp. 5–6, expenditures for meetings in 1989 totaled 43.7 billion dollars and 94 million people attended those meetings. That's big business! Those who control dollars of that magnitude certainly need organized planning.

THE MEETING BUDGET

Once the purpose and goals for a particular meeting have been determined and the broad outline agenda or program have been set, the next step is to put together a financial plan. This financial plan is demonstrated and controlled through the drawing up of a meeting budget. The basic meeting budget consists of three major parts: the expense budget, the income budget and the spreadsheet. Accountants will talk about balance sheets, statements of income and expense, charts of accounts, and supplementary schedules— and if you are well-versed in accounting, all of these records are of inestimable value. However, the planner can work well with the basic expense and income budgets and a spreadsheet, to have a working knowledge of the meeting's financial condition at all times, and be well in control of the meeting finances. Leaving the more finely tuned accounting records to the accounting department, the planner can keep a day-by-day "finger" of control on the finances of a meeting with simple income and expense budgets and accompanying spreadsheets.

The planner must know some of the basic concepts of the organization for which he/she is planning a meeting; such as: Is the meeting supposed to make a profit? Is the meeting planner only responsible for seeing that the meeting breaks even? Or is the organization "underwriting" the entire expense, so that the benefits of the meeting are intangible instead of financial, and the meeting is not even expected to pay for its own expenses?

THE EXPENSE BUDGET

For our purposes, let's presume that the meeting needs only to break even. Our first chore then is to set up the projected expense budget. This budget will include all of the monies needed to produce the meeting. The budget should be constructed such that every possible expenditure has been foreseen and is included. Each heading in the expense budget has detailed sub-items that cover every possible cost. For example, the first item may be "Program Expense," and sub headings would include: program committee expenses; speaker fees and expenses; composition and printing of any hand-outs to be used in the program; and finally, writing, layout and printing (including photos and artwork if applicable) of the program booklet. Note the expense budget sample in Appendix D, and be particularly aware of all of the line items in this expense budget. This is a sample for an imaginary meeting. Every meeting may have these line items plus or minus items or events, which must be reflected in the budget.

To support each line item, the planner should have a single sheet of paper attached to the budget, indicating how that cost was calculated. If the item "Printing of Program" is listed at $2,000, then an attached sheet should show that the program is projected to be 8 double-sided pages (16 pages), printed in 2 colors on fine sixty pound slick magazine stock, with an eighty pound colored card stock cover, and that the quote from the printer for 400 copies is to be $2,000. To explain an item for "Air Fares— Corporate Personnel" at $5,260, there should be an attached sheet delineating that this figure covers round-trip air fare, tourist class, of $526 each for 10 corporate personnel from Philadelphia, PA. to the meeting destination Phoenix, AZ. Thus, backup information is available, so that if it becomes necessary to reduce expenses, the planner can immediately see how all of the figures were arrived at and where a few dollars might possibly be cut.

The first preliminary expense budget should include all of the things that the planner would like to see included in the meeting format. Then, after the income budget is developed, if there is a shortage of funds the planner can go back and start paring down any frills that aren't absolutely necessary and that won't really affect the quality of the meeting if they were to be eliminated.

The last item in the expense budget should be an amount of money called a *contingency fund*. This item (generally from 2% to 5% of the total expense budget) creates a "cushion" for the planner against going over budget. In the event of any estimated cost increases between the time of the budget and the actual meeting, or if some additional item is added to the program once the meeting is on-site, the contingency fund allows for payment without exceeding the budget. Should the Chairman of the Board decide at the last minute that a photographer is needed to cover the golf tournament, in order that candid slides can be shown at the golf awards luncheon, the costs for this service would then be taken from the contingency fund.

THE INCOME BUDGET

Once the ideal expense budget is complete, the planner turns to the income budget. This budget demonstrates by line items every possible source of funds for running the meeting. It may include: meeting registration fees; hotel reservation monies (if the planner is handling hotel reservations); ticket purchases by attendees for special meals or events; exhibit booth rentals (if an exhibit is part of the meeting); and/or monies provided by suppliers to host a special dinner, party or sports event. If start-up monies are being provided from a previous meeting, these too would be a part of the income budget, as would any special grants or gifts. (See Appendix D for a sample income budget.)

BALANCING THE BUDGET

When both expense and income budgets have been completed, the planner then compares the bottom line figures to be sure that expenses will not exceed income. And, in the case of our imaginary meeting, which needs only to break even, special events, tours or gifts might be added to absorb any income overage.

THE SPREADSHEET

When both income and expense budgets have been reviewed and the planner is satisfied that the meeting can be created and produced within those budgets, a spreadsheet is constructed. This is merely a chart of all projected income and expenses divided up into each month between the time the planning process begins and the end of the meeting. (See Appendix D for a sample spreadsheet). By studying the spreadsheet, the planner can tell each month whether or not the financial condition of the meeting is on target. If the planner perceives some problem area, adjustments can be made by either cutting costs or increasing income. Thus, the financial management responsibility for a meeting is handled.

THE MEETING PLAN

The meeting plan is just what the name implies: the meeting planner's written, detailed blueprint of the meeting. Every planner has developed a favorite meeting plan format, but the basic contents of every plan are very similar. We will look at one such plan in detail (See Appendix D), keeping in mind that it may be altered, expanded or adjusted to fit a particular meeting or the style of a certain meeting planner.

Let's consider the basic components of a good meeting plan:

1. Index page — directions to all of the detailed information
2. Data on site city, property, DMC being used et al
3. Detailed list of property staff with inside phone numbers
4. Information on property, insurance, unions, front desk registration, meeting rooms, general data
5. List of dining facilities within the property
6. Information on sports facilities/amenities on property
7. Attendee registration list with room and arrival/departure information
8. Detailed day-by-day plans of each meeting or event
9. Final meeting closure information and checklist
10. Meeting evaluation data

The meeting plan is begun just as soon as the site-selection process is over and continues through final evaluation report. Concurrently with the development of a meeting plan, the planner should begin the progress calendar, which details each facet of the plan, illustrating the status of each task day by day. (See Chapter 15 for examples of a progress calendar.) In order for any executive to maintain management control of any project or event, a written organized plan must be developed. In the case of a meeting plan, it should be complete and comprehensive enough that any experienced travel staff member could run that meeting from the plan. Immediately after the location has been determined and the site property selected, the first pages of the plan can be filled in. That is, the information about the property and its personnel. Then as the program itself is developed, all corresponding information is filled in on the pages of the plan. (See examples in the Meeting Plan, Appendix D.) By studying the sample meeting plan, one can see just how the meeting plan carries all detailed information on the property, the program of the meeting, all meals and extracurricular activities and the attendant costs.

Concurrent with the development of the meeting plan is the finalization of the budgets as previously discussed. As more and more detail is finalized for placement in the meeting plan, those more accurate costs can be put into the budget.

Also, as the meeting plan is constructed, the calendar, which will keep it all on schedule, is annotated and placed on the meeting manager's wall in a conspicuous place. By color-coded dots and progress lines, every task preparatory to the meeting is scheduled and its current status followed graphically. (See sample in Chapter 15.) By having this tracer method prominently displayed, the planner can detect any trouble spots in the progress and completion of various tasks, and handle any problems before they become critical.

WHAT NOW? PROMOTION!

The planner has finalized the programming, set the expense and income budgets, and begun the process of putting together the meeting plan. Next, thoughts must turn to encouraging attendance at the meeting. To this purpose, a mailing piece should be designed. This might be a one page letter describing the meeting, a multipaged but simple brochure (Figure 10-1) or a very sophisticated multicolored production. No matter which format is used, the purpose of the mailing piece is to "lure" attendees, and the following information should be included:

❑ Dates of the meeting
❑ City/state selected as the site
❑ Hotel or hotels being used for the meeting, together with hotel brochure(s) and full information on kinds of rooms available and the corresponding rates being charged (including any service charges, telephone charges and applicable taxes)
❑ Amenities offered by each hotel might include: nightly turndown service; bonded babysitters; dry cleaning and pressing services; beauty and barber shops; boutiques; house doctor on call; personalized stationery or matchbooks; morning newspaper delivery; refrigerators containing juices, snacks, and other beverages which are charged upon usage
❑ Distance of hotel(s) from headquarters hotel and meeting locations
❑ Full program detail: dates, times, speakers or other presentations
❑ Meals and breaks included in registration fee
❑ Meals, theme parties, special banquets *not* included in the registration fee, including full descriptions, menus and ticket prices
❑ Optional events or sports *not* included in registration fee, together with costs per person
❑ Full information on handling of airplane tickets, official carrier if one is designated, classes of tickets available, discounts arranged for meeting group if any
❑ Ground transportation available for transfer from airport to hotel(s), and whether special transportation is being arranged and at what price
❑ Also, information on the destination city, its culture, points of interest, temperature, expected rain or snow (if applicable), clothing suggestions— if casual or formal clothes are appropriate at meetings, parties and special events. Send city and attraction brochures if available in quantity at no cost. Any other special information applicable to this particular meeting

Remember this brochure or letter is the communication which will sell people on attending the meeting.

COORDINATED COSMETICS ANNUAL SALES MEETING

APRIL 3–6
El Paso, Texas

RIO GRANDE RESORT

Fig. 10–1. Coordinated Cosmetics Annual Sales Meeting Brochure.

COORDINATED COSMETICS ANNUAL SALES MEETING

April 3–6
El Paso, Texas

RIO GRANDE RESORT

The resort is located on 45 acres, 15 miles from the El Paso Airport, fronting on the Rio Grande River and boasting 18 challenging holes of golf, and 15 grass tennis courts, lighted for night play.

While a guest at the Rio Grande, you may enjoy swimming in their enormous, Olympic-style lap pool, or sunning around the social pool, which is constructed in the shape of the great state of Texas, with a Texas-sized swim-up bar for refreshments.

All rooms are complete suites, with double-double bedroom, luxuriously appointed living room, compact breakfast room with prestocked wet bar, electronically operated coffee service, and a refrigerator stocked with your favorite mixes, fruit juices and spring water. Every suite is designed with its own, flower-screened patio and private jacuzzi.

Fig. 10–1. Coordinated Cosmetics Annual Sales Meeting Brochure (Continued)

You will find El Paso to be a completely friendly, casual city. Sports or casual clothing is entirely appropriate for all meetings and activities, in the hotel or in the city, except for the final banquet for which more unique attire is suggested. (See information on final theme party.)

In April, this area of Texas should be sunny and warm during the daylight hours, with a very light wrap or sweater sufficient for the slightly cooler evenings. Bring comfortable walking shoes for any sightseeing you might plan to do.

PROGRAM

APRIL 3—ARRIVALS
All guests will be met at the airport by uniformed hosts in western attire and escorted to the hotel in stretch limousines. Please look for the greeters in the baggage area with signs bearing our corporate logo.

Please register at the hotel front desk, relax and freshen up for our swinging Western Welcome Party beginning in the Acapulco Room promptly at 7 P.M. Get ready to enjoy cocktails, full hors d'oeuvres buffet and dessert table. We'll have music and entertainment for your enjoyment.

Fig. 10—1. Coordinated Cosmetics Annual Sales Meeting Brochure (Continued)

APRIL 4 — MORNING BUSINESS MEETING

A continental breakfast will be set up in the foyer of
the Saguaro Room at 7:30 A.M. Our Annual Sales Meeting will follow at 8:00 A.M. in the Saguaro Room. Please
be prompt!

SPOUSE/COMPANION ACTIVITIES

Please sign up for any of these activities at the meeting
registration desk:

A) Vans will be provided for those who wish to go on a
   shopping excursion to Ciudad Juarez, Mexico. Escorts will conduct a brief orientation at breakfast in
   the Ocotillo Room at 8:00 A.M. Transportation will
   leave promptly at 9:00 A.M. and will return to the
   hotel in time for luncheon at 12:30 P.M.

B) A sightseeing tour of the Tiqua Village near downtown El Paso will afford us a look at the lifestyle of
   these ancient Indians. We will have time to shop for
   Indian jewelry and art objects before boarding our
   buses for the Old Town area and an opportunity to
   shop in the many boutiques, gift shops, and galler-
   ies. We will return to the resort in time for luncheon at 12:30 P.M.

Fig. 10–1. Coordinated Cosmetics Annual Sales Meeting Brochure (Continued)

APRIL 4 — LUNCHEON AND AFTERNOON

Luncheon will be served in the Joshua Room promptly at 12:30 P.M.

The afternoon will be devoted to golf and tennis tournaments. Please sign up to participate at our registration/information desk.

Those who do not wish to join in the organized tournaments may wish to relax around the pool or enjoy the "behind the scenes" tours of the resort property — these will include the art collection, the kitchens, the front desk/registration area and the office complex.

APRIL 4 — EVENING

Sports awards banquet — with cocktails in the convention lobby foyer promptly at 7 P.M. Dinner will follow in the Golden Desert Ballroom at 8 P.M.

Awards for tennis and golf tournaments will be presented by surprise touring pros.

The awards program will be followed by dancing until 1 A.M.

Fig. 10–1. Coordinated Cosmetics Annual Sales Meeting Brochure (Continued)

APRIL 5—GENERAL SESSION MEETING
  (Spouses/companions welcome to attend)

A full American breakfast will be served in Meeting
Room C promptly at 8:00 A.M.

General Session begins in the Saguaro Ballroom immediately following at 9:00 A.M. Our featured speakers will
be a panel of well known high fashion models who will
demonstrate the newest of our avant garde cosmetics
"look" for the coming season.

Luncheon will be on your own. Either enjoy one of the
dining rooms in the resort, or we will provide van
shuttle service to several downtown restaurants. Vans
will begin service at noon.

APRIL 5—EVENING

This evening will be our final banquet and theme
party, "Dream Fashions of the Year 2020." Please
come as you imagine the "yuppies" of that year will
look! There will be prizes for the most imaginative costumes. After dinner and the "Grand Costume Parade"
we will have a complete musical show, a medley of
Broadway's newest musical offerings in rehearsal for
next season.

Cocktails 7 P.M.
Dinner 8 P.M.
Grand Costume Parade 9:30 p.m.
Show 10:30 P.M.—11:15 P.M.
Dancing to follow until 1 A.M.

Fig. 10—1. Coordinated Cosmetics Annual Sales Meeting Brochure (Continued)

APRIL 6 – FINAL BREAKFAST

Please have your luggage outside of your room door prior to coming to Meeting Room B for breakfast.

9:00 A.M.: Western Farewell Breakfast, featuring a menu of regional treats. There will be a brief but intriguing video presentation on the site for next year's meeting! Don't miss this one!

APRIL 6 – DEPARTURES

10:30 A.M.: Vans and buses begin leaving for the airport. Please read the instruction sheet, which will be delivered to your room on April 5, giving you details of transportation to your flight.

DON'T FORGET TO TURN IN YOUR MEETING EVALUATIONS. DROP THEM AT THE REGISTRATION DESK BEFORE YOU DEPART.

VAYA CON DIOS, AMIGOS!

Fig. 10–1. Coordinated Cosmetics Annual Sales Meeting Brochure (Continued)

❏ *SUMMARY*

The income and expense budgets and spreadsheet, together with the meeting plan and progress chart really constitute the skeleton of any meeting, upon which the planner can flesh out the finished body with creativity and imagination. Budgets, meeting plan and progress chart are begun just as soon as the destination and site property have been chosen.

Financial management is critical to the success of any meeting and the planner is responsible for seeing that a quality meeting is produced, which will meet the purposes and goals set by the organization, within budgetary guidelines. To this purpose then the meeting planner works closely throughout the planning process with the budget, spreadsheet and progress chart, even altering them periodically to keep the meeting on target and within monetary limits.

Full income and expense budgets, spreadsheet and meeting plan are exhibited in Appendices D and F. An example of the progress chart will be found in Chapter 15.

❏ *PROJECTS*

1. Make up a mock income and expense budget for a luncheon meeting for 50 persons. Obtain banquet menus from local hotels or restaurants. In the expense budget include the cost of:

    1. production and mailing of meeting notices
    2. one speaker (including speaker's luncheon)
    3. centerpieces or floral arrangements
    4. luncheon menu
    5. attendee name tags
    6. one staff member to check in guests

    In the income budget include a 20% mark-up on total costs as the price of meeting.

    When this is completed make up a meeting plan for the luncheon, using the format shown in the meeting plan in Appendix D. You will need only the page for luncheons.

2. Call a local association meeting planner and ask if you might have a copy of the type of forms they use for meeting budgets. Bring them to class for discussion.

3. Call a local corporate meeting planner and ask if the planner would send you a copy of the forms used in the meeting plan for their company. Bring them to class for discussion.

❏ *DISCUSSION QUESTIONS*

1. **Put in the proper sequence these first steps in beginning the process of meeting planning: income budget, progress chart, outline of agenda or program, meeting plan, expense budget, spreadsheet.**

2. **What is included in the first draft of the expense budget?**

3. **What are the detail sheets which must be attached to the expense budget? Why are they necessary?**

4. **List some of the expenses that might be listed under the item "Program Expense."**

5. **What is the final item to be listed in the expense budget? Explain its purpose.**

6. **List some of the items that might be included in an income budget.**

7. **Describe a spreadsheet and what its purpose is.**

8. How does the text describe the meeting plan?

9. List the ten basic components of the average meeting plan.

10. Describe the progress chart, its purpose and how it is constructed.

11. Discuss how the budgeting process and putting together the total meeting plan represent the real "core" of the meeting planner's job.

LIABILITIES AND INSURANCES

OBJECTIVES

After reading this chapter, you will be able:

❑ To demonstrate awareness of potential legal liabilities associated with meetings
❑ To understand the various types of insurance protection available
❑ To understand the concept of "reasonable care"

Anyone in business must be concerned about the things which can go wrong during the course of conducting everyday activities. In the business of meetings, things that can go wrong may occur in the office prior to the meeting, or during the meeting at the hotel or at some off-property location. They may take the form of personal injury, property damage, monetary loss or errors and omissions. Since the corporation/association, or the meeting planner, may be held personally liable, those involved in meetings must be concerned about being insured against any of these eventualities.

Let's consider some of these potential mishaps, under which insurance each of them would fall and the meeting planner's responsibility in each case.

PERSONAL INJURY, PROPERTY DAMAGE AND LOSS OF PROPERTY

If any of the above involve the company/association's employees, the meeting staff or outside attendees, it could be disastrously costly. For this reason, all meetings must be covered by general liability insurance.

IF . . .
❑ A conference coordinator, in the association's own office trips over the computer's electrical cord and falls
❑ A fire in the office destroys the master meeting plan and all attendee kits for the meeting
❑ A visiting meeting speaker, who has just stopped in at the office, has a metal box of photographic slides dropped on his hand

... These accidents would be covered by general liability insurance carried by any business or organization. The meeting planner is then only responsible for seeing that the company *is* covered by such liability insurance.

IF ...

- ☐ An attendee at the meeting slips and falls on a wet floor in the hotel's public restroom
- ☐ A speaker's chair slips from the podium during a general session in the hotel ballroom
- ☐ A musician at one of the meeting banquets has an expensive sound system damaged by a waiter dropping a carafe of hot coffee into a speaker
- ☐ A meeting coordinator has luggage, containing a minicomputer, disappear from the bellman's storage area
- ☐ The hotel/resort has a disastrous fire that results in death or injury involving any meeting employee, attendee or participant

... These mishaps may be covered by liability insurance carried by the hotel or resort, *if* the property or any of its employees can be considered negligent or responsible in any way. The meeting planner, prior to contracting with a property, asks to see "proof of insurance," to be sure that the hotel is adequately protected. However, the organization sponsoring any meeting should also carry Convention Liability Insurance to cover any unexpected legal action expense. Many convention centers and hotels will have "Hold Harmless" clauses in their contracts, confirming that the facility is not responsible for any and all damages or destruction to, including theft of, any materials or equipment owned or rented by the organization. The property may also require proof that the meeting sponsor is covered by insurance to a certain dollar amount.

In all cases, it is up to the meeting planner to be aware of the potential for liability and be sure that the company/association and the planner, personally, are adequately protected.

ERRORS AND OMISSIONS INSURANCE

This type of insurance is generally carried by travel agents, and planners may have to search for an underwriter who is familiar with this particular type of policy. It is almost mandatory that an independent meeting management company carry such insurance, but it is a good idea for any organization with an in-house meeting management department. This insurance will pay for any damages incurred due to errors or omissions committed by a member of the planning group.

IF ...

- ☐ A meeting coordinator makes a mistake and books too few seats on a flight from one point of origination, causing several attendees to miss the first day of sessions. These sessions happened to be those which introduced the sales group to new products for the season, and several sales personnel missing these meetings could cost both the individual salespersons and the company money.

❏ A typist in the meeting department omits several attendees names from the hotel rooming list, and when they arrive the hotel doesn't have rooms for them, causing them to stay at another property some distance away, resulting in substantial daily taxi fares to meetings.

❏ A tour operator has gone out of business without notifying the meeting planner, and without returning the required deposit monies. The planning staff has neglected to check on the arrangements just prior to arrival. On-site, the planner must arrange for a substitute activity, for which the meeting sponsor must again pay deposits.

. . . Each of these "disasters" was the fault of some error or omission on the part of a member of the planning staff. Errors and omissions insurance, while not solving the problems, would take some of the monetary "sting" out of the mistakes in the event of legal action; or ready cash may allow provision for extra labor hours to correct the error. These examples are another good indication of why a meeting planner must check, check, and double check each and every detail of a meeting.

PLANNER'S PROFESSIONAL LIABILITY

It is a good policy for any meeting planner to carry planner's professional liability insurance. It protects the planner personally in the event that any person involved in a meeting should name the planner as a defendent or codefendent in a legal action. This insurance pays for fees charged by an attorney or it may pay for bonds, expenses incurred in the investigation, adjustment, and appeal of a claim by the insurance company, and all other reasonable fees.

Some companies or associations may pay the premiums to provide this type of insurance for their meeting planners. However, even if it means paying for the insurance personally, it is well worth the money!

LIABILITY OF OUTSIDE CONTRACTORS

This type of liability is also a concern of the sponsor of every meeting. Co-insured "riders" should be requested of all contractors. This means that the meeting sponsor and/or independent meeting planner will be named as an "insured" on the liability policies of all bus companies, limousine suppliers, attractions, restaurants, or other contractors involved in the meeting. Certificates of insurance, including the rider, should be supplied to the meeting sponsor, and become a part of the permanent file on a specific meeting.

Fig. 11–1. "Risk Management" describes the function of managing an insurance program and avoiding liability, as described in the "Four Basic Rules of Risk Management." Reprinted with permission from *Meeting News* magazine, a Gralla publication.

FOUR BASIC RULES OF RISK MANAGEMENT[1]

Avoiding liability is probably impossible these days, but there are ways to minimize your chances of ending up in court. Atlanta-based attorney, John Foster, offers these four basic rules:

1. Avoid risk. Evaluate every situation for possible problems. Find potential risk, then make an effort to avoid it: "It may not be a good idea to have a fun-run for senior citizens or a beach Olympics at a resort that's far from medical

---
[1] Source: "So Sue Me!" by Geoffrey Brewer, *Meeting News,* pp. 19, March 1991

facilities," Foster said. "It's also important that on site inspection, you check not only numbers of rooms and rates, but also for safety features."

2. Transfer risk. "Whatever risk you can't avoid, transfer to other parties. Get 'hold-harmless' clauses; planners shouldn't be held responsible for acts of the suppliers—if there's something dangerous at the facility, the planner shouldn't be liable. Or get attendees to sign release/waiver clauses, in which the attendee in effect says, 'I'm assuming the risk of a physical activity, and if I hurt myself because of something I've done—as opposed to some unseen hazard the planner has subjected me to—then I am responsible.' "

3. Retain part of the risk. "Purchase insurance with a high deductible, keeping, say, the first $5,000 or $10,000 as a deductible for any damages. By doing this, you're assuming part of the risk, but not all of it."

4. Buy insurance. Generally, follow rule 3. However, if it's going to cost more to have a deductible than not, don't purchase a policy with a high deductible. Usually, though, it's more cost-effective to have as high a deductible as possible. If you can afford to take, say $10,000 loss, then have a deductible."

THIRD-PARTY LIQUOR LIABILITY

This has become a concern of all persons involved in meetings and conventions. "Dram Shop" laws have been passed by many states in the U.S. and the laws vary from state to state. These laws make the "third party," that is the person supplying, serving or buying alcoholic beverages, responsible for the acts of any inebriated guest during or after any event. The meeting planner should inquire of the hotel or other catering service or facility whether their service is covered by "host liquor legal liability," and, if so, request a written statement to that effect and request that the meeting sponsor be named as an additional insured on that policy. If, for some reason, the planner cannot obtain coverage in this way, a separate policy for this coverage should be obtained from the organization's own insurance agent or broker.

MEETING CANCELLATION INSURANCE

This insurance is also available, which will compensate the company/association for revenue lost as a result of cancellation of the meeting through no fault of the organization, and may also cover expenses incurred as a result of non-appearance of a principal speaker or entertainer, or even the costs involved if the organization does not vacate the convention facility as contracted. Some illustrations are:

❏ For an off-shore meeting, the entire meeting group is stranded at the port of embarcation when a hurricane develops at sea. The meeting will have to be quickly switched to an alternate site (but that is another problem). Off-shore hotel reservations for the meeting cannot be honored, so meeting cancellation insurance will come into play and pay the necessary penalties for the group's "no show" at the off-shore site.

❑   In a reverse situation, a tornado watch in a Midwestern city causes all airplane flights to be cancelled. The meeting attendees were scheduled to depart, but cannot obtain transportation and therefore must stay at the hotel for another night. The corporation holding the meeting therefore incurs the additional cost of 125 rooms for an additional night at $140 per room or $17,500 and will also be responsible for additional meals at considerable cost. These additional monetary outlays can be covered by insurance.

OTHER INSURANCES

Many other types of insurance are available to cover almost any eventuality, including the loss or theft of money while at the convention property or while directly en route to a local bank or other secure facility. Bonds can be obtained to cover theft of monies by employees. Or special policies will be issued to cover any particularly valuable item involved with the meeting, against theft or damage; for example, art items, jewels, gems or furs on display as part of the event; expensive computers, boats, cars or other equipment, which are part of a trade show.

REASONABLE CARE

In case of any suit, the issue that is considered is "reasonable care." In planning a meeting, it is the responsibility of the planner and staff to see that "reasonable care" is exercised to protect everyone involved.

For example, when planning a meeting at which the majority of attendees might be in a "senior citizen" category, it will be wise to arrange for paramedic teams and ambulance to be on stand-by at any large group activity. Hopefully, there will be no need for their services, but in the event of a heat stroke, heart attack or other medical emergency, the planner has exercised "reasonable care" and concern for attendees.

If a meeting or incentive group will be participating in any possibly hazardous activity, such as mini-rodeo, hiking in the mountains or Olympic-type swimming pool activities, it might be wise to have paramedics along. This would demonstrate "reasonable care."

❑ *SUMMARY*

Every meeting and every company or association has its own unique insurance needs. The meeting planner needs to be aware of what liabilities exist and what insurance may be available for protection. Then, the planner should consult with an insurance broker who is familiar with these unique policies.

Types of Insurances to be Considered for Meetings

Personal injury	Property damage
Loss of property	Errors and omissions
Planners professional liability	Liability of contractors
Third-party liquor liability	Meeting cancellation
Other miscellaneous insurance	

❑ *PROJECTS*

1. Call a local meeting management company or a destination management company and ask if they will tell you what kinds of insurances they carry. List them here.

2. Call a hotel or resort in your region and ask what kinds of insurances they carry which might have an impact on meetings. Ask particularly about Third-Party Liquor Liability.

3. Call an insurance broker and find out what kinds of insurance he/she suggests for meeting planners. Does it include the types of insurance discussed in the text?

❏ *DISCUSSION QUESTIONS*

1. Cite some examples of personal injury at a meeting.

2. Cite some examples of property damage at a meeting.

3. Cite some examples of loss of property at a meeting.

4. What is meant by "errors and omissions" insurance. Cite some examples of errors and omissions.

5. Why should every meeting planner carry Planner's Professional Liability Insurance? Who pays for this insurance?

6. How should liability of outside contractors be handled? Explain.

7. What is "Third-Party Liquor Liability" or "Dram Shop Laws"? What is the insurance against this possible liability called?

8. What does meeting cancellation insurance cover?

9. What other insurances should concern the planner?

10. Describe "reasonable care" and explain its importance in running a meeting.

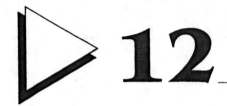

12

TAXES

By Mark J. Mitchell, C.P.A.
Partner-In-Charge
Henry & Horne
Tucson, Arizona

OBJECTIVES

After reading this chapter, you will be able:

❏ To enumerate the various taxes impacting on the meetings industry
❏ To illustrate the cost of transaction taxes on meetings
❏ To show how income tax deductions effect meeting attendees
❏ To describe how selection of "foreign sites" or cruise ships can effect the meeting tax picture

The cost of operating any business includes a variety of fees, licenses, and taxes, which are assessed by federal, state and local taxing authorities. The taxes items can be broken down into three main categories:

1. Payroll taxes
2. Transaction Taxes
3. Income Taxes

Payroll taxes, which are calculated as a direct percentage of payroll, will not be discussed here. The latter two categories, which affect the meeting planning business as a whole as well as each meeting, will be the focus of this chapter.[4]

---

[4] Note: The tax information included in this chapter is based on current tax laws at the time of publication. Since tax laws are constantly revised, the reader is advised to consult his or her tax advisor.

TRANSACTION TAXES

Transaction taxes are those taxes levied by state and local jurisdictions on the purchase of products and services. While the laws in each jurisdiction vary, transaction taxes normally includes "sales and use" taxes on the purchase of goods or services, as well as "bed" taxes charged on hotel rooms. Also included are "duty" charges for bringing certain items back into the country. Unlike other convention costs, taxes are not negotiable and it is extremely important to be aware of them during the budget process of every meeting planned. Although the simplest way of including these costs in your budget is to request all-inclusive quotations from suppliers and subcontractors, you may wish to receive a breakdown of the transaction taxes. This breakdown is often important when submitting your proposal to management or a client for purposes of comparing bids.

The comparison of Fig. 12-1 is a hypothetical example of a business meeting budget. It is obvious that, if the meeting planner is not aware of the financial consequences of the transaction taxes, a shock may be in store at the final outcome. The financial consequences will be most harshly felt by the independent planner who charges a fee based on the total anticipated cost. The 6% average transaction tax may take away the planner's entire profit on the engagement.

The payment requirements for the transaction taxes vary from state to state and country to country. Some authorities require payment at the time of purchase by the planner, while others require payment by the vendor. Where the vendor pays the tax, the tax will be included in the base charge quoted to the planner. In any event, planners should do their homework and inquire as to what the tax rates are for each item in their budget.

For those planners working in the international arena, including the Caribbean Basin, particular care should be taken to inquire into duty fees for taking supplies and equipment in and out of the United States and its possessions.

	Proposal A	Proposal B	
Transportation	$5,000	$5,250	5% Tax
Supplies	200	214	7% Tax
Meals	500	535	7% Tax
Lodging	1,000	1,120	12% Tax
Subtotal	6,700	7,119	
Transaction taxes	419	N/A	Avg. 6%
Total	$7,119	$7,119	

Fig. 12–1. Two Proposals Showing Breakdown of Transaction Taxes

INCOME TAXES

The *income tax* consequences may have a more traumatic effect on the participants of meetings and conventions than transaction taxes. Taxpayers may deduct expenses incurred in attending domestic and foreign meetings and conventions only if directly related to the active conduct of a trade or business. For meetings held outside of North America it must be as reasonable for the meeting to be held within North America. These basic rules apply both to the traveler and to any other person claiming the deduction.

The prerequisite for claiming the cost of attending any meeting or convention is that it is "... reasonable and necessary in the conduct of the taxpayer's business and directly attributable to it..." (IRC Reg.1.162-2(a)). This prerequisite is emphasized by IRC 274(h)(7) which states in part that no deduction is permitted for the costs of attending such conventions for investment purposes, for example, discussing real estate, limited partnerships, stock market strategies, fine art, etc.

Once the active business-relationship test has been satisfied, the task of accumulating documentation to substantiate the expenditures begins. The following is a suggested list of supporting items:

❏ Written itinerary and list of activities
❏ Business purpose of the meeting
❏ Receipts for lodging, meals, and any other costs exceeding $25
❏ List of attendees

These records should be kept with other tax records and saved for six years from the date the tax return is filed.

The importance of adequate documentation can be seen from the following exhibit:

Cost of convention	$ 3,000
Less: taxes saved by deducting cost of convention on tax return. Maximum corporate rate of 34 %	(1,020)
Net cost of convention	**$ 1,980**

Here the net cost of the convention is substantially reduced, because of the tax saved by deducting the convention expenses. A well-substantiated deduction should hold up to IRS scrutiny, if required. The tax savings will vary of course, depending on your federal and state income tax rates.

For meetings outside the United States or on cruise ships, additional requirements must be met. The more stringent rules apply if the meeting, convention or seminar is outside "the North American area." Thus, a convention is not considered a foreign convention if it is held anywhere in the U.S. or its possessions (Puerto Rico, Guam, the U.S. Virgin Islands), in Canada or Mexico. Also excluded

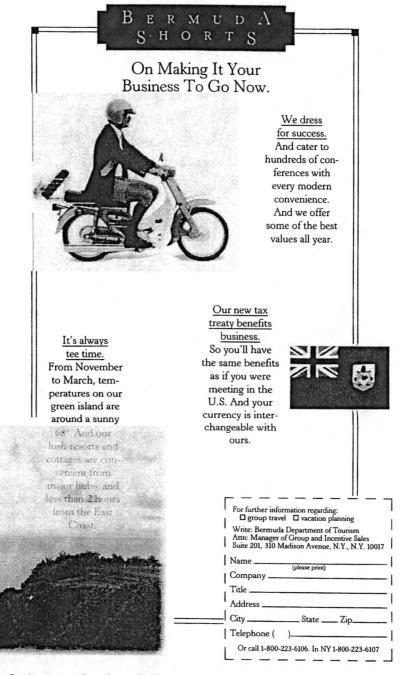

Fig. 12–2. Among the beneficiary countries is Bermuda, and this ad stresses the tax treaty that exists with the U.S. (Courtesy of the Bermuda Department of Tourism.)

Table 12-1 Beneficiary Countries

Anguilla	Honduras
Antigua and Barbuda	Jamaica
Bahamas, the	Nicaragua
Barbados	Panama
Belize	Saint Lucia
Bermuda	St. Vincent and the Grenadines
Costa Rica	Suriname
Dominica	Trinidad and Tobago
Dominican Republic	Cayman Islands
El Salvador	Montserrat
Grenada	Netherlands Antilles
Guatemala	St. Christopher-Nevis
Guyana	Turks and Caicos Islands
Haiti	Virgin Islands, British

---

from the foreign convention rules are those countries listed above as "Beneficiary countries." A beneficiary country is considered within the North American area if at the time a convention, seminar or similar meeting begins:

1. There is in effect a bilateral or multilateral agreement providing for the exchange of tax information between the United States and such country.
2. There is not in effect a finding by the U.S. Treasury Department that the tax laws of such country descriminate against conventions held in the United States (IRC 274(h) (6) (A)).

Under the foreign convention rules, the taxpayer must still establish the active business purpose of the trip and substantiate the deductions claimed. In addition, he or she must also establish that it is "reasonable" for the meeting to be held in a foreign location. Establishing a "reasonable" purpose hinges on the business purpose for traveling to a foreign country versus staying in the North American area. For example, a convention of wine vendors might be able to establish that a convention in France was reasonable because certain expertise or facilities relevant to the convention are only available in France. Similarly, business people who export their products or services to foreign countries may be able to establish reasonable purposes for holding a convention or meeting in foreign country.

The maximum deduction for conferences on a cruise ship is $2,000 per taxpayer per year. The ship must be registered in the United States, and all ports of call must be located in the U.S. or its possessions. In order to obtain the deduction, each taxpayer must attach two written statements to his or her tax return concerning the

Celebrities come and go. When are you coming?

State of Vaud, Switzerland

Why do celebrities flock to the Lake Geneva region? The reasons are identical to your objectives for your next incentive trip. The lake of Geneva region is simply the most cosmopolitan European scene and scenery. The infrastructure for prominent visitors has been in place since the turn of the century. A liberating experience for the discriminating meetings and conventions planner.

The incentive environment varies from the sophisticated old world resort to the fairytale alpine village. And the catalog of activities goes beyond comprehension, especially when considering the strategic geographic location. Give us a call, we are used to dealing with celebrities. Whether it concerns a cast of thousands or the board meeting. We treat them all as the celebrities they are.

State of Vaud Tourist Office Switzerland
P.O. Box 242
CH-1000 Lausanne 6

Tel. 01041-21-617.72.02
Fax 01041-21-617.72.40

Lausanne – Vevey – Montreux

Château-d'Oex – Les Diablerets – Leysin – Villars – Yverdon-les-Bains

Fig. 12–3. The concept of a "foreign" meeting, especially at a location where you might find celebrities, is attractive to many groups. International meetings have a wealth of exotic destinations from which to choose. (Courtesy of State of Vaud Tourist Office, Western Switzerland.)

cruise. The first statement is an affidavit by the taxpayer stating the total number of days spent on the cruise, the amount of time devoted to scheduled business activities and a program of those activities. The second statement must contain the same information, but should be signed by an officer of the sponsoring organization.

AN ADDENDUM BY THE TEXT AUTHOR

Bed Taxes

Bed taxes are really a kind of sales tax levied by state, county and/or city, however they are very specifically important to the budget for a meeting.

Many state legislators, county supervisors and city council persons have levied a tax on each room-night in hotels and resorts, some of these funds being earmarked to assist in promoting tourism and meetings to the area, others going to the general fund. These taxes may range from 1% or 2% to 20% to 28% in some of the larger metropolitan convention sites.

Consider a room rate of $125 per night: adding 4% or 5% sales tax and 12% or 15% bed tax, may increase costs by $25 per room, per night—a hefty jump in the total meeting expenditure. In terms of only 100 rooms, costs are thus elevated by $2,500 per night or $7,500 for a three night stay. The meeting planner must be sure to ascertain the total tax figure which will be added to the quoted room rate at the time of negotiating the original contact with a possible site-hotel, or risk an unpleasant surprise upon receipt of final billing.

☐ *SUMMARY*

In conclusion, taxes play an important role in the cost of any convention or meeting. While transaction taxes add to the cost of the meeting, income tax deductions are available to substantially offset the total cost of the convention. All business meeting planners should be aware of the costs and benefits entailed.

Taxes can constitute a major item in the meeting budget. Each of these taxes impacts upon the meeting and may be a consideration in selecting a site for a meeting. These fees can be broken down into three main categories: payroll taxes; transaction taxes (which would include bed taxes); and income taxes.

In addition to the direct and indirect taxes, which may be imposed by the various governmental bodies, we must also consider the deductibility of some meeting expenses from the taxes paid by corporations or attendees subsequent to a meeting. This factor becomes a consideration particularly when thinking of the possibility of a foreign country or off-shore island as a meeting site.

The professional meeting planner must be cognizant of these tax questions and the impact they may have on a meeting.

❏ *PROJECTS*

1. Talk to any business people of your acquaintance who regularly attend meetings, and ask what kind of documentation they keep to support the deductibility of meeting expenses.

2. Discuss with a local independent meeting planner his/her experience in arranging meetings held out of the country, with regard to taxes. Have they had experience with beneficiary countries?

❏ *DISCUSSION QUESTIONS*

1. **What are the three main categories of taxes in operating any business?**

2. **Define "transaction taxes." Name three kinds of taxes (in the meetings business) which would be considered transaction taxes.**

3. What is the simplest way to include these transaction taxes in your budget?

4. What is the determining criteria as to whether taxpayers may deduct meeting expenses from their income tax?

5. What kind of documentation will be required to substantiate such expenditures?

6. How many years must these records be saved, with regard to income tax?

7. Define a "foreign convention," from the viewpoint of an American planner.

8. What rules must be followed in order to allow an attendee to deduct expenses of a foreign meeting?

9. What is meant by a "beneficiary country"? Name some beneficiary countries of the U.S.

10. What is the maximum deduction for meetings on cruise ships? Give two requirements for tax deduction on a cruise ship meeting.

11. What documentation is required to prove to the IRS that a cruise ship meeting's expenses should be tax deductible?

12. Define a "bed tax." What kinds of percentages are charged in various cities?

13. How does the bed tax effect the meeting planner's site selection? How can it affect the meeting budget?

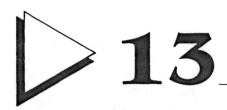

THE FINANCIAL IMPACT OF MEETINGS

OBJECTIVES

After reading this chapter, you will be able:

❏ To emphasize the impact of meetings on the corporations and associations holding them
❏ To describe the impact of meetings on the suppliers to the industry
❏ To illustrate the impact of meetings on the communities in which they are held
❏ To emphasize the impact of meetings on governments, both local and national, through increase in tax revenues

As with all businesses, the purpose of the meetings industry is to make money. It is true that meetings are held to inform, educate, inspire or motivate—but that doesn't preclude the desire to make money. Consider why the company or association wants to inform, educate, inspire or motivate. Employees must be informed and educated to perform better in their jobs, and thus make money for their companies. People must be inspired or motivated to produce more, to be more enthusiastic, to do a better job, and thus make more money for their organizations. And, not only do meetings have a financial impact on the company or association producing them, but on the suppliers to the industry, the hotels/resorts and those other companies directly involved in servicing the meetings industry, and ultimately on the communities in which meetings are held and even the nation as a whole.

In this chapter we will take a look at the financial impact of meetings on the corporation and on the association; on the hotels/resorts and other suppliers to the industry; and then on the community, the nation, and of course the individuals employed in the business of meetings.

THE IMPACT ON THE CORPORATION

Corporations hold meetings as an investment, which will subsequently pay monetary dividends. Let us look at the kinds of meetings held by companies and how they effect the bottom line.

The employee orientation meeting or continuing training program both have one primary objective: improving the performance of employees. The orientation introduces new employees to the company and its policies, its products and services, its rules and regulations; and then to the requirements of his or her specific job. The continuing training program reinforces the original training, updates the employee on new products, procedures or markets, further educating the employee in the employer's business.

If employees are thoroughly cognizant of what the company has to sell, are convinced that "their company" is one of the very best in their industry, and understand what the company is trying to accomplish, then they will be greater assets to the firm and will perform the jobs assigned much more efficiently than if they have not attended an orientation meeting. Since every job within a company contributes to its financial success, the efficacy of each and every employee ultimately contributes to the total income of that company. Hence, the orientation meeting helps increase the monetary gains of the firm.

The Board of Directors meeting reports the status of a company to its top decision makers. It also serves to inform Board members of future plans and to seek their approval. The Directors meeting can be a brainstorming session that looks at new and innovative ways of diversifying the company's activities or to broaden its base of operation. The Board (at Board meetings) also elects the officers who will direct the day-to-day operation of the firm. Every facet of the Board's deliberations is targeting one final result: making of money to be able to pay dividends to the stockholders who have financed the operation as an investment, for profit.

The motivational meeting is designed to get employees "fired up," enthusiastic and to create a "go out and conquer the world" attitude. In sales, this will translate into a greater number of customers and/or larger, more profitable orders from each client. With production personnel, highly motivated employees will produce more, have less down time, manufacture a better product or develop cost-saving methods; all of which translate into better profits and more money for the corporation.

Incentive meetings are rewards for service well-rendered and are designed for fun! How can this possibly translate into more money for the company, when it costs a lot of money to hold an incentive program? Think back to what an incentive program really is: a program developed to motivate people to produce more sales or greater production, in order to *win* the privilege of attending an incentive meeting and participate in all of that fun! So, we see that money is produced for the company, prior to the incentive meeting, in quantities sufficient enough to pay for the employees' attendance at the incentive and still leave profits for the firm. Note that in this case, the money is earned by the company before it is spent on the incentive trip.

Informational meetings are just what the title implies. They inform executives, employees and everyone on a corporate payroll of what is happening, what new products may be introduced, and how new methods of production may be utilized. By informing people of the true situation and avoiding the rumor mill, a company makes the personnel feel involved in what is happening. Anytime you can show workers their part in an organization and make them feel important to the ultimate outcome, you will have employees who work harder, smarter and *care about the success* and profitability of the company. In a word, people who are invited to informational meetings will try harder to make money for the company.

THE IMPACT ON THE ASSOCIATION

Associations, as we have discovered in the text, are generally not-for-profit entities. However, not producing a profit does not mean not producing money. It only indicates that the *profitability* of the association does not show up as bottom line monies to the organization. The association still must cover its own costs, fund its programs or purposes and *assist its membership in making more money!*

By attending association meetings, the membership must feel that they are obtaining some benefit, or they will not continue to be members and will not attend meetings. The association can provide information and education to its membership, which will translate into their being more knowledgeable or efficient in their own individual jobs or endeavors, and therefore make more money for their companies and themselves. Association get-togethers also provide the membership with an opportunity to meet with their peers, potential clients and competitors, to network and to keep abreast of what's happening in their particular industry, business or profession. All of these reasons for belonging to an association and attending their monthly meetings and their regional or national conventions, eventually translate into some type of profit and money derived.

Often the sentiment is expressed after an association meeting that, "I really didn't get anything out of that convention, but I would have been conspicuous by my absence." The unhappy attendee is merely saying that although the content of the program wasn't particularly informative or useful, clients or potential clients would have missed his or her presence and would have perhaps interpreted the absence as a lack of interest in the profession, or an indifference toward meeting with them at the conference. Or, the attendee may be concerned that many competitors would be very visible at the meeting in his/her absence. Therefore, networking at these meetings *is* a prime consideration.

We have seen how meetings make money for the corporations and associations holding them. What about direct benefits derived by those involved in the meeting itself? How do meetings financially impact on hotels/resorts and all of the many suppliers who are called upon?

THE IMPACT ON HOTELS/RESORTS

Hotels/resorts naturally profit from holding conventions in their properties. But why would they rather have a meeting in-house than just rent a series of bedrooms to traveling businessmen or the general touring public?

Meetings result in a large group of people in a single mass, producing more concentrated income in a short period of time. The sales effort that goes into bringing meetings to a property is more cost effective than sales of rooms to individuals. A single sales call (or maybe two or three) on one decision-maker can fill 300 rooms for a four night period, while months and years of advertising, sales calls on travel agents and word-of-mouth reputation may be required to produce the same number of room nights with the individual or family traveler.

Per diem expenditures by the meeting attendee are historically higher than the casual traveler. Since the company or association is scheduling luncheons, dinners and cocktail parties in the hotel, the food and beverage dollar is more consistent. The individual tourist probably will eat more meals and spend more time out of the hotel than one who is being scheduled in-house by a meeting planner. Also, since the meeting functions are paid for on a master account by the entity holding the meeting, the attendee is more prone to spend extra dollars in the restaurants, in the lounges and in the gift shops.

Thus, we see that meetings are certainly a money-making piece of business for the hotels and resorts. The hotel designed for meetings may derive as much as 75% to 80% of their bottom-line dollars from meetings; while even smaller commercial hotels can impact their bottom lines by 25% to 30% by holding a few overnight meetings and many local luncheon and dinner meetings.

THE IMPACT ON SUPPLIERS

Suppliers to the meetings industry certainly profit from conferences and conventions using their services. Many would not be in business at all if it were not for meetings.

Airlines

Let's start with airlines, who transport people to a meeting city. Like the hotels, their sales efforts to be a "primary carrier," or the "official carrier" for a major meeting certainly take less energy and time, than filling that many airliner seats through advertising and sales to travel agencies and individuals. Almost all major airlines have a license to service the most popular convention cities, and may have made the decision to service those cities based on the great volume of meeting traffic.

Their interest in servicing this kind of business is evidenced by the "extras" they will provide to meeting attendees. For the clients' convenience, a toll-free "800 number" will be designated just for reservations by those planning to attend a particular meeting. Special group rates are granted at considerable discounts off the regular tariff. An airline representative may be assigned to the flight origination cities to assist with baggage tagging, to facilitate loading and to be of general assistance to the attendees. An airline rep may be assigned to be at the hotel, to assist attendees with baggage that may not have arrived and/or to be on hand for any changes in return reservations. Often the airlines supply carry-on canvas bags, beach umbrellas and balls, "shells" (folders with colorfully printed outsides and blank insides) in which the meeting planner may print program agenda or promotional material, or other gifts.

If the meetings business were not so lucrative for the airlines, they would not be able to afford to offer these "extra" accommodations.

Ground Handlers

Ground handler companies have long provided limousine service at major airports, or provided van transportation for individuals. But the proliferation of these companies, and their expansion into charter services, is directly attributable to the growth of the meetings industry. With the largest percentage of their business now coming from meetings, these companies can very definitely be said to profit from meetings. They transport all of the attendees from the airport to the hotel or resort, they provide meet/greet personnel in the airport baggage areas, and provide escorts on the bus or van transportation to make the ride more enjoyable.

Ground Handlers frequently work for a meeting planner with a smaller meeting by supplying transfers to restaurants and shopping and are sometimes hired by destination management companies to supplement their staffs on very large meetings.

Entertainment Bookers

Entertainment bookers, whether they be individual agents, large agencies, or individual performers, are certainly getting much of their business from the convention and meeting market. Entertainment providers will book business into major hotels on a regular basis, or will arrange music for a wedding or Bar Mitzvah, Christening or other special occasion, but by and large the major portion of their business comes from meetings, conferences, conventions and incentive programs. If there is a fall-off in the number of conventions booked into a particular destination, the entertainment bookers will certainly be financially hurt.

Decorators/Party Planners

Although theme parties may be planned by individuals not connected with conferences, conventions or meetings, for instance at Halloween or for a Charity Event, the majority of business for party planners comes from the meetings industry. Not only do they do more business with conventions, but will generally work with larger budgets. Without meetings, the numbers and quality of the decorators would certainly lessen.

Transportation Companies

Transportation companies derive the greatest part of their incomes from the large numbers of people attending meetings, as do the local attractions and tour guide companies. All of these suppliers plan on booking large groups for their services from the conventions and meetings booked into their communities. This business is not only frequent but also proves quite lucrative.

The Individual Who Works in the Industry

Having discussed the various types of hotels, resorts and other suppliers who benefit financially from the meetings business, there is one more important cog in the wheel—the individual who works in the conventions and meetings business. Every person who works for a hotel, a resort, a conference center, or for the ground handler or decorator or DMC, receives their paycheck because of the meetings business.

But what about the gas station attendant who has a job because service stations are so busy during the meetings season in that town? What about the drugstore clerk, the medical office personnel and the waiters and waitresses in the restaurants in a town where the main business "in season" is meetings? Each and every one of these people profits financially because of meetings. If we extend this thinking, every one of these employees pays rent, buys cars, visits the grocery store, goes to the beauty shop and sees a movie on money earned because of meetings. In turn, all of these employees spend their meeting-earned dollars within the community. The cycle goes on and on. Meetings are profitable for everyone! This process is called the *multiplier factor*.

THE IMPACT ON THE COMMUNITY

Meetings and conventions have a major financial impact on the businesses which are directly involved in the industry of meetings, but what about the financial impact of meetings on the community?

It seems that every settlement of people, from huge metropolitan areas to small towns, is now focusing on the economic development of their area; that is, the attracting of new industry to the area to provide jobs and a more stable economy.

With the focus on ecology and recycling, every town is seeking out those industries which do not pollute their air, their water sources and the very ground they live on. In searching for new industry, what better clean business can you encourage than tourism and meetings? The people come, use your local facilities, give work to in-town suppliers and then after leaving their dollars, they go home!

Meetings are a clean, non-polluting, non-invasive industry and their dollar impact on any community is a sizeable one. We know that meetings bring money to our airlines, our hotels, our ground operators and destination management companies—but think of how the numbers of people who come to our area for meetings spend money in our grocery stores, restaurants, department stores, gift and souvenier shops, gasoline stations and car rental companies! All of this money circulating in our towns increases the stability of our economy.

The Multiplier Factor

And we talk about the *multiplier factor,* which describes how people directly employed in the meetings and conventions industry go out and spend their dollars in the community for food and clothing, for dry cleaning and prescription drugs. The employees of those establishments then receive their wages and go out and buy necessities and entertainment. Thus the meeting dollar circulates over and over and over again, demonstrating how important meetings are to the financial well-being of our communities.

THE IMPACT ON THE NATION

Still, we haven't finished illustrating the financial impact of meetings and conventions on all of us! What about our governmental entities and the tax dollars that it takes to run them? The sales and use taxes paid, by companies who hold meetings and the people who attend them, to hotels, suppliers, restaurants and other businesses in the community, make a major contribution to the tax resources of our cities and states.

Almost every city airport pays taxes, based on the number of flights and landings, to the local government agency. The hotels and motels pay bed taxes based on the number of room-nights they sell, and the suppliers pay sales taxes on every item they buy for use at a convention or meeting; therefore, the more meetings that are booked into a city, the more tax dollars that are generated for the local economy. Without those convention/meeting tax dollars, residents would have to pay greater taxes to support the government, to pay for schools and to afford fire and police protection.

The financial impact of conventions and meetings on our tax bills is enormous.

THE IMPACT ON BUSINESS

What about other businesses in a community? How do they profit from conventions/meetings? Many cities would not have as many restaurants, as many hotels and resorts or as many gas stations for the use of local residents, if it weren't for the number of people that are brought into their communities by meetings. More newspapers are sold, more liquor is purchased, more cosmetics are bought and more groceries and snacks are consumed because of the numbers of persons attending meetings. We must also remember that the wholesale food purveyors, the mattress companies, the beer distributors and even the churches will benefit from the people visiting the community for meetings.

❏ *SUMMARY*

Meetings mean *money*. Anytime that money circulates, it has a major impact on the people spending the money and on the people, companies, communities and governments receiving the money.

Thus the impressive amount of money spent upon meetings circulates in the geographic locations where the meetings are held. It impacts on the business and lives of the corporation or association holding the meeting; on the hotel/resort companies supplying the accommodations; on the suppliers of various services for the meetings; and on the employees of all of the entities involved in the meeting. Then that money sifts down to the companies providing goods and services bought for the hotel or by the individual employees. From these expenditures, the government taxing agencies receive their portion and from these taxes many of the community services, like schools, refuse collection and fire protection, are supported.

Meetings are a clean, non-polluting, non-invasive industry, which can profit everyone!

❏ *PROJECTS*

Talk to a hotel employee who benefits from meetings. Then from information supplied, talk to employees of the businesses from whom that person purchases goods and services, and find out where they spend their paychecks. Then talk to employees of those businesses; and thusly, follow some of the meeting money through the multiplier factor right in your own community. This should give you a feel for the "pebble in the pool" effect of the meetings and convention industry dollars.

❏ *DISCUSSION QUESTIONS*

1. Why do hotels and resorts find meetings profitable?

2. Would hotels/resorts rather have meetings than individual guests? Why?

3. **How do airlines profit from meetings?**

4. **What profits do ground handlers derive from meetings?**

5. **When might a ground handler work for a meeting planner?**

6. **Do Entertainment bookers do more business with local weddings, bar mitzvahs and other parties? Why or why not?**

7. **Would most transportation companies be in business if it were not for meetings?**

8. What about individual employees who work somewhere in the hospitality industry—how do they impact on other economies?

9. How are meetings described in this chapter?

10. What is "the multiplier factor"? Illustrate how it works.

11. How do meetings impact on *your* community?

12. Who in your community promotes meetings? Why?

13. **Illustrate the benefits of meeting-destination resorts and hotels to your community.**

14. **How are tax dollars generated by the meetings and convention industry?**

15. **How do these tax dollars benefit the average resident?**

16. **What other non-tourist businesses are impacted by the meetings industry? How are they impacted?**

17. **What can we conclude from this chapter about the profitability and economic impact of meetings?**

ETHICS IN THE MEETING WORLD

OBJECTIVES

After reading this chapter, you will be able:

❑ To recognize the potential for unethical behavior in the meetings industry
❑ To stress the importance of ethical behavior on the part of both planner and supplier
❑ To address the question of the propriety of "gifts" in the hospitality industry

Ethics in government, business and our personal lives is being brought into focus today more than ever. We see the nation's moral standards and ethical behavior coming into question daily in Senate hearings, police internal affairs investigations, Wall Street Security and Exchange Commission cases and individuals in the local police blotter. All are making front page headlines in the nation's newspapers and full coverage on the TV evening news. The meetings and convention industry, by its very nature, produces situations that are highly prone to unethical behavior. And many meeting managers and planners will disagree as to just what is ethical and what is not. Let us look at some of the situations in which unethical behavior can occur.

FAMILIARIZATION TRIPS (fam trip)

When cities, convention bureaus and individual properties invite meeting planners to visit gratis, they are obviously hoping to influence the planner to hold a future meeting at their site. Planners with a real potential of booking a meeting there are perfectly legitimate in accepting the free trip. However, ethics come into play when a planner, who has either no potential or no intention of taking a meeting to that particular location, accepts the invitation as a method of obtaining a no-cost fun weekend, perhaps even taking spouse or friend along. Some planners actually consider these free trips as an industry "perk" to which they are entitled. However, most planners understand the true ethics of the situation, and respect the fact that the host site has every right to anticipate a possible return for their "fam trip" expenditures.

SUPPLIER RELATIONS

There was a time (and not only in the meetings industry) when a handshake was as binding as a written contract. The old adage that "man's word was as good as his bond" unfortunately is too infrequently true in today's world. Some planners feel that suppliers, by and large, are out to get the most they can for their firms and are not above shading the truth to get what they want. In turn, when speaking with numerous suppliers, their feelings can all too often be the same. The natural caution that exists between buyer and seller, it seems, has developed into downright distrust. Many planners now deal with all suppliers only on the basis of a legal contract. Reputations do get around in the industry, and a really ethical supplier is heralded throughout the business. However, no matter how highly regarded, in today's market it is wiser and safer for all concerned to operate on the basis of a mutually agreeable, written plan of action. With the seller's product or service described in detail and the buyer's financial responsibility spelled out, there will be no room for question.

Regardless of the written contract, however, both planner and supplier *should* deal with each other with only direct, forthright honesty. The planner should describe the needs and financial expectations accurately and in turn the supplier should put forth only those items which can be realistically and accurately supplied within the planner's financial bounds.

When the supplier submits a detailed, creative and unique proposal, it is the planner's ethical duty to either accept the proposal and negotiate a contract for the services, or return the proposal and refrain from using, copying or "borrowing" any of the ideas or activities that had been proposed. The activities, events and ideas contained in that proposal are the property of the supplier, and the planner cannot, in good conscience, use any part thereof, without full payment to the supplier.

GIFT GIVING

This has come to be a touchy, questionable practice. Gifts from a simple fruit and cheese basket to an expensive piece of jewelry are commonplace. Strictly defined perhaps no gift is truly ethical. The practice of "gifting" potential or present clients has become traditional and perhaps even expected.

To re-establish ethics in this business of giving and receiving gifts will take the cooperation and mutual understanding of both the giver and the receiver. When does a business gift become a bribe? This is an extremely gray area of judgement, but it would seem that a gift of a basket of fruit or upgrading of a vacation room (for which the planner has personally paid) might be an acceptable level, whereas expensive or personal gifts would not be. The planner might well expect to be wined

THE MOST ETHICAL TRAVEL WRITER

Marguerite L. Weirich, Meeting Manager
Arizona Connection, Inc.

I rather enjoyed an incident that happened a few years ago. As a representative of the local convention and visitors bureau, I had volunteered to escort a very prestigious travel writer around our community, showing him our accommodations and attractions and places of interest. Of course, it was our hope that he would write a very complimentary article on our city for the well-read travel section of his newspaper, which happened to be a major West Coast publication.

We had visited several of our major resorts and hotels, and it was about lunch time. We stopped at a historic old Inn, with a well-deserved reputation for fine food. When the check came, however, my guest insisted upon paying for his own lunch. Each time we stopped for some cool refreshment on that very warm day, he was also adamant that he pay his share. I was both pleasantly surprised and a little amused at the lengths to which he carried this code of ethics—thinking to myself, tongue in cheek, that he had not as yet offered to pay for the gasoline!

Late in the day, I delivered the gentleman to the airport to catch his flight home, and escorted him to his boarding gate. Upon returning to my car, I found a bottle of very fine scotch, with a note of thanks for my time and the use of my private car for his "fam trip"! In repeating the story to my peers in the industry, I was not surprised that they already knew of this gentleman's penchant for strictly ethical behavior. He was well-known for his adherence to a strict code, and deservedly so. Meeting this gentleman was really refreshing, and it restored my faith that there really are honest people with great integrity in an industry in which true integrity can be so rare.

P.S. We got an excellent, rave article about our community—one that was truly deserved, not purchased.

and dined on property during a site-selection trip, but a very expensive dinner at an off-property five-star restaurant is a different matter.

Some companies have now ruled that persons in a position to make purchasing decisions may not accept any gifts, and this would seem to settle the question! However, pending the passage of this kind of ruling throughout the industry, the decision would seem to come down to the ethical behavior of every individual involved.

These are but a couple of situations in which ethics come into play. Also, charges should be equitable, and clients should always get what they pay for;

outright thievery or disappearance of equipment while in a hotel should be stopped; the planner should always closely estimate the room requirements and give honest guarantees for meals and breaks. In every instance, ethics depend upon honesty, integrity and courtesy adhered to by all parties. Both planner and supplier are suspect where unethical behavior is concerned.

❏ *SUMMARY*

Unethical behavior is evident all around us: in scholastic circles, in the corporate world, in local and state government and even in our nation's capital. This is no less true in the business of meetings and conventions.

Familiarization tours are accepted by planners who have no real intention to use a particular location for a meeting; suppliers and planners recognize the need for "ironclad" contracts, in order to assure delivery of all that was promised; and a supplier's ideas are sometimes "pirated" by planners to whom a proposal was submitted. Gifts (above and beyond the value of goodwill or a simple thank you) are given, accepted and even expected.

Only by the cooperative efforts of those in the industry can these questionable practices be eliminated. Those who truly behave according to a strict, honest code of ethics, and there are a number of them, should be models to others. It is up to the industry to police their own!

❏ *PROJECTS*

1. Call a few local hotels/resorts and ask if they have a code of ethics published for their employees. Also ask the same properties if they have any ruling on the acceptance of gifts from business associates.

2. Call the convention and visitors bureau and ask what their experience has been with regard to "fam trips." Do they feel that all of their acceptees have been ethical and true potential customers?

3. Call a local DMC and ask if they have any tales of either truly ethical or unethical behavior of some clients. How do they generally feel about ethics in the meetings industry?

4. Talk to a meeting manager for a local association, and ask if they find the behavior of suppliers in the industry strictly ethical. What is the meeting manager's feeling about ethics in the industry in general?

☐ DISCUSSION QUESTIONS

1. What is a "fam" or familiarization trip?

2. When is it ethical for a planner to accept an invitation to a "fam trip"? When is it considered unethical?

3. **Why does a prudent planner consider a written contract a necessity in dealing with suppliers and subcontractors?**

4. **What is the planner's unspoken committment to the supplier regarding a detailed proposal?**

5. **Why is "gifting" a potential client a questionable activity? In your opinion, at what level is a gift a "gift" and at what level does it become a "bribe"?**

6. **From your own knowledge and experience, describe a situation in which ethics comes into play.**

7. **Why do you think ethical behavior is important in all business dealings?**

MEETING MINUTIAE

OBJECTIVES

After reading this chapter, you will be able:

❏ To demonstrate the importance of badges and registration kits
❏ To describe the various kinds of audio/visual equipment
❏ To introduce the concept of seating plans
❏ To demonstrate the use of a "progress calendar"

This chapter is a miscellany of small but important details, which the meeting planner must consider.

BADGES

Meeting badges have one purpose: to identify attendees. They may be very sophisticated metal, picture badges, or paper badges, handwritten from the registration list and inserted into plastic pin or clip carriers, which are affixed to the attendee's clothing. Some are written using caligraphy on plain white cards; others are typed in bulletin type on a typewriter set up for just this purpose; and still others are computer-generated labels glued on to shiny card stock. Ribbon paste-ons are frequently used to indicate members of the host group, speakers, chairpersons, members of the Board of Directors or guests. Other planners will identify these VIPs by using different colored badges, or brilliant dots of different colors. If there is a trade show in conjunction with the meeting, exhibitors should be clearly identified by some unique character of the badge, which may be its color, its shape or an attached ribbon.

There are a wide variety of badge styles available. The meeting planner should contact a badge company and ask for samples (and prices), before deciding upon the badge to be used. In addition to the basic badge, the planner must consider the ease or difficulty of making up the badges, any equipment that might be required, and the potential for adding or correcting badges on-site.

Whatever kind of badge the planner decides upon, there are several important things that *every* badge should have:

❑ Logo or other identification of the meeting group
❑ Person's name, large enough to be read at a short distance
❑ Attendee's city and state—and if there is no objection, identification of the company represented
❑ Some method of identifying VIPs, members, nonmembers, exhibitors, guests, speakers, planning staff, etc. This identification is important for security purposes, as well as to keep nonregistered persons out of the meeting.
❑ Make sure meeting planning staff are *clearly* identified, so people know whom to ask, if they have questions.
❑ A device for attaching the badge to the attendee's clothing—often the "clip-on" or "bolo tie" variety is preferred to any kind of pin which might make marks on lapels or fine dresses.

Badges should be prepared and placed in registration kits well before the meeting, but there should be some method of making up additional badges or making changes in spelling, etc., at the meeting registration desk.

REGISTRATION KITS/MATERIALS

All information about the site city and hotel, full data on the meeting program, informational lists of all attendees, note pads, pens/pencils, registration receipt, any necessary function tickets, meeting badge and any "freebies" or giveaways should be assembled in some kind of packet for each attendee to pick up at registration for the meeting.

All of this meeting information can be delivered in a number of ways, such as those listed below, and every meeting planner tries to create new and different ways of handling these packets:

1. A simple manila *envelope,* with or without the company logo and with the name of each attendee affixed to the outside—These envelopes, which are inexpensive, can be purchased in "office beige," brown, white, and a rainbow of colors.
2. A stiff paper *folder,* with pockets inside to hold meeting program, pads of paper, pencils, badge—Folders may also be imprinted with the name of the meeting or of the company sponsoring the meeting, and will sometimes bear a logo and perhaps the theme of the meeting. These, too, are available in various grades of paper and come in many colors.
3. A loose-leaf *notebook* (the 8½ × 5 size is popular)—Some come in blue denim or other materials, or are covered with a loose plastic sheet, behind which the planner may slip a pre-printed sheet of paper bearing logo, name of meeting, etc. If budget permits, these notebooks may even be purchased in pigskin or other fine leather, imprinted in gold leaf if desired. The loose leaf pages are a detailed program, attendee lists, descriptions of extracurricular activities and blank pages for notes; the interior of the notebook usually has pockets for writing implements and badges, plus any required tickets.

4. A *portfolio* (with interior pockets) of either inexpensive vinyl or beautifully tooled calfskin. These may also be imprinted with information of the planner's choice.
5. *Brief cases* in cloth, vinyl or leather, imprinted in gold leaf with the attendee's name, name of the meeting, dates and hotel/city
6. Plastic or cloth drawstring *bags* are sometimes available free or very inexpensively from the site city convention and visitor bureau. In the event of a very tight budget, these may serve to hold registration materials.

Registration kits may either be utilitarian, serving only the purpose of delivering information to each attendee, or they may represent a souvenir of the meeting, to be taken home and used in the future. The determination as to which usage best fits a meeting will be based on the kind of meeting, the budget, and the best judgement of the meeting planner.

AUDIO/VISUAL AIDS

A strictly visual medium, simple and easy to use is the flip chart mounted on an easel and written on with a crayon or grease pencil. The flip chart tablet of paper may be preprinted, in order to present a more professional looking chart, or the presenter may write on the pages as he/she speaks. Flip charts are often used at the registration desk to call attention to an event, to give instructions, or to simply list the day's activities.

A/V has become an integral part of most meetings, and ranges from a simple overhead projector to very sophisticated, multiple-screen/multiple-projector, computer-operated equipment. The meeting planner should be acquainted with the technology that is available, but for all but the most simple projection should employ the technical expertise of a professional to assure quality audio/visual production.

Projection is Divided into Two Basic Types

Front Screen.   The projector is placed amid the audience or behind the seating area, and projected on a screen at the front of the meeting room. With this method, people may not be seated or standing in an area in a direct line between the projector and the screen. People arriving late or walking across the room and crossing the projection line of sight will cast shadows on the screen. (See Fig. 15-1.)

Rear Screen.   The projector is located behind the screen and the image is projected from the rear. The room need not be dark with this type, but the space behind the screen must be enclosed or draped so as not to admit light in this area. The screen must also be placed further out into the seating area, to allow room behind the screen for the projecting equipment, and thus will reduce the number of persons who may be seated in the room. However, persons walking around the room do not interrupt projection. This is a more professional, but also more costly way, to show visual images at a meeting. (See Fig. 15-2.)

Screens

Screens come in various sizes and materials. The surface of the screen determines many of its other characteristics:

Matte White.   A common cloth screen surface, allowing a wide viewing angle, for which the room must be darkened.

Glass-Bead.   Producing three times the brightness of matte white screens, but with only half the viewing angle. These screens also require darkness.

Lenticular.   A small screen surface, which may be used in normally lit rooms and has a lesser viewing angle.

Rear Projection.   Translucent material screens, requiring complete darkness in the projection area (behind the screen), but permitting normal light in the viewing area.

Screen placement is determined by room set-up, audience size and the type of projection being utilized. But a basic rule of thumb is that the front-row audience should be at a distance of 1 ½ times the screen height from the screen, and the back row should be no further away than 6 times the screen height.

Screen size also has some rule of thumb guidelines. Naturally, the screen must be of sufficient size to be clearly visible from all seats in the room. The bottom of the screen must be 5′ from the surface of the floor, so the planner should double check to be sure the ceiling height is sufficient to accommodate the size of the screen, plus this five-foot allowance.

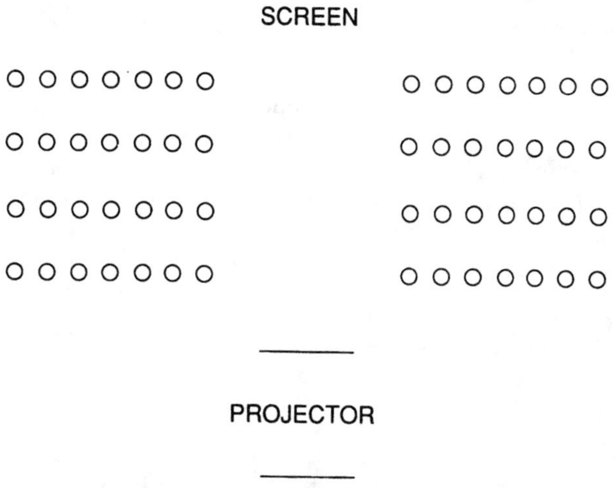

SCREEN

O O O O O O O   O O O O O O

O O O O O O O   O O O O O O

O O O O O O O   O O O O O O

O O O O O O O   O O O O O O

————   ————

PROJECTOR

————

Fig. 15-1. Front Screen Projection

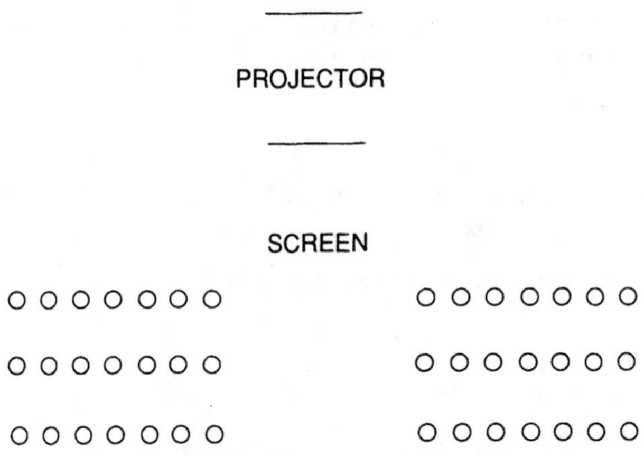

PROJECTOR

_____

SCREEN

O O O O O O   O O O O O O

O O O O O O   O O O O O O

O O O O O O   O O O O O O

Fig. 15-2. Rear Screen Projection

For viewing quality in a particular meeting room for a specific meeting, consult an A/V expert, who has worked with meetings in the past. Rely on the counsel and assistance of pros, and employ an expert to operate the equipment if it is not fully within the purview of someone on the meeting staff to set up and operate such technologically advanced equipment.

The Medium to Be Used

Now that the projection equipment has been overviewed, just what does the planner have to know about the medium? Whenever planning equipment, whether for an in-house presentation or for an outside contracted speaker, be sure to know what medium has been chosen, in order to determine the necessary projection equipment.

35 mm Slides. Slides used for professional production are just like the 35 mm slides produced by a personal camera. They give good, clear, quality images and are easy to edit. Anything can be produced on slides from photos of charts and tables to pictures of buildings, landscapes and people. These are used most frequently in a rotary tray called a carousel and this tray may be used in front or rear projection, on simplistic or computer-operated multiple-projector equipment.

Motion Picture Film. The most common motion picture film used in professional projection is 16 mm. For the operation of the projection equipment you will probably need a professional. Projectors may be automatically threaded with film, or the operator may need to load the projector manually.

Video. Video tape has become the most popular medium of choice. Video productions will most often need professional operators. However, the planner should know the rudiments of this medium. VHS and Beta are the two types of equipment used, with VHS being the most common. In addition, VHS tape comes in several sizes, which use different kinds of projection equipment.

The VHS tape itself can range from that in a mini-casette using a light weight camera, to ½″ used in most amateur-run home video cameras, to ¾″ professional or 1″ television-camera sizes. The planner should be aware of the differences in tapes and be sure to ask every speaker or presenter just what kind of equipment will be needed, and what size tape will be used.

Video tape is shown on a monitor (better clarity but slightly more expensive) or on a regular television screen. If the room is large, the planner may want to have monitors located throughout the seating area, to provide better viewing for all participants. If the meeting is a very large one, and the room expansive, the planner may want to arrange for a large video projection unit, usually operated from an elevated projection booth, with the unit itself mounted on the ceiling of the room. The picture is then projected on to a large screen in the front of the meeting room and sound is "piped" through a central system already installed in the room. From the projection booth, the picture can be enlarged or made smaller to fit the size of the screen available, and the volume of sound can be controlled.

 AUDIO/VISUAL NIGHTMARE!

By Marti Lorenzen
Denver, Colorado

As Communications Director for a regional bank holding company, I was responsible for many types of meetings. The most important meetings I arranged were those for the Board of Directors of our lead, or flagship bank.

These were monthly meetings in our own boardroom. As part of the agenda, we showed more than 150 slides of financial statements about our loan customers. This basically was the purpose of the meeting, to review our loan portfolio.

We had a rear-screen projection system that was orchestrated by an older model synchronizer. As audio/visual support I had two long-time employees from the graphics department. Each month I would collect the information from our line departments and give it to graphics. They were responsible for formating the information along established guidelines and proofing. We always had a rehearsal on the afternoon before the board meeting, where we would identify errors in slides and senior management could change the order or omit certain slides.

I had been managing these meetings less than a year, yet I had heard horror stories about equipment that had malfunctioned in this room. We had several backup systems in place, such as extra bulbs for the six projectors that were used. We had extra lenses and time frames established so we did not leave one slide on so long that it would melt.

Although I thought we were glitch-proof, I soon found out how wrong I was. In February, all had gone well during rehearsal. We had made minor changes and were ready early on board day. About ten slides into the show, the synchronizer froze up. We apologized to the audience (the Chairman of the Board, the President, several other officers and twenty board members who were important executives in the community) and started on the backup plan.

I can still remember how it felt. Within three minutes, the graphics team beeped me on my intercom. They had switched to the second synchronizer and it was also frozen. They could not project the slides *at all.*

My boss, who was also in the room, assumed control, informed the board of the problem and asked them to continue with the off-screen items while we worked on the system.

Off I ran to make copies of the originals, which we had used to shoot the slides. It took thirty-five minutes to make sufficient copies of the multiple pages. Returning to the boardroom was not something I looked forward to doing. The board continued the meeting, finishing almost two hours later than expected.

As a remedy for future meetings, we always brought copies of the originals and an opaque projector in case of other equipment failures. Of course, in the following three years, the synchronizers did not quit again. And, my comfort level took at least six months to return. I learned two important lessons: First, when you think you have enough backup systems, think again. Second, if you hear rumors or talk of prior problems, double and triple check those areas.

Opaque Projection Materials. The opaque projector is a simple magnifying glass projector, which will allow the speaker to show pages of a magazine, typewritten charts or other already printed material. It is very simple to operate and can be run by the speaker or an assistant at the podium.

Overhead Transparencies. The overhead projects any material which has been transferred onto a transparent plastic sheet. The advantage of this is not only its ease of operation, but also that the speaker can point to items on the plastic sheet or write with a grease pencil on the sheet, in order to illustrate a point or call a certain piece of data to the attention of the audience. This can also act as backup equipment, in the event of failure of one of the other types of projector.

Multimedia and Multi-Image Presentation. With a multitude of 35 mm slide trays and a good sound system, all interconnected and synchronized by computers, the planner can present the most sophisticated programs. Up to thirty projectors at a time can be controlled in this manner. Although somewhat expensive, this method creates dynamic and impressive audio/visual productions.

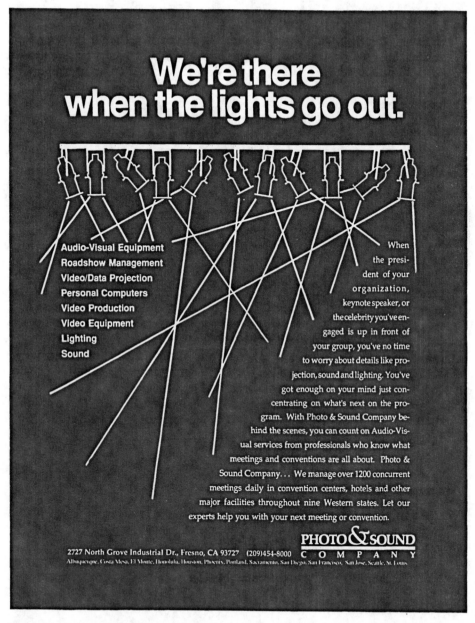

Fig. 15–3. When handling audiovisual effects, it is always intelligent to hire professionals. This ad for Photo & Sound Company, one of the prominent A/V companies, stresses all of the lights and sound they will handle for a meeting. (Courtesy of Photo & Sound Company.)

SEATING ARRANGEMENTS AND ROOM SET-UPS

Whenever a planner is considering a meeting session, whether it be for a large general session or a small break-out meeting, consideration must be given to the comfort of the attendee. Chairs must be well constructed so as to support the back, seat surfaces should be covered with comfortable seating material and the chairs must be well spaced [5″ to 6″ between each chair] to avoid the "sardine syndrome" among the audience. The room itself must be well-ventilated, and properly heated or cooled as the temperature demands. Controls for operation of heating/cooling equipment should be in each room, accessible to the planning staff for making adjustments, as the temperature may vary during the meeting. Posts, pillars or other supports must not obstruct the line of sight from the attendee to the stage, dais or front table. Line of sight for any projector is critical, so that everyone has a clear and direct view of any materials being shown on screen. Lights should be on a rheostat for better control. After the planner has checked out the room itself, chairs must be placed according to a preset plan that will best complement the type of meeting. Instructions for the seating arrangement must *never* be given verbally to the hotel set-up staff. For each and every session, meal or event, the planning staff should draw up a seating chart and attach it to instructions to the hotel personnel. These can be done on graph paper to make spacing simpler, or a kit for making seating charts (complete with templates for chairs, tables, dais, podiums, etc.) called "The Perfect Fit" is available from the offices of Meeting Planners International. The kit also includes "The Arranger, A Comfort Calculator," which will assist you in determining the number of persons a room will accommodate in any of the seating arrangements. The basic styles of seating arrangement are: theatre, schoolroom and conference. There are many variations on these set-ups, but we will illustrate some of the basic layouts in Fig. 15-4, Fig. 15-5, and Fig. 15-6.

Spacing Notes

There should be at least 2′ between the rows of chairs in theatre seating, to allow comfortable space for knees, and for passage of people through the aisles. And there should be approximately 5″ to 6″ between chairs.

In order to allow space for people to walk around tables, and for servers to have access, there should be approximately 4′ between tables in a classroom set-up and 6′ for a banquet.

THEATRE SEATING:

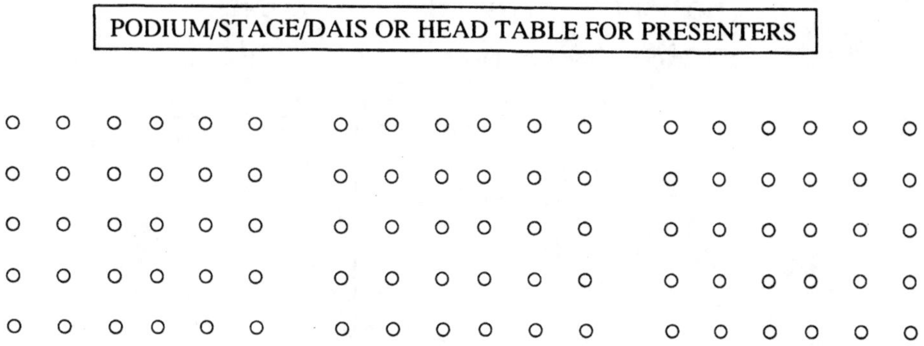

PODIUM/STAGE/DAIS OR HEAD TABLE FOR PRESENTERS

O O O O O O   O O O O O O   O O O O O O

O O O O O O   O O O O O O   O O O O O O

O O O O O O   O O O O O O   O O O O O O

O O O O O O   O O O O O O   O O O O O O

O O O O O O   O O O O O O   O O O O O O

SCHOOLROOM:

PODIUM/STAGE/DAIS OR HEAD TABLE FOR SPEAKERS

O O O O   O O O O   O O O O

O O O O   O O O O   O O O O

O O O O   O O O O   O O O O

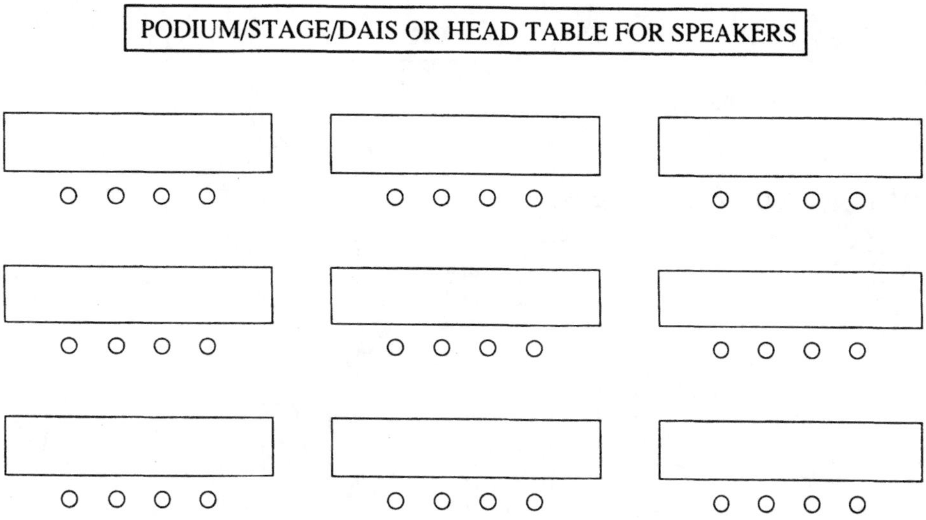

Both of these seating arrangements lend themselves well to large groups, and either of them can be adapted to variations, such as the chevron or semicircle.

Fig. 15–4. Seating Arrangements/Room Set-ups

CONFERENCE STYLES:

NO PODIUM/STAGE/DAIS OR HEAD TABLE

BOARD OF DIRECTORS (either oblong or oval):

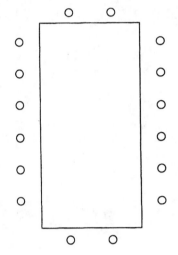

U-SHAPED CONFERENCE: (variations on this can be an "E" or "T")

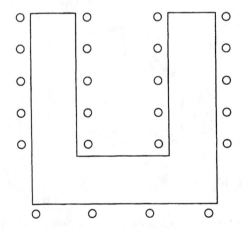

Fig. 15–5. Seating Arrangements/Room Set-ups

HOLLOW SQUARE: (may also be a hollow circle using serpentine sections to round the corners)

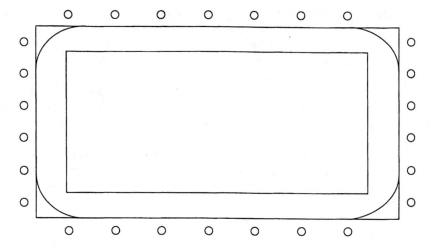

ROUNDS: (Seating often used for group discussions, workshops or food functions)

Fig. 15–6. Seating Arrangements/Room Set-ups (Continued)

THE PROGRESS CALENDAR

As a planner, the meeting professional should certainly have a fool-proof scheduling mechanism, to keep all of the various facets of the meeting plan on time. One of the better methods is a calendar wall chart. On this chart are listed all of the chores to be performed, their start and finish dates and some visual method of quickly ascertaining whether or not each phase is on schedule.

By using colored dots with matching grease pens, every task can be shown on this calendar. A dot is placed on the start date of a specific task (such as program preparation and printing) and another dot of the same color at the targeted finish date. Then a grease pencil of the same color is used to draw a line from the "start" dot to the date on which each chore or portion of the task is completed, until the colored line ends at the finish dot when the entire task has been completed.

A color key is written on the bottom of the calendar to designate each task thus illustrated and scheduled. By this method, the planner has an instant visual representation of exactly where each phase of the meeting is and whether it is on schedule. (See Fig. 15-7.)

☐ *SUMMARY*

The major portion of planning a meeting seems to be taken up with expense and income budgets, developing and setting the full program of events, selecting a site, and creating an all-inclusive meeting plan. However, there are many less impressive but nonetheless critical details that go into producing a successful meeting.

Every year new and creative methods of identifying meeting attendees are coming on the market. Badges are necessary and their selection and production are a part of every meeting.

When registrants arrive at a meeting, they are almost always presented with materials and information. The development of innovative and interesting ways of packaging these items falls to the creative abilities of the planner.

Audio/Visual materials for meetings are becoming ever more sophisticated. Although the planner need not become an A/V technician, nevertheless it is expected that he/she will be knowledgeable about the technology, know what is available, how to use it and where to find the personnel to produce and operate it.

When participants come to a meeting, they have every right to expect that they will be able to hear and see all presentations from comfortable seating, in well-lighted and heated or air conditioned rooms. To this end, the planner must understand the various seating arrangements and rooms set-ups with their advantages and limitations. Correct lines of sight, equipment placement and seating space considerations are all necessary parts of the planner's job.

In order for the planner to stay on top of the multitude of deadlines necessitated in putting together the parts of a meeting, a method of tracking each task

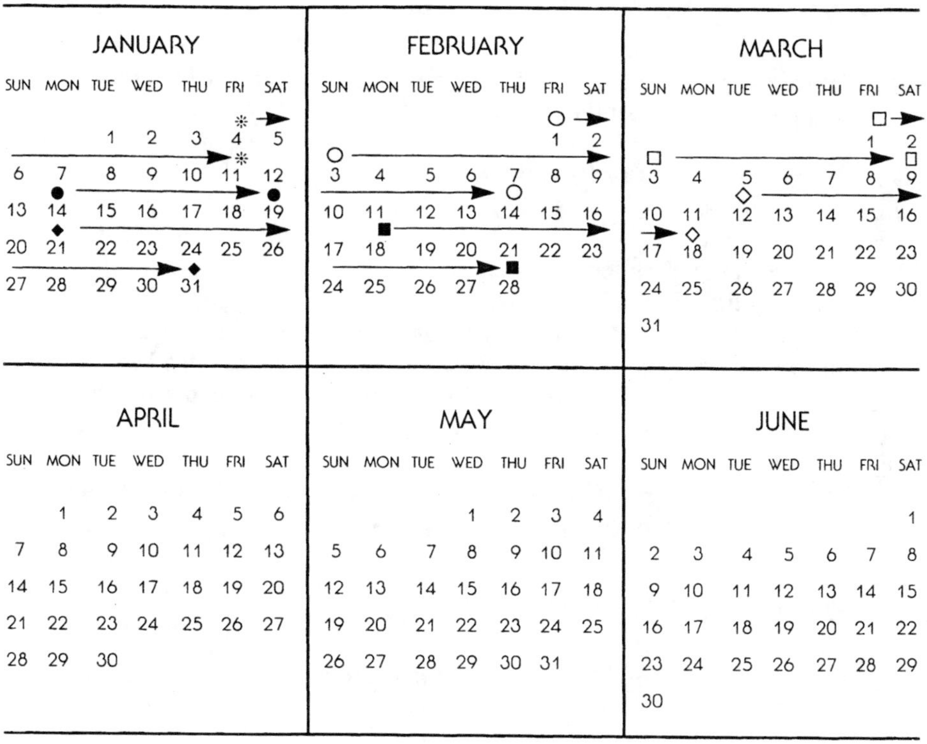

※ January 4-11: Compose, layout, print-registration/promo
● January 14-19: Mail registrations to potential attendees
◆ January 21-31: Speaker details finalized
○ February 1-14: Receive and process registrations
■ February 18-28: Room lists delivered to hotel
□ March 1-9: Food and beverage finalized with hotel
◇ March 12-18: Meeting on-site

Fig. 15—7. A sample progress calendar.

must be developed. One good, visual method is a progress calendar. A wall calendar with each job's beginning and completion dates inserted is one way to follow the time schedule.

Although each of the items discussed in this chapter by themselves may seem minor, they nevertheless are necessary to enhance the whole when producing a meeting. The innovative ideas and creativity that go into these smaller pieces of the meeting can mean the difference between a simply adequate meeting and an outstanding and memorable experience.

❏ *PROJECTS*

1. Visit your convention and visitors bureau and gather up all of the materials you would put into a convention attendee's kit:

❏ A sample badge and badge holder
❏ City brochures
❏ Hotel brochures
❏ Pamphlets describing local attractions
❏ A dining guide (if one is available)
    Ask someone at the bureau if they have any giveaways you might have to add to your kit. The bureau may also have a folder or logo-bearing bag in which to put all of your items. A local hotel might have pads of paper and pencils/pens. Now add a "mock" convention program and you have completed your registration kit.
    If everyone were to bring their "kit" to class, it might be interesting to see the variety of items collected with no cost.

❏ *DISCUSSION QUESTIONS*

1. **What is the purpose of badges at a meeting?**

2. **Discuss some of the badge styles used.**

3. **Name some of the ways of identifying VIPs, speakers, meeting staff, members and guests through badges.**

4. **What are some things that must be considered when choosing a badge type?**

5. **What are some of the items that must be on *every* badge?**

6. **Name some of the devices used to affix badges to the attendees. What are the pros and cons of each?**

7. **What is a registration kit?**

8. **Name some of the registration kits in current usage. List their good and bad points.**

9. In discussing A/V, what are the two basic types of projection? Describe each.

10. What kinds of screens are available for projection? What are their good and bad points?

11. Generally, how far should the front row of the audience be from the screen? How far should the last row be?

12. Why is ceiling height important when considering screen size?

13. Why are 35 mm slides a good medium for projection?

14. **What is the most commonly used size of motion picture film for meetings?**

15. **What types of video equipment are used? Which is the most common?**

16. **What sizes of VHS tape are there? Why must the planner be aware of these sizes?**

17. **Where is the picture seen when using video tape?**

18. **What is an opaque projector? What are its advantages?**

19. What is an overhead transparency? How is it different from an opaque projector?

20. What system will produce the most sophisticated program? Describe it.

21. Why are seating arrangements important? Name the three basic seating arrangements for a meeting.

22. What distance should be left between rows of chairs in a theater seating arrangement? What distance should there be between the chairs?

23. How much space should be left between tables in a classroom set-up? How much space should be left between tables in a banquet?

24. **Name some of the variations of the conference style and describe them.**

25. **Why should a planner have a progress calendar?**

26. **Describe the wall calendar method and how it works.**

APPENDIX A ASSOCIATIONS OF INTEREST TO THOSE IN THE MEETING INDUSTRY

These are only some of the associations in which meeting industry people are involved. For additional information, check with your local library or with someone in the meeting industry in your area.

AMERICAN HOTEL & MOTEL ASSOCIATION (AH&MA)
1201 New York Avenue, N.W., Washington, D.C. 20005-3917

AMERICAN SOCIETY OF ASSOCIATION EXECUTIVES (ASAE)
1575 Eye Street, N.W., Washington, D.C. 20005

CONVENTION LIAISON COUNCIL (CLC)
1575 Eye Street N.W., Washington, D.C. 20005

INTERNATIONAL ASSOCIATION OF CONVENTION & VISITORS BUREAUS (IACVB)
P.O. Box 758, Champaign, IL 61820

INTERNATIONAL EXHIBITORS ASSOCIATION (IEA)
5103 B. Backlick Road, Annandale, VA 22003

MEETING PLANNERS INTERNATIONAL (MPI)
1950 Stemmons Freeway, Dallas, TX 75207

NATIONAL ASSOCIATION OF EXPOSITION MANAGERS (NAEM)
334 E. Garfield Road, Aurora, OH 44202

PROFESSIONAL CONVENTION MANAGEMENT ASSOCIATION (PCMA)
2027 First Avenue North, Suite 1007, Birmingham, AL 35203

SOCIETY OF COMPANY MEETING PLANNERS (SCMP)
2600 Garden Road, #208, Monterey, CA 93940

SOCIETY OF INCENTIVE TRAVEL EXECUTIVES (SITE)
271 Madison Avenue, New York, NY 10016

APPENDIX B PERIODICALS OF INTEREST TO THOSE IN THE MEETING INDUSTRY

This list represents only a sampling of the magazines and newspapers dedicated to subjects of interest to those in the meetings and conventions business. Additional information might be available from your local library, or by writing one of the meetings associations.

ASSOCIATION & SOCIETY MANAGER (bimonthly)
Barrington Publications
825 S. Barrington Avenue, Los Angeles, CA 90049

BUSINESS TRAVEL NEWS (semimonthly)
CMP Publications, Inc.
600 Community Drive, Manhasset, NY 11030

CORPORATE MEETINGS & INCENTIVES (monthly)
Edgell Communications Inc.
7500 Old Oak Boulevard, Cleveland, OH 44130
Note: *Corporate Meetings & Incentives* publishes an annual suppliers directory listing names, addresses and phone numbers of: hotels, resorts, airlines, DMCs, incentive management companies, auto rentals, wholesale tour operators and cruise lines, both domestic and international.

CORPORATE TRAVEL (monthly)
Gralla Publications
1515 Broadway, New York, NY 10036

INCENTIVE/MANAGING & MARKETING THROUGH MOTIVATION (monthly)
Bill Communications, Inc.
633 Third Avenue, New York, NY 10017

INCENTIVE TRAVEL MANAGER (monthly)
Barrington Publications
825 S. Barrington Avenue, Los Angeles, CA 90049

INSURANCE CONFERENCE PLANNER (published six times per year)
Bayard Publications
1234 Summer Street, Stamford, CT 06905

MEDICAL MEETINGS (published eight times per year)
Medical Meetings
20 Central Avenue, P.O. Box 700, Ayer, MA 01432

MEETING NEWS (monthly)
Gralla Publications
1515 Broadway, New York, NY 10036

MEETINGS & CONVENTIONS, including INCENTIVE WORLD (monthly)
Ziff-Davis Publishing Co.
One Park Avenue, New York, NY 10016

SUCCESSFUL MEETINGS (monthly)
Bill Communications
633 Third Avenue, New York, NY 10017

MEETINGS & INCENTIVE TRAVEL (bimonthly)
Southam Communications, Ltd.
1450 Don Mills Road, Ontario M3B2X7

RESORTS & INCENTIVES (bimonthly)
Gralla Publications/United Newspapers Group
1515 Broadway, New York, NY 10036

THE MEETING MANAGER (monthly)
Meeting Planners International
1950 Stemmons Freeway, Dallas, TX 75207

TOUR & TRAVEL NEWS (weekly)
CMP Publications Inc.
600 Community Drive, Manhasset, NY 11030

APPENDIX C FORMS UTILIZED IN PLANNING MEETINGS

The multiplicity of details involved in planning a meeting, putting together a budget, keeping all of the registrants' and their information straight while on site, demand the use of forms: forms for a budget, forms for registrations, forms for extracurricular activities, forms for transportation information, forms for arrival/departure data, forms for evaluations, ad infinitum. While most meeting planners' forms are a compilation of needs and experience over many meetings and differ from one another in format, there is certain basic information that must be included on each. To this end, this appendix will endeavor to exhibit a few basic forms.

Form 1 – Preliminary Budget
Form 2 – Estimated Income Budget
Form 3 – Speaker Information
Form 4 – Registration for Meeting
Form 5 – Rooming List
Form 6 – Meeting Budget (Expense Only)

Form 1 — PRELIMINARY BUDGET PAGE—1 OF 2

This is an *expense budget* outlining the estimated costs of the meeting. When working with a corporate or company-paid meeting, this is the only budget used, since there would be no direct *income* to this meeting. (See completed sample expense budget pages 226-229.)

MEETING BUDGET

PROGRAM DEVELOPMENT AND PRODUCTION $ _____
    Programs:
        Copy
        Layout
        Production and Printing
    Internal speakers and participants — expenses
    Outside speakers — honoraria, travel, lodging
PROMOTIONAL MAILINGS $ _____
    Brochures:
        Copy
        Layout
        Production and Printing
        Distribution/mailing costs
    Promotional letters (2)
        Production
        Mailing costs
    Registration forms
        Copy
        Layout
        Printing
        Mailing costs
        Return prestamped envelopes
EXHIBITS (Equipment) $ _____
    Decorator
        Drayage
        Poster boards (signage)
        Security
        Space rental for equipment
TRANSPORTATION: $ _____
    Air fares for estimated number of attendees (round trip)
    Airport transfers
        At point of origination — estimated round trip
        At meeting site — estimated round trip
    Luggage transfer — (if applicable)
REGISTRATION $ _____
    Registration form processing
        Registration kits on-site
        Badges — purchase and processing
        Personnel on site
        Miscellaneous equipment at registration desk
ACCOMMODATIONS (Rooms) (including service charge and/or tax) $ _____
    ____ Singles @ $ _____ per night ____ night(s)
    ____ Doubles @ $ _____ per night ____ night(s)
    ____ Double/doubles @ $ _____ per night ____ night(s)
    ____ Suites @ $ _____ per night ____ night(s)

Form 1 – PRELIMINARY BUDGET PAGE – 2 OF 2

AUDIO/VISUAL EQUIPMENT $ _____
    Projectors – rental
        Operator fees
        Stock film costs

MEETING SPACE (including tax or gratuities applicable) $ _____
    Largest ballroom – room rental (if any)
        Break-out rooms – room rentals (if any)
        Hospitality suites – room rentals (if any)
        Exhibit space – room rental (if any)

SOCIAL FUNCTIONS (including tax or gratuities) $ _____
    Tickets – production for all functions
        Opening reception:
            Food
            Beverage
            Entertainment
        Banquet:
            Food
            Beverage
            Entertainment
            Decor/centerpieces/tables/gifts/miscellaneous costs
        Breakfasts:
            Food
            Beverage
            Entertainment
        Luncheons:
            Food
            Beverage
            Entertainment
        Breaks:
            Food
            Beverage

SPORTS ACTIVITIES $ _____
    Spa costs
    Golf – greens fees/cart fees
    Tennis – court time costs
    Misc. purchases in the pro shops
    Equipment rentals (where necessary)
    Transportation to sports areas

OPERATIONS AND OVERHEAD $ _____
    Staffing and office overhead for meeting
    On-site telephone expenses
    Duplicating and printing costs on site
    General postage expenses
    Insurance
    Staff air and other transportation expenses
    Staff lodging and road expenses
    Extra set-up breakdown costs
    Additional microphone charges
    Meeting miscellaneous gratuities
    Contingency fund

SPECIAL OR EXTRAORDINARY EXPENSES: $ _____

                TOTAL ESTIMATED EXPENSES: $ _____

Form 2—ESTIMATED INCOME BUDGET

If the planner is working for an association or other meeting where there will be registration fees and other income, an income budget would be constructed.

MEETING ATTENDEES:

Air fares for _____ attendees $ _____

Transfers on site (round trip) $ _____

Room/accommodations income $ _____

     _____ Singles @ $ _____ for _____ night(s)

     _____ Doubles @ $ _____ for _____ night(s)

     _____ Double/doubles @ $ _____ for _____ night(s)

     _____ Suites @ $ _____ for _____ night(s)

Meeting registration fees: $ _____

     _____ Members @ $ _____ per person

     _____ Spouses/companions @ $ _____ per person

     _____ Nonmembers @ $ _____ per person

     _____ Students @ $ _____ per person

Special events not included in registration fee: $ _____

     _____ tickets for theme party @ $ _____ per person

     _____ tickets for final banquet @ $ _____ per person

     _____ tickets for golf tourney @ $ _____ per person

     _____ tickets for tennis round-robin @ $ _____ per person

     _____ Sightseeing tour tickets @ $ _____ per person

Sales of speaker tapes: $ _____

     _____ tapes @ $ _____ per tape

Sales of photographs: $ _____

     _____ Individuals @ $ _____ per photo

     _____ Group photos @ $ _____ each

EXHIBITS: $ _____

Sales of exhibit booths: _____ booths @ $ _____ each

Exhibitor sponsorship of breaks—estimated:

Exhibitor sponsorship of cocktail party

OTHER SPONSORSHIPS: $ _____

Program/advertisements

Underwriting badge expenses

Underwriting entertainment

Miscellaneous

OTHER MISCELLANEOUS INCOME: $ _____

                 TOTAL ESTIMATED INCOME: $ _____

                 TOTAL ESTIMATED EXPENSE: $ _____

                 PROJECTED PROFIT <LOSS>: $ _____

NOTES AND COMMENTS:

Form 3 — SPEAKER INFORMATION

NAME
_____

COMPANY OR ASSOCIATION
_____

MAILING ADDRESS
_____

CITY   STATE   ZIP
_____

DEGREES/TITLES
_____

BIO/BACKGROUND:
_____
_____

PRESENTATION DATE: TIME: LOCATION:
_____

SPECIAL INFORMATION FOR INTRODUCTION:
_____
_____

TITLE OF PRESENTATION:
_____

SCRIPT/AUDIOVISUAL MATERIALS HAVE BEEN SUBMITTED
      YES   NO
_____

ARRIVAL DATE: TIME:
_____

METHOD OF TRANSPORT: PVT. CAR   TRAIN   BUS   AIR
_____

AIRLINE AND FLIGHT NUMBER IF APPLICABLE:
_____

WOULD LIKE TRANSPORTATION TO HOTEL PROVIDED:
      YES   NO
_____

ACCOMMODATIONS DESIRED AT HOTEL: SINGLE   DOUBLE
_____

(If double, who will be accompanying?)
_____

DEPARTURE DATE: TIME:
_____

WILL REQUIRE TRANSPORTATION TO DEPOT/AIRPORT:
      YES   NO
_____

SPECIAL REQUESTS:

SPEAKER'S FEE:

OR SPEAKER'S HONORARIUM:

NOTES:

Form 4 — REGISTRATION FOR MEETING

DATES OF MEETING: CITY:
OFFICIAL HOTEL:

Name _____

Address _____

City _____ State _____ Zip _____

Spouse or companion name (as it should appear on name badge):

_____

Please check appropriate box: (SEE RATES IN ENCLOSED BROCHURE)

    SINGLE ROOM ____ nights @ $ _____ per night

    DOUBLE ROOM ____ nights @ $ _____ per night

    DOUBLE/DOUBLE ROOM ____ nights @ $ _____ per night

    SUITE ____ nights @ $ _____ per night

    I HAVE ENCLOSED MY CHECK FOR
        ACCOMMODATIONS FOR $ _____

Registration fees: (SEE RATES IN ENCLOSED BROCHURE)

    ____ Members @ $ _____

    ____ Nonmembers @ $ _____

    ____ Students @ $ _____

    I HAVE ENCLOSED MY CHECK FOR
        REGISTRATIONS FOR $ _____

Special events fees: (SEE RATES IN ENCLOSED BROCHURE)

    ____ tickets for theme party @ $ _____

    ____ tickets for final banquet @ $ _____

    ____ reservations for golf tourney @ $ _____

    ____ reservations for tennis tourney @ $ _____

    ____ reservations for day 1 city tour @ $ _____

    ____ reservations for day 3 city tour to historical sites
        including lunch @ $ _____

    I HAVE ENCLOSED MY CHECK FOR SPECIAL
        EVENTS FOR $ _____

Please handle my air reservations from _____ to site city.

    Preferred arrival date   A.M.   or   P.M.

    Preferred Departure Date   A.M.   or   P.M.

I require reservations for ____ persons (names listed below):

_____

_____

Unless otherwise indicated, **XYZ** airline — our official meeting airline — will be used whenever possible. When reservations are confirmed you will be billed for air fares.

TOTAL MONIES ENCLOSED FOR ALL ABOVE RESERVATIONS: $ _____

Form 5 — ROOMING LIST

NAME OF GROUP: _____

NAME OF HOTEL: _____

DATES OF MEETING: _____

GUEST NAME	ROOM TYPE	ARR. DATE	ARR. TIME	DEPT. DATE
M/M John Doe	Double	04/01/93	4:30 P.M.	04/05/93
Mary England	Single	03/31/93	8:00 P.M.	04/05/93
Jerry Earl	Single	04/02/93	7:30 A.M.	04/06/93

This list is filled in as the registration forms are received by the meeting planning staff. It is then submitted to the hotel by the deadline agreed upon. If the meeting is for over 200 attendees, the planner may elect to send these lists to the hotel every few days, as the registrations are received.

Form 6 — MEETING BUDGET (EXPENSE ONLY) PAGE—1 OF 2

This expense budget represents the final budget devised for the imaginary meeting shown in the Meeting Plan, Appendix D.

FOR: CONYER & WRIGHT BROKERAGE FIRM	DATES 4/3 TO 4/6/92	
LOC: DESERT CANYON RESORT, PHOENIX, AZ		
ITEM GROUP/ITEM	COST	GRAT. 18%
PROGRAM DEVELOPMENT AND PRODUCTION		
Printed Programs — Production Outside Speakers, honoraria, travel lodging	2,000.00 21,999.10	
PROMOTIONAL MAILINGS		
Brochures/letters/regis. forms (3) 750 pcs.	1,500.00	
EXHIBITS (Equipment)		
Decorator Drayage Poster boards Security Space for equipment		
AIRPORT TRANSFERS	4,390.40	790.00
REGISTRATION		
Badges and forms Personnel — on-site Conv. & Visit. Bureau Misc. Equip. at Regis. Desk	498.00 360.00 1,000.00	80.00
ROOMS Rates S— $\frac{195}{8}$ D— $\frac{175}{121}$ SU— ___	68,205.00	
Qty.— Rate avg.— _____ +Tax 9%	6,138.45	
AUDIO/VISUAL Operators	1,250.00	225.00
Projector/operator rental stock film	360.00	65.00
SOCIAL FUNCTIONS		
Tickets N/A Opening reception food 5504.25 Bev. 3075 Banquets (2) Luncheons Qty. 1 Coffee Breaks Qty. N/A Breakfasts Qty. 3	 7,323.75 44,580.00 4,158.00 6,858.15	 1,255.50 8,024.40 712.80 1,212.00
PAGE 1 SUBTOTALS		
COMMENTS—		
SIGNATURE _____ DATE __/__/__		

Form 6 — MEETING BUDGET (EXPENSE ONLY) PAGE — 2 OF 2

FOR: CONYER & WRIGHT BROKERAGE FIRM	DATES 4/3 TO 4/6/92	
LOC: PHOENIX, AZ		
ITEM GROUP/ITEM	COST	GRAT. 18%
OPERATION & OVERHEAD		
Staffing and office overhead	21,000,00	N/A
Sales Qty. ___ for ___ days @ $_____		
Clerical Qty. ___ for ___ days @ $_____		
Genl. OH @ $_____		
Phone on site long distance	97.00	
Duplication	300.00	
Gen. postage	369.24	
Insurance	3,000.00	
Staff lodging and road expenses	6.026.30	
Meeting room rental/Set-Ups	3,800.00	684.00
Extra microphones	200.00	36.00
Misc. gratuities		500.00
Contingency	12,400.00	
PAGE 2 SUBTOTALS		
OTHERS — ?		
Tour — day 3, 125 persons × $40	5,000.00	900.00
Tennis, bev. cart + lunch 138.42 × 24 players	3,322.08	598.00
Golf, bev. cart + luncheon $250.00 × 64 golfers	16,000.00	2,880.00
GRAND SUBTOTAL PAGE 1, 2, OTHER	241,135.37	17,962.70
TOTAL BUDGET COST INCLUDING GRATUITY	259,098.07	
COST PER PERSON ATTENDENCE # 250	1,036.40	

See attached notes on individual items.

COMMENTS —

SIGNATURE _____ DATE __/__/__

ADDENDA TO BUDGET

PROGRAM $2,000 inclusive of taxes
> Minimum 400 copies—XYZ Printer
> 8 double-sided pages/2 colors/60# slick magazine stock
> 80# colored stock cover

OUTSIDE SPEAKERS	TOTALS	$21,999.10
Golf pro		
Fee		12,000.00
Air, 1st C., R. T. Atlanta-Phoenix		560.00
Room		212.55
Transfers to and from airport		
Pt. of origin		30.00
Destination		30.00
TOTAL		$12,927.55
Tennis pro		
Fee		8,000.00
Air, 1st C., R. T. Miami-Phoenix		687.00
Room		212.55
Meals—L, D, B		95.00
Transfers to and from airport		
Pt. of origin		47.00
Destination		47.00
TOTAL		$9,071.55

PROMO MAILINGS	TOTALS	$1,500.00	
Letter advising of meeting		250.00	(250 copies)
Brochure w/regis. form		1,000.00	(250 copies)
Confirmation letter w/receipts		250.00	(250 copies)

AIRPORT TRANSFERS	TOTALS	$4,390.40
IN 3 bus trips @ 357.20/ea.		1,071.60
12 van trips @ 105.00/ea.		1,260.00
OUT 4 bus trips @ 357.20/ea.		1,428.80
6 van trips @ 105.00/ea.		630.00
STAFF—LIMO—COMPED		
TOTAL		$4,390.40

REGISTRATION	TOTALS	$ 498.00
Badges 300 @ 1.36		408.00
Forms		60.00
Golf/tennis sign-ups		30.00
TOTALS		$ 498.00

PERSONNEL ON SITE   TOTALS $ 1,360.00

C & VB Personnel (2) @ $6/hr
   4 days/15 hrs per day   360.00
Equipment—typewriter rental   200.00
Telephone N/C—hotel   — — —
Computer/printer rental   500.00
Miscellaneous items   300.00
   TOTAL $1,360.00

AUDIO/VISUAL   TOTALS $ 1,475.00

Own equipment—operator Exp.
   $800 + $150 + 300   1,250.00
   Gratuity   225.00
   TOTAL $1,475.00

MEALS   TOTALS $ 74,124.60

Welcome Reception	$ 4,698.75 food	2,625 bev.	1,255.50 grat.		
Banquets (2)	44,580.00 food &	bev.	8,024.40 grat.		
Luncheons (1)	4,158.00 food &	bev.	712.80 grat.		
Breakfasts (3)	6,858.15 food &	bev.	1,212.00 grat.		
TOTALS	$60,294.90	2,625	11,204.70		

POSTAGE   TOTALS $369.24

Speakers—3 contacts
   2 × 3 × .29   1.74
Promos   750 × .29   217.50
Misc.—hotel, suppliers, etc.   150.00
   TOTALS $369.24

STAFF EXPENSES   TOTALS $ 27,026.20

Salaries $21,000.00
Air fares   1,520.00
Ground—car rent/gas/ins.   275.00
Food   395.00
Rooms—2 singles   2,340.00
     1 double   1,050.00
     Tax   271.20
Miscellaneous   175.00
   TOTAL $27,026.20

APPENDIX D   THE MEETING PLAN

As mentioned at the beginning of Chapter 10, the meeting plan is the final, total word on any meeting. It is started as soon as the decision is made to hold a meeting and is completed only after the meeting is over. The plan used in this appendix is only one possibility. Every planner composes, borrows ideas and constantly alters and adds to the meeting plan. It almost becomes a living thing, ever moving and shifting to fit the meeting which is being planned at that moment. Some planners now have computer software with which to construct their entire meeting plan, including rooming lists, arrival/departure information, sporting events, and tours.

I have included a rather full plan in this appendix to give you an opportunity to go through each step of the planning process, and to think about the multiple pieces that make up an entire meeting.

DATES OF MEETING:
APRIL 3, 4, 5 and 6   Attendees: 250 persons

COMPANY/DEPARTMENT HOLDING MEETING: CONYER &
WRIGHT BROKERAGE FIRM, PHILADELPHIA, PA—ANNUAL
SALES MEETING

DAY/DATE	EVENT	ROOM	PAGE
All	City/Property/suppliers list		1
All	Property staff w/phone numbers		2
All	Property insurance/registration/meeting rooms		3
All	Dining/other facilities on-property		4
All	Golf/tennis/spas et al, Gratuities/Acctg.		5
All	Attendees/room and arrival information		6–11
1-4/3	Airport meet/greet and transfer schedules		12–16
1-4/3	Registration date/information desk—lobby		17
1-4/3	Welcome reception—Conv. foyer		18
2-4/4	Breakfast/general session—Foyer/ballroom		19–20
2-4/4	Luncheon	Patio A	21
2-4/4	Afternoon breakout sessions:		
	1. Subject/title	Mtg. Rm. A	22
	2. Subject/title	Mtg. Rm. B	23
	3. Subject/title	Mtg. Rm. C	24
2-4/4	Dinner/evening entertainment—Grand Ballroom		25–26
3-4/5	Breakfast—poolside		27
3-4/5	Sightseeing tour w/lunch		28
3-4/5	Golf tournament		29
3-4/5	Tennis tournament		30
3-4/5	Awards banquet—Grand Ballroom		31–33
4-4/6	Breakfast/departures/transportation sched.		34–36
4-4/6	Planning staff meeting/dinner	Mtg. Rm. A	37
5-4/7	Meeting shut-down info.		38
5-4/7	Meeting evaluation data		39

MEETING PLAN CITY/PROPERTY/SUPPLIERS

MEETING MANAGER: Phyllis Congdon ROOM # Sgl. #224

TRAVEL STAFF: John Bowen, Julia Wright, ROOM # Sgl. #222
and Marge Jeffers ROOM # Dbl. #226

CITY: PHOENIX, AZ

PROPERTY: DESERT CANYON RESORT
121 double rooms @ $175; 8 single rooms @ $195

SUPPLIERS:

AIRLINE: DELTA AL CONTACT: William Miller
PHONE# 666-4444

DMC PHOENIX CONNECTION CONTACT: Sue Leslie
PHONE# 602-747-333

TRANSPORTATION CO.: Gray Line CONTACT: through DMC
PHONE# 602-747-7373

TOUR GUIDE CO.: Desert Guides CONTACT: through DMC
PHONE# 602-747-6469

OTHER SUPPLIERS:

Spencer Clerical Services 602-777-9132
Computer Operators 602-747-7890

MEETING PLAN	PROPERTY STAFF
STAFF NAMES	PHONE NUMBERS
GENERAL MANAGER John Gillespie	Ext. 1212
SALES MANAGER George Montgomery	Ext. 1215
CONVENTION SERVICES MANAGER Judy Smith/ Asst. Jill	Ext. 1279
RESERVATION MANAGER Barbara Brody	Ext. 3433
CATERING MANAGER George Jennings	Ext. 6561
BEVERAGE MANAGER Jim Goeffries	Ext. 7675
EXECUTIVE CHEF Chef Rene Lesault	Ext. 9843
DINING ROOM CAPTAINS Paul Rosseau, Vincent Westmoreland, and Richard Frostmore	Ext. 9982
ROOM SERVICE MANGER Marilyn LeBeau	Ext. 2340
BELL CAPTAINS Day/Jerry and Chip Night/Monty and Phil	Ext. 5555
TRANSPORTATION MANAGER Carl German	Ext. 9670
HEAD HOUSEMAN Charles St. Amant	Ext. 1776
ELECTRICIAN John Light	Ext. 6265
SECURITY OFFICER Lt. Harold Watson	Ext. 1111
A/V PERSON Jim Johnson	Ext. 43
SET-UP PERSON FOR MEETING ROOMS Chuck Roe	Ext. 1777
HEAD HOUSEKEEPER Janice Forester	Ext. 66
SOCIAL DIRECTOR FOR HOTEL Jessica Best	Ext. 30
HOTEL PUBLIC RELATIONS Gladys Generet	Ext. 33
CASHIER Victor Verdugo	Ext. 277
AUDITOR Virginia Fortes	Ext. 278

MEETING PLAN   PROPERTY INSUR./REGIS./MTG. RMS

INSURANCE COVERAGE: With Prudential—policy copy to come
    THEFT AND INJURY   Yes
    GEN. LIABILITY   Yes
    PERFORMANCE BOND   Yes

REGISTRATION: INDIVIDUAL   X
                 CONTROLLED BY MTG. PLANNER   X
                 LIST REQUIRED: 21 Days in advance of arr.
                 LOCATION OF REGISTRATION DESK
                    Main lobby
                 GUESTS ARE PREREGISTERED or   No
                           REGISTER ON ARRIVAL   Yes
                 CONVENTION BUREAU PERSONNEL
                 AVAILABLE   Yes

MEETING ROOMS: FLOOR PLANS AVAILABLE   (attached)
                  USE CHARGES   YES   X   NO
                  IF SO AMOUNT $3,800

NAME	SIZE	THEA.	SCRM.	RECP.	BANQ.	A/V	A.C.	STAGE
Conv. foyer	2500 sq. ft.	277	143	499	250			
Ballroom	4000 sq. ft.	444	229	799	400			
Mtg. Rm. A	850 sq. ft.	94	49	166	80			
Mtg. Rm. B	900 sq. ft.	100	51	177	90			
Mtg. Rm. C	1050 sq. ft.	116	60	200	100			

TYPE OF ROOM DIVIDERS   Air walls
NEARBY WORKROOM   Adjacent to   SIZE   20 × 20
    LOCATION   ballroom
EXHIBIT AREA AVAILABLE Yes
NOTES:

MEETING PLAN   DINING ROOMS AND OTHER FACILITIES

NAME	HOURS	CAPACITY	MAP, FAP	MEALS SERVED A LA CARTE	BAR B LD

CAFÉ AU LAIT (Coffee shop)
____   6 A.M. to 11 P.M.   250   X   XXX

GOLDEN CACTUS (Fine dining)
____   5 P.M. to 1 A.M.   178   X   −XX

THE DUNES (Poolside)
____   11 A.M. to 5 P.M.   80   X   XX−

MEALS   FAP OR MAP FOOD PORTION OF RATE:
      BKFST: N/A
      LUNCH: N/A
      DINNER: N/A

SURCHARGES   8% tax + 18% gratuity

SPECIAL PRINTED MENU   On request   COST $1 per person

BUFFET BKFST. AVAILABLE   On request

CONTINENTAL BKFST. AVAILABLE   On request

VARIETY OF SELECTION DAILY   Yes

SPECIAL DIETS ACCOMMODATED   Yes

SPECIAL OUTDOOR MEALS   Yes

ROOM SERVICE CHG.   20% gratuity and Serv. Chg.

COFFEE BRK. CHG.   W/PASTRY $7   W/O PASTRY $4

COCKTAIL PARTY CHG. PER DRINK $3.50
   PER HOUR $6/pp   PER BOTTLE   On quote

FINAL GUARANTEE TIME FOR FOOD FUNCTIONS   72 hr.

WINE LIST   attached   STUDENT MENU   Attached

MEETING PLAN   OTHER

POOLSIDE SNACK BAR   Yes
BAR-LOUNGE   Yes
LOBBY BAR   Yes
GIFT SHOPS   NUMBER 3   LOCATION   On Parada
HAIR SALONS   NUMBER 1   LOCATION   3rd floor
FLORIST   Yes   LOCATION   Parada
BOUTIQUES   NUMBER 2   LOCATION   Parada
CONCIERGE 3   HOURS 7 a.m. to 11 p.m. LOCATION   Lobby
TOUR DESK Yes HOURS 7 a.m. to 5 p.m. LOCATION   Lobby
CAR RENTAL CO. Yes   LOCATION   Parada
GAME ROOM   Yes   LOCATION   3rd floor
NURSERY/BABYSITTING   Yes   LOCATION   3rd floor
                  HOURS   By arrang.
SWIMMING   NUMBER 3   LOCATION   Rear patio
  POOLS   LIFE GUARDS   6
JACCUZZIS   NUMBER 3   LOCATION   Side court-
                                         yard adjacent to pools

OTHER FACILITIES:
   SPA — 3rd floor
   Masseuse — Spa — 3rd floor
   Nail Salon — 3rd floor
   Card room w/hostess — 3rd floor

NOTES:

MEETING PLAN   GOLF/TENNIS/SPAS/ET AL

GOLF COURSE ON PROPERTY?   YES x   NO

NUMBER OF HOLES 36   LOCATIONS Adjacent to patio

GREENS FEES $75   CART FEES inclu.   CADDIES $10/hr.

CLUB RENTAL RATES $20/set   PRO SHOP Yes

GOLF CLUB PRO NAME Jim Gleason   PHONE Ext. 10142

WILL COURSE BLOCK TEE TIMES FOR MEETING GUESTS? Yes

WILL PRO STRUCTURE TOURNAMENTS FOR GROUPS? Yes; no chg.

TENNIS COURTS ON PROPERTY?   YES x   NO

NUMBER OF COURTS 10   LIGHTED FOR NIGHT PLAY? Yes

COURT FEES $10/hr.   RAQUET RENTAL FEES $10

TENNIS PRO NAME Jennifer Guest   PHONE Ext. 10157

WILL PRO BLOCK TIMES FOR MEETING GUESTS? Yes

WILL PRO STRUCTURE TOURNAMENTS FOR GROUPS? Yes; no chg.

IF GOLF OR TENNIS NOT AVAILABLE ON PROPERTY, WILL HOTEL MAKE SPECIAL ARRANGEMENTS FOR OFF-PROPERTY PLAY?

DISTANCE TO COURSE   TRANSPORTATION COST

IS SPA AVAILABLE ON PROPERTY? Yes

ARE THERE TRAINED EXERCISE SPECIALISTS? Yes

TYPE OF EXERCISE EQUIPMENT Nautilus

IS MASSEUSE AVAILABLE? Yes

ARE THERE SCHEDULED EXERCISE CLASSES? By appt.

ARE GUESTS WELCOME TO USE EQUIPMENT INDIVIDUALLY? Yes

SPA MANAGER NAME: Craig Barry   PHONE: Ext. 10198

MEETING PLAN   GRATUITIES/ACCOUNTING

                          GRATUITIES

BLANKET   YES X NO   AMT

SPECIAL LIST   YES X NO   AMT

BELL PERSONS   YES X NO   AMT

WAIT PERSONS   YES X NO   AMT

MAIDS   YES X NO   AMT

SWITCHBOARD   YES X NO   AMT

CONCIERGE   YES X NO   AMT

ALL FOOD PERSONNEL   YES X NO   AMT

ALL BEVERAGE PERSONNEL   YES X NO   AMT

GOLF/TENNIS CLUB
   PERSONNEL   YES X NO   AMT

CONVENTION SERVICES
   PERSONNEL   YES X NO   AMT

HOUSEMEN ON MEETING
   SET-UPS   YES X NO   AMT

SPECIAL SERVICES   YES X NO   AMT

Amt. of Gratuties to be awarded after meeting _____

in case of special services _____

OTHERS

GRATUITIES TO BE PAID INDIVIDUALLY   CK.   CASH X

GRATUITIES TO BE PAID IN BULK TO CONV. COORD.
    YES   NO X

MEETING PLAN			ATTENDEE ARRIVAL/ROOM INFO		
NAME	DATE	FLIGHT	AIRLINE ETA	HOTEL ETA	ROOM #

This list contains the names and arrival information of all expected attendees.

MEETING PLAN   PRE-CONVENTION MEETING

STAFF MEMBER IN CHARGE OF SETTING UP WITH HOTEL
CONV. COORD.

_____ Julia Wright

TIME: 8 a.m.   DATE: April 2   PLACE: Board rm. 5

ATTENDEES:

ALL PLANNING STAFF MEMBERS: Congdon, Bowen, Wright,
Jeffers

HOTEL PERSONNEL	NAME	DEPARTMENT
	George Montgomery	Sales mgr.
	Victor Verdugo	Acctg./cashier
	Judy Smith	Conf. coord.
	Barbara Brody	Reserv.
	George Jennings	Catering
	Jim Goeffries	Bev.
	Chef Lesault	F & B
	Jerry and Monty	Bell Capts.
	Charles St. Amant	Houseperson

DMC PERSONNEL: Sue Leslie
                Joe McIntosh

OTHER SUPPLIER PERSONNEL:
Computer operators Gordon Jellison

ALL STAFF MEMBERS BRING YOUR COPY OF MEETING PLAN
—THIS WILL SERVE AS AGENDA FOR MEETING.

MEETING PLAN   AIRPORT MEET/GREET & TRANSFERS

DATE:4/3   STAFF MBR. IN CHG: JEFFERS

                  STAFF ASSIGNED: DMC personnel

FLIGHT	ARR.	SCHEDULE	# PAX	VEHICLE ASSIGNED:
AAL 0034	4/3	10:27 a.m.	11	VAN #1
Delta 97	4/3	11:02 a.m.	39	BUS #1
AW 149	4/3	11:32 a.m.	41	BUS #1
AAL 0076	4/3	1:44 p.m.	9	VAN #1

(Here are listed all flights on which you expect passengers, together with number of passengers deplaning and the van, bus, or limousine which has been assigned to transport those passengers to the hotel. To this sheet should be attached a passenger manifest, which is a detailed list of flights with passenger names, arrival times et al. The manifest is usually supplied by the travel agent or airline with whom the meeting planner has been working. The same information is put on a separate sheet for departures from the hotel including the number of passengers with vehicle assignments.)

NOTES:

AW 149 — 30 minutes late

MEETING PLAN   REGISTRATION/INFORMATION

REGISTRATION/INFORMATION DESK FOR MEETING:

LOCATION: Convention foyer   DATES OPEN: April 3–6

HOURS DESK STAFFED: 7 a.m. to 10 p.m.

MEETING STAFF MEMBER IN CHARGE: Marge Jeffers

CREW TO OPERATE DESK: Jeffers, Wright + 2 Convention and Visitors' Bureau Personnel

MATERIALS TO BE AT DESK:

REGISTRATION PACKETS TO BE AT DESK PRIOR TO FIRST ARRIVALS. TO INCLUDE: Name badges; programs; brief-case kits

TOUR/GOLF/TENNIS SIGN-UP SHEETS:

FLIP CHART FOR DAILY INFORMATION NOTICES/MESSAGES:

CORK BOARD ON EASEL AND PUSH-PINS FOR SAME:

PHONE MESSAGE PADS: YELLOW LEGAL PADS: PENS/PENCILS

TYPEWRITER: (Paper, ribbons)

BADGE TYPEWRITER: Badge stock

TELEPHONE w/OUTSIDE LINE AND LONG DISTANCE CAPABILITIES

LOCAL TELEPHONE BOOKS

HOTEL STAFF TELEPHONE DIRECTORY – EMERGENCY NUMBERS

COMPUTER TERMINAL

COMPUTER PRINTER CAPABILITY

DESK-TOP COPY MACHINE   ELECTRONIC MESSAGE BOARD

LOCAL SIGHTSEEING BROCHURES AVAILABLE   CITY MAPS

MEETING PLAN   WELCOME RECEPTION

DATE: 4/3   ROOM: Convention foyer

MEETING STAFF MEMBER IN CHARGE: Congdon

TIME OF RECEPTION: 7:00 p.m. to 10:00 p.m.

TIME HOTEL TO HAVE ROOM SET: 6:45 p.m.

NO. OF ATTENDEES EXPECTED: 250

TABLE SET UP INSTRUCTIONS: Number   Size   Type
   Small cocktail-size tables to seat 100 only—skirted

ROOM SET-UP CHART ATTACHED:

BARS SET-UP: 5   LOCATIONS: Distributed around room away
                                    from entries to room

   NO. OF BARS: 5   NO OF BARTENDERS: 10

   WELL BRANDS:

   PREMIUM BRANDS REQUESTED: Chivas Regal, Canadian Club,
   Jack Daniels, Absolute, Beefeaters, Johnny Walker Red,
   St. Emilion, Pouilly Fusse

   STANDARD MIXES TO BE PROVIDED: Yes

   SPECIAL MIXES REQUESTED: Perrier

   HOSTED BAR: x   TICKET BAR: CASH BAR:

FOOD REQUIREMENTS Yes   (See menu attached.)

NO. OF SERVERS REQUIRED: 8   NO. OF BUS PERSONS: 6

TIME OF ACTUAL FOOD SERVICE: 7:00 p.m. —9:00 p.m.

COST PER PERSON: $22

ENTERTAINMENT: Local Mariachi group 10/person

SET-UP TIME: 6:30 p.m.

PERFORMANCE TIMES: 7:00 p.m. to 10:00 p.m.
                     10 Min. breaks every 45 min.

MUSIC TO BE PROVIDED: Celebratory Mexican standards/quietly

LIGHTS: No Special   SOUND: Not required

PAYMENT ARRANGEMENTS: DMC to handle

MENU

Welcome Reception

Convention foyer	7 p.m. to 10 p.m.
Buffet format	250 persons

8 White gloved servers behind buffet to serve guests
6 bus persons to keep tables cleared, pick up glasses/plates
Additional food to be added as needed at direction of meeting planner during evening, substitutions will be made if necessary

Shrimp, shelled, deveined, cleaned in crystal bowls on ice @ $200/bowl × 3 service to be staged in 3 stages	$ 600.00
Stone crab legs, shelled in crystal bowls on ice w/cocktail sauces @ $280/bowl × 3 service to be staged in 3 stages	$ 840.00
Mini roast filet of beef sandwiches, miniature seeded rolls, horse radish sauce, sliced to order by chef at buffet @ $3/ea. × 300	$ 900.00
Imported cheeses tray/water wafers staged throughout evening @ $90/tray × 5 trays	$ 450.00
Exotic tropical fruits in mellon baskets spaced along buffet, 5 boats @ $90/ea.	$ 450.00
Assorted raw vegetables w/green goddess dip and gruyere cheese dip on platters, 4 platters @ $90/ea.	$ 360.00
Hot coffee/hot tea in silver service, waitress to pour, accompanying crystalline raw sugar, heavy cream, lemon and orange wedges, $50/pot × 10 pots	$ 500.00
French pastry trays—assorted, 5 trays @ $75/ea.	$ 375.00
FOOD TOTAL	$4,475.00
Taxes @ 5%	223.75
Gratuities @ 18%	805.50
TOTAL	$5,504.25

$22.017/per person + bar

SEATING CHART
Opening Reception

250 persons, possible — cocktail style
25 tables of four only to encourage mixing
5 bars/double

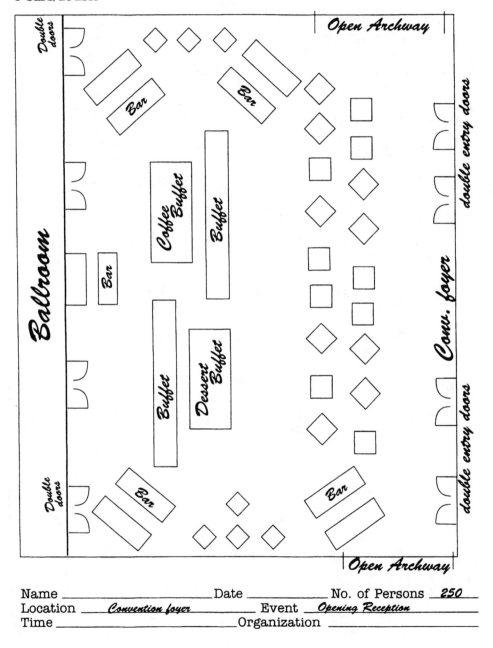

Name _____ Date _____ No. of Persons _250_
Location ___*Convention foyer*___ Event ___*Opening Reception*___
Time _____ Organization _____

MEETING PLAN   BREAKFAST

STAFF MEMBER IN CHARGE: Wright

DAY/DATE: 2-4/4   LOCATION: Conv. foyer

NO. OF ATTENDEES: 200   GUARANTEE DUE   72 hr.

NO. OF TABLES: 22 of 10   ARRANGEMENT: Chevron
   ROOM SET-UP CHART ATTACHED

TIMES OF SERVICE: 7:30 a.m. to 8:30 a.m.

NO. OF SERVERS: 12   NO. OF BUS PERSONS: 8

FOOD (SEE MENU ATTACHED):   COST PER PERSON: $12

HEAD TABLE REQUIRED?   Yes   LOCATION: Front/center

LECTERN REQUIRED? Yes   FREE-STANDING?   Yes
   TABLE TOP?

MICROPHONE? Yes ON STAND?   ON LECTERN? Yes
   LAVALIERE?

LIGHTING: Usual room lights
   FOLLOW SPOT?   No

BACKGROUND MUSIC?   No   LIVE?   TAPED?

NOTES:

MENU

BREAKFAST—DAY 2

Sitdown   7:30 a.m. to 8:30 a.m.

Convention foyer   200 persons

1/2 Grapefruit or 1/2 Melon or choice of juice

Eggs Benedict

Assorted mini-danish/toast/croissants,
    warmed and on tables

Assorted muffins, warmed and on tables

Coffee, tea, milk

$12 per person × 200	$ 2,400.00
+ Sales Tax @ 5%	120.00
+ 18% Gratuity	432.00
TOTAL	$ 2,952.00

200 persons @ $14.76/ea.
(Original quotation in meeting plan neglected to add tax and
gratuity.)

SEATING CHART
DAY 2 BREAKFAST

200 persons, possible
22 tables of 10 persons each in Chevron pattern, focus on head table front
and center

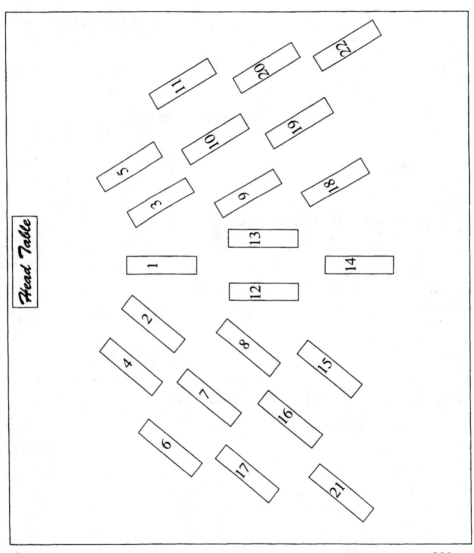

Name_____ Date _____ No. of Persons __200__
Location ____*Conv Foyer*____ Event_____ *Breakfast Day 2*
Time_____ Organization _____

MEETING PLAN   OPENING GENERAL SESSION

DAY/DATE: 2-4/4   LOCATION: Grand Ballroom

SEATING ARRANGEMENT: THEATRE: x   SCHOOLROOM:
  CONFERENCE: SEATING CHART ATTACHED:

STAGE: Yes   DAIS:

STANDING LECTERNS: 2   LIGHTED? YES

TABLE LECTERNS: LIGHTED?

PROJECTORS: 1   SPECIFY TYPES AND NO.: Rear projection,
computer operated — 30 trays, 2 video tape players — VHS 1/2",
monitors both front corners
  LOCATIONS: Rear view on stage

PROJECTION SCREENS: SPECIFY TYPES AND NO.: 1 Rear view
  LOCATIONS: On stage

MICROPHONES: 2   SPECIFY TYPES AND NO.: On lecterns

POINTERS?   FLIP CHARTS?   EASELS?

BLACKBOARDS?   BULLETIN BOARDS?

CLOSED CIRCUIT TELEVISION?   NO. OF MONITORS

  LOCATIONS?

SOUND SYSTEM: Voice only   OPERATOR: 1

SPECIAL LIGHTING: Follow spot   OPERATOR: 1

  UNION OPERATORS REQUIRED? No
  COST: $15/hr./worker

FIRE EXITS? Marked
  LOCATIONS: Left and right of stage; foyer

IS EMERGENCY MEDICAL EQUIPMENT AVAILABLE? Yes
  COST: $25/hr.

NOTES: EMTs not required at this session

SEATING CHART
Opening General Session

Grand Ballroom   Theatre style
250 persons, possible
2 lecterns—front, stage right, and stage left (w/microphones)
Rear-view projection on stage, 2 VHS monitors on stage, on stage right
and left outside lecterns

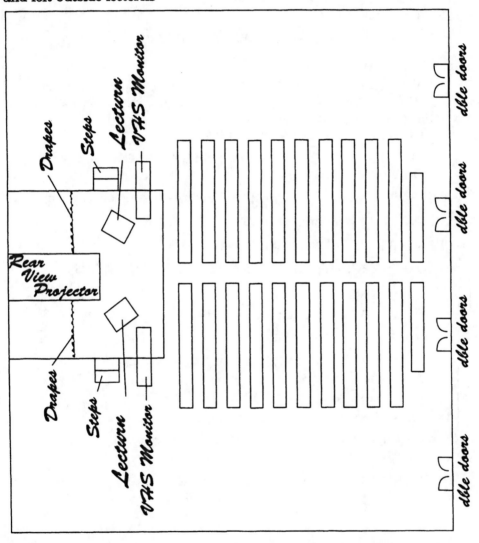

Name _____ Date _____ No. of Persons _250_
Location _Grand Ballroom_____ Event _Opening Sessions_
Time _____Organization _____

MEETING PLAN   GENL. SESSION PROGRAM

(If the meeting planner is responsible for the program itself, then this page would be added.)

IS NEWS RELEASE ON GENL. SESSION AND SPEAKERS APPRO-PRIATE? Yes DONE? Yes SENT TO: Local/hometown papers

WELCOME AND INTRODUCTIONS:

SPEAKER   Co. President/CEO

BIOGRAPHICAL INFO. FOR PROGRAM RECEIVED
  YES x NO

DOUBLE-SPACED SCRIPT TO BE ATTACHED WHEN
  AVAILABLE

ARRIVAL INFO. RECEIVED?   YES x NO

TO BE PICKED UP AT AIRPORT: TIME: FLT #

WHO ASSIGNED TO MEET AND TRANSPORT?   CAR LIMO.

REHEARSAL: TIME 8 p.m.; 4/3 LOCATION: Ballroom

ROOM REQUIRED? Yes   RM. # 1434

KEYNOTE SPEAKER: tba

BIOGRAPHICAL INFO. FOR PROGRAM RECEIVED: YES   NO

DOUBLE-SPACED SCRIPT TO BE ATTACHED WHEN AVAILABLE.

ARRIVAL INFO. RECEIVED? YES   NO

TO BE PICKED UP AT AIRPORT: TIME: FLT. #

WHO ASSIGNED TO MEET AND TRANSPORT? CAR   LIMO.

REHEARSAL: TIME   8:30 p.m.; 4/3 LOCATION: Ballroom

ROOM REQUIRED?   ROOM #:

INFORMATION IMPARTED TO SPEAKERS ON THEIR FLIGHTS, PICK-UP, AND ACCOMMODATIONS. THEY HAVE BEEN NOTI-FIED OF REHEARSAL TIMES, TIME OF APPEARANCE AT OPEN-ING GENERAL SESSION, AND TIME ALLOTTED FOR THEIR PRE-SENTATION.   YES x NO

MEETING PLAN   LUNCHEON

DAY/DATE: 2-4/4   LOCATION: Patio A

TIME OF FUNCTION: 12:15 p.m.

STAFF MEMBER IN CHARGE: Wright

NO. OF ATTENDEES ANTICIPATED: 220
   GUARANTEE DUE: 72 hr

TABLE SET-UP: CHART ATTACHED:

BAR SERVICE? No   BAR LOCATIONS
  WELL BRANDS?   PREMIUM BRANDS?
  COST PER PERSON: PER DRINK: PER BOTTLE:

TIMES OF SERVICE: 12:30 p.m.

FOOD (SEE MENU ATTACHED):   COST PER PERSON: $18

HEAD TABLE REQUIRED? No   LOCATION:

NO PROGRAM AT LUNCHEON; NO AUDIO/VISUAL EQUIPMENT;
  NO LIGHT OR SOUND EQUIPMENT

BACKGROUND MUSIC? Yes   LIVE? x TAPED?

NOTES: Music fee $350

MENU

Day Two Luncheon

Cold gaspacho soup topped with fresh cilantro

Desert salad

Served in taco shell bowls (edible)

Bottom of bowl lined w/Mexican refried beans, choice of lemon-pepper chicken breast chunks or carne asada (seasoned shredded beef), crisp shredded lettuce, diced tomatoes, chopped mild green chiles, topped with finely shredded yellow cheese. Both hot and mild salsa in condiment bowls on all tables

Flan—a light Mexican custard, with burnt carmel topping

Dos Equis Mexican beer or margarita*

Coffee, tea, milk, soft drinks

220 @ $18/per person	$ 3,960.00
+ 5% tax	198.00
+ 18% gratuity	712.80
TOTAL	$ 4,870.80

*Limit 2 beers or 2 margaritas at luncheon.

SEATING CHART
Luncheon Day Two

Sit-Down
220 persons
No bars
No head table
Background music

Patio A
Rounds of 10

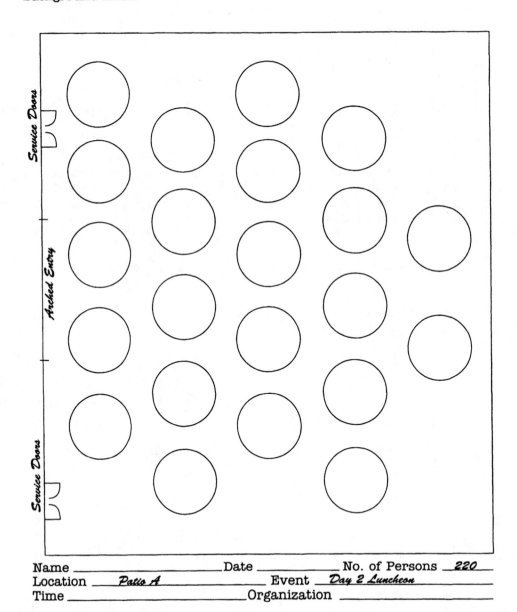

Name _____ Date _____ No. of Persons __*220*__
Location ____*Patio A*____ Event __*Day 2 Luncheon*_____
Time _____ Organization _____

MEETING PLAN   BREAKOUT SESSION #1

PLANNING STAFF MEMBER IN CHARGE: Bowen

TIME: 2:00 p.m.   LOCATION: MTG. RM. A

SUBJECT: New profit bonds

TITLE: Above

SPEAKER: VP Sales/Mktg.
  SPEAKER'S SCRIPT AND/OR SLIDES TO BE DELIVERED?   Yes
  WHEN AND WHERE?   Ballroom 4/3, 9 p.m.

EQUIPMENT None

STAGE PLATFORM?   YES   NO x

STANDING LECTERNS   YES x NO   LIGHTED? x

TABLE LECTERNS   YES   NO   LIGHTED?

	NUMBER	SIZE	TYPE
TABLES	7	6 '	
CHAIRS	42		

SEATING ARRANGEMENT:
  SCRM.   THEAT.   CONF.   (seating chart attached)

EASELS	1	
BLACKBOARDS		
FLIP CHARTS	1	
POINTERS	1	
A/V EQUIPMENT		
PROJECTORS		
SCREENS		
T.V. MONITORS		
MICROPHONES	1	

SEATING CHART
Breakout Session One — Day Two

Schoolroom Seating   42 persons
7–6' tables/42 chairs

Standing lectern front and center of room w/microphone/light
easel/flip chart/pointer + 6 markers   42 pens/pads on tables

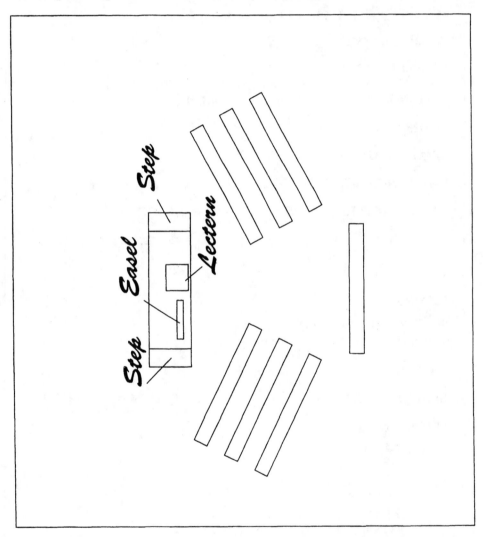

Name_____ Date_____ No. of Persons_____
Location __*Mtg. Rm. A*_____ Event_*Breakout Session 1*_____
Time _____ Organization _____

MEETING PLAN   BREAKOUT SESSION #1

	NUMBER	SIZE	TYPE
PIANO			
FLAGS			
GAVEL			
PENS/PADS	42	reg.	
CHALK			
MARKERS	6		
SPECIAL LIGHTING			
SOUND SYSTEM			

OTHER EQUIPMENT:

UNION OPERATORS REQUIRED   YES   NO   COST

EQUIPMENT OPERATORS ASSIGNED?

NOTES:

(Similar sheets are made up for each breakout session.)

MEETING PLAN   BREAKOUT SESSION #1

SUBJECT: See previous page

SPEAKER/MODERATOR: VP Sales/Mktg.

BIOGRAPHICAL MATERIAL FOR PROGRAM REC'D   YES x   NO

DOUBLE-SPACED SCRIPT TO BE ATTACHED WHEN AVAILABLE.

ARRIVAL INFO.   RECEIVED: YES   x   NO

TO BE PICKED UP AT AIRPORT? No TIME: FLT. #

WHO ASSIGNED TO MEET AND
TRANSPORT?   CAR: LIMO

   ROOM REQUIRED?   YES   ROOM #:   1200

REHEARSAL: TIME: 4/3; 9 p.m.   LOCATION: Ballroom

SPEAKER HAS BEEN ADVISED OF FLIGHT, PICK-UP TIME, AND
ACCOMMODATIONS. HAS BEEN NOTIFIED OF REHEARSAL
TIMES, TIME OF APPEARANCE AT BREAKOUT SESSION #1 AND
TIME ALLOTTED FOR PRESENTATION.

NOTES:

(Similar sheets are made up for each breakout session.)

MEETING PLAN   DINNER/ENTERTAINMENT

DAY/DATE: 2-4/4   ROOMS: Foyer/ballroom

MEETING STAFF MEMBER IN CHARGE: Congdon and Bowen

NO. OF ATTENDEES EXPECTED: 270
   GUARANTEE DUE: 72 hr.

TIME HOTEL TO HAVE ROOMS SET: 6:45 p.m.

TIME OF COCKTAIL PARTY: (Conv. foyer):   7 p.m.
(For setup and location of bars and buffet tables, see attached
chart.)

NO. OF BARS REQUIRED: 5   NO. OF BARTENDERS: 10

CHARGE: BY BOTTLE: PER PERSON: $10   PER HOUR:

WELL BRANDS:

PREMIUM BRANDS REQUESTED: Same as welcome reception

STANDARD MIXES TO BE PROVIDED: Yes

SPECIAL MIXES REQUESTED: Perrier

BUFFET HORS D'OUEVRES CHARGES: $10 per person; light
   dinner to follow

COCKTAIL ENTERTAINMENT: Baby grand

   SET-UP TIME: 6:00 p.m.   PERFORMANCE TIME: 6:45 p.m.

   ARRANGEMENTS HANDLED BY: DMC

   COST: $150   HOW PAID?   DMC

FOOD REQUIREMENTS (See attached menu.)
   COST: $40 per person
(Table and seating chart and locations attached.)

NO. OF SERVERS REQUIRED: 25   NO. OF BUS PERSONS: 10

TIME OF ACTUAL FOOD SERVICE: 8:30 p.m. promptly (seated
   at 8 p.m.)

MEETING PLAN   DINNER/ENTERTAINMENT

SPECIAL NOTES REGARDING DINNER SERVICE:

    LINEN   COLOR?   Mauve cloths,
                                    peach napkins

    CENTERPIECES?   FLORAL?   Desert-type
                                    WHO TO SUPPLY?   DMC

    FAVORS?   WHAT? Cactus garden/Indian pot
                                    WHO TO SUPPLY? DMC

    PLACE CARDS?   CALLIGRAPHY?   Yes
                                    WHO TO SUPPLY?   DMC

    SEATING PLACEMENTS   WHO TO SUPPLY?   Sales dept.

    SOUVENIR MENUS?   No

ENTERTAINMENT DURING & AFTER DINNER: Destination management company to handle complete magic/illusion show, including background music during dinner and after dinner dance combo. Obtain detailed plan from DMC and meet with representative to go over all detail.

NAME OF DMC: Phx. Connection—Sue Leslie
                  PHONE NO.: 747-3333
  CONTACT:

SPECIAL LIGHTS, SOUND ETC. FOR ENTIRE COCKTAIL/DINNER PARTY TO BE HANDLED BY DMC.

NOTES: DMC cost for evening entertainment $8,000.00

MENU
Dinner Day Two

Cocktails—ballroom foyer	Dinner—ballroom
270 persons	

Cocktail hors d'oeuvres—chef's choice
Light, since dinner will follow immediately
Hot and cold canapes—finger foods only

$10 per person × 270	$2,700.00
+ 5% tax	135.00
+18% gratuity	486.00
TOTAL	$3,321.00

Dinner:
Thinly sliced Nova Scotia salmon, rolled
  w/prosciutto ham and thin cantaloupe strips
  drizzled w/vinaigrette
Caesar salad—tossed by captains—one between
  each four tables
Veal Oscar
Baked Alaska—paraded in flaming by waiters,
  w/house lights out
Coffee, tea, milk

$40 per person × 270 persons	$10,800.00
5% tax	540.00
18% gratuity	1,944.00
SUBTOTAL	$13,284.00
+ Cocktail menu	$3,321.00
TOTAL	$16,605.00

270 persons @ $61.50 per person
(Original quote in meeting plan does not include tax and gratuity.)

SEATING CHART
DAY 2 DINNER

Cocktails—ballroom foyer   Dinner—ballroom
270 persons
5 double bars/10 bartenders

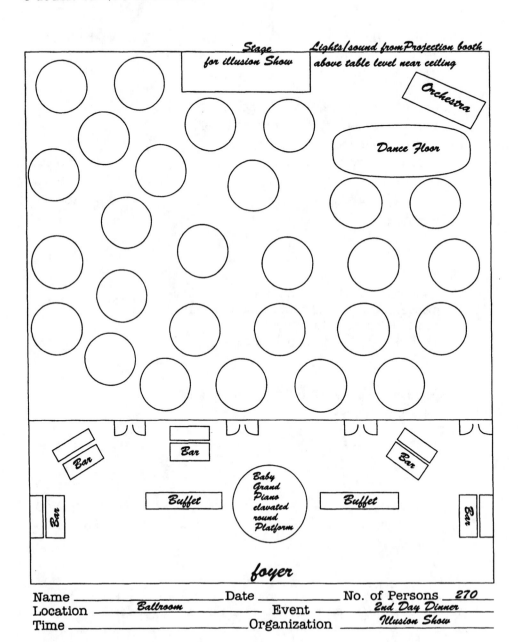

Name _____ Date _____ No. of Persons _*270*_
Location ____*Ballroom*____   *2nd Day Dinner*
                              Event _____ *Illusion Show*
Time _____ Organization ____

MEETING PLAN   BREAKFAST

STAFF MEMBER IN CHARGE: Wright

DAY/DATE: 3-4/5   LOCATION: Poolside

NO. OF ATTENDEES: 200   GUARANTEE DUE: 48 hr.

NO. OF TABLES: 20 of 10   ARRANGEMENT: Around pool
   SEATING CHART ATTACHED   No chart—random arrangement

TIMES OF SERVICE: 7:30-8:30 p.m.

NO. OF SERVERS: 10   NO. OF BUS PERSONS: 6

FOOD: (See attached menu.) COST PER PERSON: $13

HEAD TABLE REQUIRED? No   LOCATION:

NO PLATFORM, LECTERN, MICROPHONE OR OTHER EQUIP-
MENT.   NO PROGRAM AT BREAKFAST TODAY.

BACKGROUND MUSIC? Strolling violins LIVE? x TAPED?

NOTES: DMC to arrange 6 violins @ $175

MENU
BREAKFAST DAY 3

Poolside   200 persons

5 omelette stations w/chefs — guests to pick up omelette cooked to order on outdoor grills; assorted ingredients at station for omelettes, all other service at tables

Juice of guests' choice

Tropical fruit compote

Baskets of assorted bread on tables: nut bread, banana bread, bran muffins, orange bread, corn bread sticks

Coffee, tea, milk

200 persons @ $13 per person inclusive $2,600.00

MEETING PLAN   SIGHTSEEING TOUR

STAFF MEMBER IN CHARGE: Bowen

SIGN-UPS DUE BY: 4 p.m.; 4-4

DAY/DATE: 3-4/5   TOUR TO: City/museum/old town

DEPARTURE TIME: 9 a.m.   RETURN TIME: 5 p.m.

NO. OF ATTENDEES ANTICIPATED: 125   NO. OF
VEHICLES: 3

BUSES DEPART PROMPTLY FROM CONVENTION FOYER
ENTRANCE. (Complete tour description/brochures attached.)

DMC HANDLING TOUR: Phx. Conn.
LEAD GUIDE ASSIGNED: Portmouth

ITINERARY: $40 per person

 9:00 a.m. Depart hotel
            city overview en route

10:00 a.m. Arrive historical museum

10:30 a.m. Coffee break—arranged with museum

11:30 a.m. Depart museum

12:00 p.m.–12:15 p.m. Drive by Capitol Bldgs.

12:20 p.m. Arrive old Indian hilltop ruins

12:45 p.m. Catered luncheon served, complete with white linen,
            flowers and appropriate wines. (See attached menu
            and set up detail.) Tables to be set amid ruins.

 1:45 p.m. Depart Indian ruins

 2:15 p.m. Arrive at old town shopping area—Scottsdale
            Allow guests 1 1/2 hr to shop and browse shops and
            galleries

 3:45 p.m. All meet at old town sidewalk cafe for refreshments

 4:15 p.m. Depart old town

 5:00 p.m. Arrive back at hotel

MEETING PLAN   GOLF TOURNAMENT

STAFF MEMBER IN CHARGE: Bowen

COURSE TO BE PLAYED   At hotel   DATE: 3-4/5

TRANSPORTATION REQUIRED?   No

CLUB PRO TO HANDLE TOURNAMENT: J. Gleason

HANDICAP/SIGN-UP/PAIRINGS SHEETS DISTRIBUTED AT LOBBY
INFORMATION DESK   MUST BE TURNED IN BY: 4/4

CARTS TO BE READY WITH SCORE CARDS/CLUBS ABOARD/
PAIRINGS BY: 8:00 a.m.

GREENS/CART FEES PER PERSON: $70

TEE TIMES: BEGINNING 8:30 a.m. every 8 minutes

ESTIMATED NUMBER OF FOURSOMES: 16

BEVERAGE CART TO CRUISE COURSE THROUGHOUT

    COST: $15 per person

AMENITIES ON ALL CARTS: 2 3-ball tubes titleists.
                                   2 company-logo visors
                                   2 club souvenir ball towels
                                   2 Pkg tees
                                   2 gold-plated ball markers

TOTAL COST PER PERSON: $150

BOX LUNCHES ARRANGED BY CLUB TO BE HANDED TO EACH
CART ON THE TURN; BEVERAGE CART TO BE STATIONED AT
TURN

COST PER PERSON: $15

CLUB PRO AND STAFF TO ARRANGE FOR LEADER BOARDS AT
9th and 18th HOLES; CLUB STAFF TO HANDLE SCORE CARDS
FOR NASSAU, AS WELL AS LOW GROSS AND LOW NET

PRIZE INFO.: AWARDS BANQ. PAGE

MEETING PLAN   TENNIS TOURNAMENT

STAFF MEMBER IN CHARGE: Bowen

COURT LOCATIONS: At hotel

NUMBER OF COURTS RESERVED: 6

ESTIMATED NUMBERS OF PLAYERS: 24

CLUB PRO: Guest

DAY/DATE: 3-4/5   TIME OF TOURNAMENT: 9 a.m.

PAIRINGS FOR SINGLES AND DOUBLES TO BE ARRANGED BY
CLUB PRO   COST PER PERSON: $30

SIGN-UP SHEETS AT CONV. INFO. DESK DUE IN BY: 4-3

BEVERAGE TABLES TO BE SET UP
COURTSIDE   COSTS: $250

LUNCHEON TO BE SERVED BETWEEN SETS IN CLUB HOUSE, AS
PLAYERS ARE AVAILABLE   COST PER PERSON: $18

AMENITIES PACKAGE TO INCLUDE (for each player):
CAN OF TENNIS BALLS   COMPANY LOGO VISOR
SOUVENIR CLUB ATHLETIC BAG   CLUB LOGO TENNIS TOWEL
CLUB LOGO RACQUET COVER
   TOTAL COST PER PERSON: Approx. $80

SCORE PROGRESS BOARD TO BE ERECTED COURTSIDE BY
CLUB FOR ELIMINATION TOURNAMENT

NOTES:

SPORTS LUNCH MENUS
DAY THREE

GOLF—Box lunches to be picked up at turn

Sliced stacked turkey (1/2 sandwich)

Sliced stacked corned beef (1/2 sandwich)

Pasta salad in 1/4 pint containers

Package of potato chips

Small package of Hershey's ™ kisses

Beverage cart stationed at turn: beer, soft drinks

Each golf cart to have 1 gallon ice water coolers
attached in club rack

Golf box luncheon $15 per person × 64 golfers $960.00

Beverage cart on course to be billed for usage

TENNIS—Luncheon in clubhouse as player available

Player's choice from luncheon menu

24 players @ $18 per person

(inclusive of taxes and gratuity) $432.00

MEETING PLAN   AWARDS BANQUET

DAY/DATE: 3-4/5   ROOM: Grand Ballroom

MEETING STAFF MEMBER IN CHARGE: Congdon

NO. OF ATTENDEES EXPECTED: 250

GUARANTEE DUE: 72 hr.

TIME HOTEL TO HAVE ROOM SET: 6:45 p.m.

TIME OF COCKTAIL PARTY (SECTION I-BALLROOM):   7 p.m.
(for set-up and location of bars and buffet tables, plus
hors d'oeuvres menu, see attached)

NO. OF BARS REQUIRED: 5   NO. OF BARTENDERS: 10

CHARGE: BY BOTTLE: PER PERSON: $10   PER HOUR:

WELL BRANDS:

PREMIUM BRANDS REQUESTED: Same as welcome reception

STANDARD MIXES TO BE PROVIDED: Yes

SPECIAL MIXES REQUESTED: Perrier

BUFFET HORS D'OEUVRES CHARGES: $19 per person

COCKTAIL ENTERTAINMENT: TO BE PROVIDED BY DMC
   REQUEST DETAIL IN WRITING BY DMC

DINNER LOCATION: (Grand Ballroom, sections II, III and IV)

DINNER FOOD REQUIREMENTS: (See attached menu.)
   COST: $47 per person

HEAD TABLE REQUIRED? Yes   NO. OF SEATS: 12
(Table and seating chart and locations attached.)

NUMBER OF SERVERS REQUIRED: 22

NO. OF BUS PERSONS: 10

TIME OF ACTUAL FOOD SERVICE: 8:15 p.m.

GOLF/TENNIS PRIZE DATA ATTACHED:

NOTES:

MENU
FOR AWARDS BANQUET
DAY THREE

Cocktails—Ballroom, section I

Grand Ballroom sections II, III and IV   250 persons

Ramaki—500 pcs.

Spiced Chicken Wings—500 pcs.

Mini BBQ meatballs—300 pcs.

Hot shrimp in butter/lemon sauce—750 pcs.

Cold vegetable trays
  2 w/appropriate dips

Melon shells filled with citrus fruit segments

Bowls of Arizona pecans

Bowls of trail mix

250 persons at $19 per person $ 4,750.00

Boullion w/angel-hair noodles

Garden salad w/avocado and tomato wedges
  Selection of dressings

Tournedos w/bernaise sauce

Restuffed baked/whipped potatoes

Fresh asparagus w/hollandaise sauce

Raspberry mousse in chocolate cups

Cordial trays passed to each table

Coffee, tea, milk

2 bottles of Piper Heidseck champagne vintage year,
  on each table

28 tables (incl. head table) × 2 × $75/btl $ 4,500.00
  (ordered by corp. pres.—last minute)

Standard menu dinner 250 persons @ $47
  inclusive of tax and gratuity $11,750.00
Hors d'oeuvres   4,750.00
TOTAL $21,000.00

SEATING CHART
SPORTS AWARDS DINNER

Cocktails — section I of ballroom   250 persons
Dinner — sections II, III and IV of ballroom
28 round tables of 10   5 double bars/10 bartenders   Head table of 12
Small stage side of cocktail area toward dinner area
Dixieland — 6 men; when air wall opens for dinner, band can turn toward
dining room without moving all equipment, mics, etc.
For awards — stage area opposite side of room from musicians
Two lecterns w/lights — rear table to hold awards (skirted)

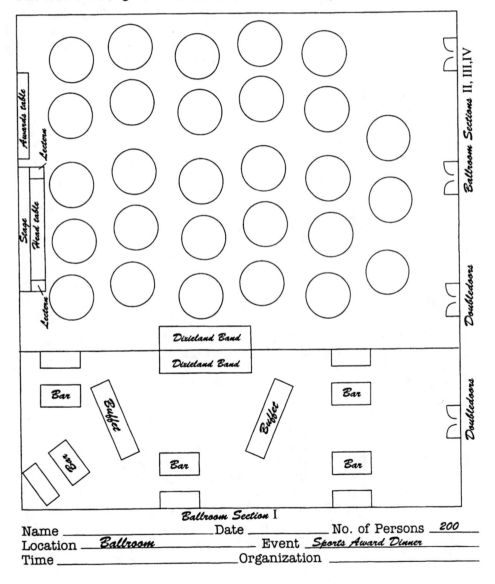

Name _____ Date _____ No. of Persons _200_
Location __*Ballroom*_____ Event _*Sports Award Dinner*___
Time _____ Organization _____

MEETING PLAN   AWARDS BANQUET

SPECIAL NOTES REGARDING DINNER SERVICE:

LINEN   COLOR? Mint green

CENTERPIECES?   FLORAL? Yes
                                    WHO TO SUPPLY?   DMC

FAVORS?   WHAT? Sports windbreakers
                                    WHO TO SUPPLY?   DMC

PLACE CARDS? TABLEMARKERS CALLIGRAPHY?   YES
   BY TEAMS   WHO TO SUPPLY?   DMC

SEATING ARRANGEMENTS?   WHO TO SUPPLY?   BY TEAMS
   SOUVENIR MENUS?   NO

GOLF AWARDS: $2400   HOW MANY? 12
                                 WHAT? Crystal trays — engraved

TENNIS AWARDS: $800   HOW MANY?   6
                                 WHAT? Crystal bowls — engraved

WHO IS ASSIGNED TO OBTAIN WINNER NAMES FROM PROS?
Golf — Bowen; tennis — Jeffers

SALES AWARDS: (Surprise!)   HOW MANY? 5 regions
   COST: $6,000 ea = $30,000   WHAT? Hawaiian trips

WHO IS ASSIGNED TO OBTAIN WINNER NAMES FROM PRES.?
Wright

DESTINATION MANAGEMENT CO. TO HANDLE AWARDS
PROGRAM DETAIL AND OBTAIN GOLF AND TENNIS
CELEBRITY — PROFESSIONALS TO GIVE OUT AWARDS. DMC TO
SUPPLY COMPLETE DETAIL AND SCRIPT, TO BE ATTACHED.
MEET WITH DMC REPRESENTATIVE TO GO OVER ALL DETAIL.

MEETING PLAN (continued)   AWARDS BANQUET

TIME SCHEDULE FOR ENTIRE EVENING PROGRAM ATTACHED.

ENTERTAINMENT: (DMC TO SUPPLY THE FOLLOWING):

  BACKGROUND MUSIC DURING COCKTAILS AND DINNER

  AWARDS CELEBRITY — PRO SPEAKERS

  MUSIC AFTER DINNER AND AWARDS

ARRANGE WITH DMC FOR REHEARSAL TIME, WHERE RE-
QUIRED.

NAME OF DMC: PHOENIX CONNECTION   PHONE NO.   747-3333

  CONTACT: SUE LESLIE

SPECIAL LIGHTS, SOUND ETC. FOR ENTIRE COCKTAIL/AWARDS
DINNER TO BE HANDLED BY DMC.

PROFESSIONAL PHOTOGRAPHER FOR AWARDS HANDLED BY
DMC

NOTES:

AGENDA

For Awards Dinner Program

6:45 p.m.   Hotel to have rooms (foyer and ballroom) set

7:00 p.m.   Cocktail party begins

7:00 p.m. to 1:00 a.m. Musicians playing—to break during presentations, and continue playing afterward, for dancing, until 1:00 a.m.

8:00 p.m.   Cocktail party ends and group moves to Grand Ballroom for dinner

8:15 p.m.   Dinner is served

9:30 p.m.   M.C. introduces golf professional and presentation of golf awards proceeds

10:00 p.m.   M.C. introduces tennis professional and presentation of tennis awards proceeds

10:30 p.m.   M.C. introduces corporation president who presents "surprise" sales awards

11:00 p.m. to 1:00 a.m. Music proceeds for dancing—bars are open

DMC to handle this entire program per agenda

Follow spots, lights and sound to be handled from projection booth at back of ballroom near ceiling

MEETING PLAN   BREAKFAST/DEPARTURES

MEETING STAFF MEMBER IN CHARGE   Congdon and Bowen
DAY/DATE   4-4/5   ROOM: Convention foyer

BREAKFAST—full detailed menu attached: to be served buffet
style—with servers on line from 6:00 a.m. to 10:00 a.m. (Minimal
seating chart—attached)
Bell staff to pull all luggage 1 hr. prior to scheduled bus departure.
list to be provided by meeting planner 36 hr. in advance. Hotel to
have sufficient bell persons to move all luggage on schedule.

NOTICE TO GO TO ALL ATTENDEES' ROOMS:

1. Luggage must be ready for bell staff pick up prior to leaving
   room for breakfast. Exact time will be indicated on notice to
   each room.

2. Personal charges must be handled with hotel cashier prior to
   breakfast on morning of departure.

3. All vehicles will leave exactly on time, so please identify luggage
   in convention foyer for departure loading 15 min. prior to departure schedule, which is to be as follows:

ATTENDEE NAME	FLT. NO.	DEPARTURE FROM HOTEL	
Joe Adams	AAL #467	BUS #1	6:35 A.M.
Marlene Tipton	UAL #2281	BUS #1	6:35 A.M.
William McGraw	AAL #467	BUS #1	6:35 A.M.
Anne Williamson	AW #2340	VAN #1	7:40 A.M.

(All attendees are thus listed, serving as a boarding checklist at
time of loading vehicles.)

BREAKFAST
DEPARTURE DAY

CONVENTION FOYER

Guests to arrive at their leisure 6 a.m. to 10 a.m.

Buffet of a selection of:

Juices

Cold cereals

Fresh fruit—berries and bananas in individual melon cups

Trays of danish—assorted

Trays of miniature "sticky buns"

Trays of croissants and muffins

Smaller portions to be displayed, but trays refilled regularly, since guests will arrive at random

Coffee, tea, milk

250 persons @ $10.00 per person $2,500.00

  (incl. tax and gratuity)

SEATING CHART

Departure Breakfast   Convention foyer
Buffet for 250 persons—from 5 a.m. to 10 a.m.
Seating for 160—20 8' banquet tables, clothed and skirted

2 buffet lines

Ballroom

Buffet   Buffet   Buffet   Buffet   Buffet

Name_____ Date_____ No. of Persons ____*250*____
Location ____*Conv Foyer*_____ Event *Breakfast Spasmodic Departure Day*
Time_____ Organization _____

MEETING PLAN   DEPARTURE MANIFEST

As a double check, this page should be a complete manifest of all departure information by flight:

PASSENGER	FLT.#/TIME	DEPT. HOTEL	ARR. DESTI-NATION
	AAL#467/ 7:35 a.m.	Bus #1/ 6:35 a.m.	1:04 p.m./ NEW YORK
Joe Adams			
William McGraw			
Sue Jefferson			
John Jefferson			
	UAL#2281/ 7:42 a.m.	Bus #1/ 6:35 a.m.	10:40 a.m./ ST.LOUIS
Marlene Tipton			
Janice Laos			
Bob Hoyt			
Margaret Hoyt			

(All passengers to be thus listed by flight.)

MEETING PLAN   PLANNING STAFF MEETING

DAY/DATE: 4-4/5   LOCATION: Hotel mtg Rm. A

TIME: 6:30 p.m.   Menu to be set with hotel banquet mgr. by
meeting planner

Meeting planner to recap general meeting, highlighting plan components that went on schedule and successfully; opening to discussion those facets of meeting which had problems or could have
been better.

Full open discussion of total meeting

AGENDA   (copy attached) TO BE SENT TO EACH MEMBER OF
STAFF ON DEPARTURE DAY.

THIS MEETING HELD IN PREPARATION FOR POST-CONVENTION
MEETING WITH HOTEL PERSONNEL AND DMC STAFF PEOPLE.

NOTES:

PLANNING STAFF MEETING

Dinner Meeting	Mtg Rm. A
Four Persons	Menu to be set by
	meeting planner (MP)

MEETING PLANNER

  Open meeting

    Recap general meeting — strong and weak points

    Outline any problems with any supplier

Each travel staff member to mention any happening with which MP may not be familiar — problems or congratulations due to any supplier — and to advise of any additional charges which may have occurred, and should be added to budget.

Discussion of exact procedure to be followed at post-con.

Brief outline of duties for tomorrow regarding packing up and leaving for home.

THANK YOU BY MP TO ALL STAFF.

MEETING PLAN   MEETING SHUT-DOWN INFO.

DAY/DATE: 5-4/7

All meeting materials to be packed for return to home office. All A/V, decor and other materials returned to owners.

   STAFF MEMBER IN CHARGE: Bowen

MEETING PLANNER TO SET UP FOLLOWING MEETINGS FOR TODAY:

WITH HOTEL CASHIER/AUDITOR TO FINALIZE BILLING AND ARRANGE PAYMENT. TIME: 10:00 a.m. PLACE: Cash. off.

WITH HOTEL CONVENTION COORDINATOR TO DISCUSS FINAL GRATUITIES DISTRIBUTION   TIME: 11 a.m. PLACE: Conv. Off.

WITH HOTEL DIRECTOR OF SALES TO SET UP POST-CONVENTION MEETING WITH HOTEL STAFF AND DMC STAFF

TIME: 12:00 a.m.   PLACE: Dining Rm.

(All Meeting Staff Members to attend post-conv. meeting.)

WITH DESTINATION MANAGEMENT COMPANY REPRESENTA-TIVE TO FINALIZE THEIR BILLING

   TIME: 2:30 p.m. PLACE: Bd. Rm. A

ATTEND POST-CONV. MEETING

   TIME: 4 p.m.   LOCATION: Conf. Rm. C

ARRANGE FOR TRANSPORTATION FOR STAFF TO AIRPORT FOR FLIGHTS HOME. PERSON IN CHARGE: Wright

NOTES:

MEETING PLAN   MEETING EVALUATION DATA

This task can be completed upon return to home office:

ALL MEETING EVALUATION SHEETS FROM ATTENDEES TO
BE STUDIED AND CONSOLIDATED RECAP SHEET TO BE
ATTACHED TO TOP:
   PLANNING STAFF MEMBER TO HANDLE: Jeffers

EVALUATION SHEETS FROM HOTEL DEPARTMENT PERSONNEL
TO BE CONSOLIDATED AND RECAP SHEET ATTACHED TO TOP:
   PLANNING STAFF MEMBER TO HANDLE: Wright

EVALUATION SHEETS FROM OUTSIDE SUPPLIERS TO BE
CONSOLIDATED AND RECAP SHEET ATTACHED TO TOP:
   PLANNING STAFF MEMBER TO HANDLE: Bowen

EVALUATION SHEETS FROM EACH MEMBER OF PLANNING
STAFF TO BE CONSOLIDATED AND RECAP SHEET ATTACHED
TO TOP:
   PLANNING STAFF MEMBER TO HANDLE: Congdon

MEETING OF ENTIRE ON-SITE PLANNING STAFF TO MEET TO
DISCUSS EVALUATION AND OUTLINE REPORT TO MANAGE-
MENT ON THIS MEETING.
   DATE: 4/15   TIME: 9 a.m.   PLACE: Planners Off.

MEETING PLANNER TO WRITE FINAL REPORT TO
MANAGEMENT
   DATE DUE: 4/20

GLOSSARY

A ACCOMODATIONS—refers to the actual sleeping and living arrangements, which are made with a hotel or resort; for example hotel rooms, resort suites or university dormitories.

ADJACENT ROOMS—are those hotel bedrooms which are next to each other and are entered separately from the main hallway or corridor.

ASSOCIATION EXECUTIVE—is generally the paid chief executive officer of an association, directly responsible to the Board of Directors.

ATTENDEES—those persons who come to a meeting or convention, but who have no part in the program.

B BENEFICIARY COUNTRIES—those countries which are either U.S. possessions or protectorates, or who have a tax treaty with this country. This enables meeting planners to hold meetings in those countries with the same income tax privileges as would apply for meetings within the U.S.

BOTTOM LINE—the net profits after all expenses, which generally appear on the bottom line of a financial statement.

BREAK-OUT ROOMS—refers to the smaller meeting and conference rooms, which might be required when a larger general session breaks up. The total group of attendees is thus broken up into smaller meeting groups.

BREAKS—times during a meeting when attendees are given a recess in the actual meeting. This permits them to stand or stretch or walk around and allows time for visits to the restrooms. During breaks, refreshments are often provided; for example, "coffee breaks."

BUDGET—a formalized list of projected income and expenses or an itemized line-by-line statement of monies allocated for the meeting.

C CITY-WIDE RATES – for a very large convention or meeting, a planner can often work with several hotels within a site-city and arrange for the same rate at all hotels being used.

CONFERENCE SEATING – an arrangement which provides for chairs on one or both sides of all tables. Since conference style does not call for a dais, stage or head table for speakers, many arrangements are possible. (See chapter on seating arrangements.)

CONNECTING ROOMS – are those hotel bedrooms which have access from both the public corridor or hallway and from an internal doorway from one room to the other.

D DEPOSIT – is a down-payment guaranteeing that the hotel must hold rooms regardless of the guest's arrival time. Deposits are generally an amount equal to one night's lodging.

DESTINATION – usually refers to the place a group is going. This might be the city of Anaheim, CA or, if the meeting is being held at a recognized self-contained hotel such as the Disneyland hotel, the hotel/theme park is considered the destination; thus the designation for some hotels as "world-class destination hotels."

DMC (Destination Management Company) – a service supplier to the meeting industry. Once a group has arrived at the site-city, this company is ready to "manage" everything within that destination (other than the meeting program itself). DMCs will assist the meeting planner by providing: airport assistance; transfers to the site hotel(s); registration desk staffing; additional personnel; and just about anything else the meeting planner requests.

DOUBLE ROOM – is room for two persons, with one bed only.

DOUBLE-DOUBLE ROOM – is a room with two queen, king, or super-king-sized beds. It may accommodate two, three or four persons and is frequently requested by families.

E EP (European Plan) – is a hotel rate, which includes room charge only. All meals are charged extra.

EXHIBIT BOOTHS – are those areas marked off generally by pipe and drape dividers, in which persons show and/or distribute either brochures or promotional materials or products during a trade show or exhibit.

F **FAM TRIP** — Familiarization trip on which meeting planners may be invited at no cost. The purpose of the trip is to introduce planners to accommodations, attractions, and points of interest of potential site cities.

FAP (Full American Plan) — is a hotel rate which offers room and three meals a day in quoted room charge.

FUNCTION — is any meal, sports activity, special event or theme party.

G **GIG** — a term usually used by musicians, meaning a job, a booking, or a performance for which they are hired.

GM — refers to the general manager. This may be the chief executive of a hotel, convention center, corporation or any business organization.

H **HIGH SEASON** — is that time of year when tourists and meetings are booked in a particular area; the busy season of the year, which varies from location to location.

HOUSE — refers to a hotel, convention hall or theatre; for example, "back of the house" refers to the inner workings or nonpublic areas while "front of the house" indicates the public areas such as lobbies, front desk, restaurants, etc.

I **IN-HOUSE** — refers to any function, activity or service which is provided entirely within the hotel in which the meeting is being held. This may also be used to refer to something entirely within a company, for example, "in-house meeting planner."

K **KING ROOM** — describes a hotel room for one or two persons, containing one king or super-king bed.

M **MAP (Modified American Plan)** — is a hotel rate which offers room and one or two meals a day in the quoted room charge.

MARKETING PLAN — is a formalized, written statement of strategy to be followed to get a product to the designated "market"; a plan to be utilized by the sales group to reach a predetermined customer segment; a program to "sell" a product.

MASTER ACCOUNT — the hotel billing account for which the meeting planner has agreed to be responsible and to which all meeting expenses will be charged.

MEET/GREET — refers to the process of meeting and greeting attendees for a meeting (generally at an airport). Staff generally stands with a "welcome" sign, including the name of the group, in order to give members a gathering point where they can be directed to baggage areas and transportation.

MEETING PLAN — is the very detailed day-by-day directions for every facet of a meeting or convention; a blueprint for the entire meeting.

MULTIPLE HOTELS — are used when a meeting is too large to be housed in a single hotel and several hotels are used within the same locale.

O **ON-SITE** — refers to an activity, which occurs at the hotel or resort property; for example: The meeting planner has asked four staff members to be on-site during the meeting.

P **PARTICIPANTS** — are all of those persons who take part in the program of a meeting, as differentiated from attendees who attend but have no official duties at the meeting.

PILLOW GIFTS — refer to individual gifts presented to each conference attendee. They are often placed upon the bed pillow at night, while attendees are at dinner.

POST-CON — refers to the meeting of all involved persons, held immediately after a meeting or convention, at which time all facets of the meeting are examined and evaluated, both good and bad, with an eye to correcting or improving all phases of the meeting.

PRE-CON — indicates the pre-convention meeting, usually called by the hotel conference coordinator and attended by everyone who has some duty to perform in connection with the meeting: meeting planner and staff; hotel personnel; DMC employees; and anyone else who may be involved.

PUBLIC AREAS — are the areas in a hotel which are ordinarily accessible to the general public; that is, the lobby, convention foyer, restaurants, lobby, restrooms, et al.

R **ROOMING LIST** — is a list of all attendees with information as to the type of accommodations requested, daily room rate, and date and time of anticipated arrival and departure. This list is prepared and sent to the hotel a specified number of days prior to the meeting.

RUN-OF-THE-HOUSE RATE — is an agreed upon price, which has been negotiated for all available rooms (not including suites), booked for a single meeting.

S   **SCHRM (Schoolroom seating arrangement)** — indicates chairs, either in a row, a semicircular arrangement, or even a chevron set-up, providing some sort of writing surface. This may mean that there are miniature sidearm tables connected to each chair, or the chairs may be arranged on one side of tables, all facing the speakers' area.

SHUTTLE SERVICE — is usually, transportation provided continuously between two or more points; for example, bus service between two or more hotels of a multiple-hotel meeting, or continuous transportation running between the hotel and a golf course.

SINGLE ROOM — refers to accommodations which will serve one person. There is generally only one bed, no larger than a standard double bed.

SITE — indicates the place where a meeting is being held. This can be used for the city chosen — or more commonly, the particular hotel/resort selected.

SITE SELECTION — is the process by which a meeting planner chooses both the geographical location and the specific property for a meeting or convention.

STANDARD LIMO — is a limousine which seats three in a back seat facing forward and two on pull-down jump seats facing backwards. As in all limos, there is a glass partition between driver and passengers.

STRETCH LIMO — is a limousine which seats three in a back seat facing forward and can seat three more on a bench seat behind the driver, facing backwards. It may have two jump seats facing forward between the two bench seats. Called "stretch" because of its greater length and seating capacity, these cars are usually luxuriously upholstered and have stereo tape/sound systems, miniature TVs and often have bar amenities. They can also be equipped with computers, videotape players, or any number of other new electronic gadgets.

T   **THEAT (Theatre Seating Arrangement)** — indicates chairs facing one direction either in a row or a semicircle, with no provision for any writing surface.

TRAFFIC PATTERN — is used to delineate the course through which a crowd is encouraged to move in order to facilitate traffic flow; the layout of a registration area or exhibit booths or meeting rooms, so that people can move more easily from place to place.

TWIN ROOM — is designed to accommodate two persons, in two single beds.

INDEX